RAISE A SMARTER CHILD BY KINDERGARTEN

ALSO BY DAVID PERLMUTTER, M.D., F.A.C.N., AND CAROL COLMAN

The Better Brain Book:
The Best Tools for Improving Memory and Sharpness and for Preventing Aging of the Brain

RAISE A SMARTER CHILD BY KINDERGARTEN

Build a Better Brain and Increase IQ Up to 30 Points

David Perlmutter, M.D., F.A.C.N., and Carol Colman

BROADWAY BOOKS
NEW YORK

PUBLISHED BY BROADWAY BOOKS

A hardcover edition of this book was originally published in 2006 by Morgan Road Books.

Published in the United States by Broadway Books, an imprint of The Doubleday Broadway Publishing Group, a division of Random House, Inc., New York.
www.broadwaybooks.com

BROADWAY BOOKS and its logo, a letter B bisected on the diagonal, are trademarks of Random House, Inc.

DISCLAIMER

Readers, please take note of the following important information.

Throughout this book certain toys, materials, and activities are recommended to stimulate your child. We urge you always to use appropriate and reasonable care in providing adult supervision for your child's activities and limiting your child's access to toys and materials that might pose a safety hazard.

In addition, while our book contains information and suggestions about the use of vitamins, supplements, and medications, whether to give these to your child, and appropriate dosages for his or her individual needs, should be discussed with your child's pediatrician. Similarly, certain charts appearing in this book, such as immunization schedules, are for general informational purposes only. Specific schedules required for your child should be determined by your child's pediatrician.

You will also encounter the names of certain toys and products in this book. When we refer to products by their brand names, those names are capitalized. Such references are not intended to suggest that this book or its recommendations are endorsed or sponsored by the manufacturers of the toys or products referred to.

Finally, although this is a work of nonfiction, some of the names and distinguishing traits of individuals described have been changed to protect their privacy.

Book design by Chris Welch

Library of Congress Cataloging-in-Publication Data
Perlmutter, David, M.D.
Raise a smarter child by kindergarten : build a better brain and increase IQ up to 30 points / David Perlmutter and Carol Colman.
p. cm.
Includes bibliographical references (p.).
1. Intellect—Nutritional aspects. 2. Children—Intelligence levels. 3. Brain—Diseases. 4. Brain—Problems, exercises, etc. I. Colman, Carol. II. Title.
QP398.P47 2006
612.8'22—dc22

2006043318

ISBN 978-0-7679-2302-6

PRINTED IN THE UNITED STATES OF AMERICA

20 19 18 17 16 15 14

Raise a Smarter Child by Kindergarten *is dedicated to parents. You have chosen to accept the most sacred responsibility of humankind.*

"You are the bows from which your children as living arrows are sent forth."

—Khalil Gibran,
The Prophet

Visit Dr. Perlmutter's blog:
RenegadeNeurologist.com

CONTENTS

PART IV
CREATING A BRAIN-ENHANCING ENVIRONMENT FOR YOUR CHILD

PART V
THE BRAIN–BODY CONNECTION: COMMON MEDICAL CONDITIONS AND VACCINATIONS THAT CAN AFFECT YOUR CHILD'S BRAIN

PART VI
FIGHTING ADHD BY BUILDING A BETTER BRAIN

Appendices

ACKNOWLEDGMENTS

I would like to thank Amy Hertz, publisher of Morgan Road Books, for her wisdom, energy, and enthusiasm, as well as her continued devotion to our goals. I have a great sense of confidence knowing that you're guiding the process along the way. Many thanks to our literary agent, Janis Vallely, for her continuing support at all stages of this process. I am grateful to Marc Haeringer and Julie Miesionczek of Morgan Road, who have worked tirelessly on this project and continue to do so. Special thanks to Rebecca Holland, publishing director and executive managing editor, for making this much needed book happen so quickly and for shepherding it through the process.

I am very grateful to Anna Belle Fore, manager of the Perlmutter Health Center, for her seemingly effortless ability to bring tranquility to the otherwise overwhelming challenges of our complex day.

Finally, I'd like to thank my wife, Leize, for her encouragement and understanding in all my endeavors, as well as our children, Austin and Reisha, for allowing us to experience the joy of parenthood. —D.P.

RAISE A SMARTER CHILD BY KINDERGARTEN

PART I

A BRIEF WINDOW OF OPPORTUNITY

CHAPTER ONE

The Smart Advantage

What does it take to raise a smarter child? What must parents do during the first five years of life to ensure that their child is primed to excel in school and in life?

The good news is, raising a smarter child is easier than you think. It doesn't require making an investment in expensive equipment or high-priced tutors. Nor do you have to devote every waking minute to demanding academic drills. There are easy (and I do mean easy) yet highly effective strategies that can vastly improve your child's brain power. It's as simple as playing the right games with your child, putting the right food on your child's plate, maintaining a brain-enhancing environment in your home, and last but not least, giving your child lots of love.

I'm a neurologist, a physician who specializes in disorders of the brain and nervous system. At my offices at the Perlmutter Health Center in Naples, Florida, I have worked with both children and adults for more than twenty years. I am also a father of two teenage children. Over the past five years, there have been incredible breakthroughs in the field of neurosciences—particularly in the area of early childhood development—that have given us a new understanding of how the brain develops.

Science now tells us that the human brain is unfinished at birth. There's a brief window of opportunity in a child's life when parents can help create a brain that is built for optimal performance. Your child's future depends on how well you do that job. If you do your job well, you will raise a smarter child who will fulfill his or her full intellectual potential.

When I was in medical school, the prevailing scientific view was that the brain you are born with is your brain for life. This belief has now been refuted. New and more effective imaging techniques have provided a window into the brain that has enabled us to see how the brain changes throughout our lifetime. We now know that the human brain is undergoing a constant and dramatic transformation from birth until about age 5 and, to a lesser extent, throughout our entire lives. The brain can be shaped and molded well into adulthood and even into old age, but the most important work is done in early childhood. And that's when parents can make the biggest impact on the lives of their children.

During the peak time of brain development, *every* activity and experience leaves an indelible mark on your baby's brain, for better or worse. The right kind of stimulation will create connections in the brain that promote intelligence and emotional stability. The wrong kind of stimulation—or lack of stimulation—can stifle intellectual development, destroy brain cells, and leave your child more vulnerable to learning or behavior problems down the road.

Some of you may be thinking: Isn't intelligence largely determined by genetics? Won't smart parents automatically have smart children? And if that's true, what can you do about your child's genes? We now know that for the most part, great brains are made, they are not born. From birth to age 3, up to 30 IQ points are up for grabs. Children may be born with the genetic potential to have a higher than average IQ, but if they are not properly nurtured and nourished during the first few years of life, they will not achieve their full potential. What parents do—or fail to do—can win or lose IQ points.

DON'T LET YOUR CHILD MISS OUT

Lots of well-meaning parents are missing key opportunities to enhance their children's intellectual and emotional well-being, not because they are derelict in their duties, but because they are not fully informed.

There are simple ways you can make your child smarter and make sure that those precious IQ points don't go down the drain.

- Breast-feeding your baby for the first twelve months of life can boost her IQ by up to 8 points. If you can't breast-feed or have to stop early, be sure to use a commercial infant formula that is fortified with brain-boosting nutrients.
- Feed your toddler an optimal diet to enhance brain growth. Even a slight deficiency in a key vitamin, mineral, or nutrient (such as iron or iodine) during the time when the brain is going through its spectacular growth spurt can result in a lower IQ, poor test scores, depression, and even teen drug abuse down the road.
- Engage your baby in mentally stimulating activities from the first few weeks of life through her entire childhood. The right games and activities can improve her memory, boost her mental capacity, and hone her critical thinking skills.
- Limit the amount of time your child spends watching TV and DVDs and playing video games. Excess time spent watching TV and playing video games during early childhood adds up to poor grades at school.
- Introduce your child to formal musical training by age 4. It will make him a stronger math and science student.
- Early training on a computer can improve your child's cognitive function and better prepare him for school.
- Protect your child from common brain toxins found in food, toys, clothing, and even your own backyard that can cause learning problems and rob her of IQ points.
- Raise your child in a warm, loving, low-stress environment with attentive caregivers.

Every choice a parent makes, from what to feed a child, to how much TV a child watches, to the choice of caregiver can profoundly affect a child's brain growth and development. And so much of your child's brain development is under your control.

SO WHAT ABOUT GENETICS?

And of course, there's a child's genetic makeup, which he gets from you, his parents. Genetics does play an important role in creating a smart brain, but not necessarily in the way that you would expect. And this is probably going to really surprise many of you—we now know that you actually have far more control over your genes than was once believed.

A healthy baby is born with the raw material to make a great brain, but there's still a lot of work to be done. The newborn brain has 100 billion brain cells (called neurons), but they are unable to communicate with each other very well. During the first one thousand days of life, neurons must learn to talk to each other by forming the vital connections—the neural "pathways to success"—that provide the foundation for language, vision, hearing, learning, feeling, and thinking. Enhancing these connections can spell the difference between a good brain and a great brain. A smart brain is hardwired to think, learn, process, and retrieve information quickly and efficiently. It's true that many of the processes of brain development are gene dependent, but it's also true that we have a great deal of say over how those genes behave.

It was once believed that if a child was lucky enough to have smart parents, he would inherit smart genes and be born with a great brain. Of course, it doesn't always work that way in real life because as we've now learned, there's so much more to this story than just pure genetics. Environment as well as genetics plays an important role in intelligence and future academic success. Babies who are loved, well nurtured, and well nourished grow up to be adults with higher IQs compared to babies who were not as well cared for. What we didn't fully appreciate in the past was the relationship between genes and environment, or more specifically, how it was possible for environment to affect genes, and therefore IQ.

We now have a much better understanding of the interrelationship between genes and the environment. Genes may determine the number and quality of brain cells you are born with, but environmental influences over which you as a parent have control turn on and off the very genes involved in brain development. More importantly, we now know that under the right circumstances, it is possible to turn on the right genes, the genes that will make a brain smarter. And I mean this literally.

Genes do their work by directing the production of proteins that are critical for brain development. These special proteins regulate the wiring between brain cells that ultimately makes the brain smarter, and they are especially important during this period of peak brain development. But what controls the smart genes in the first place? Lots of things, including regular mental stimulation, physical activity, the right foods and nutrients, and the experience of feeling loved and emotionally secure.

We also know that a negative environment can turn on bad genes and/or prevent good genes from being activated. Children who are fed a less than optimal diet, not raised in a mentally stimulating environment, exposed to dangerous chemicals in the environment, or raised in a stressful household are not as likely to achieve their full intellectual potential as children raised under better conditions.

WHAT ARE BRAIN-BUILDING ACTIVITIES?

Brain-building activities are those that challenge the brain, thereby stimulating the neurons to make more connections, which will make the brain stronger, faster, more efficient, and ultimately smarter. The point of these activities is to train the brain *how* to think, not *what* to think. It's about building up the brain's capacity so that your child will be better able to process and utilize information for her entire life. The right kind of stimulation at this pivotal time will create an optimal brain, one that will give your child better tools to perform well in the classroom.

The achievable goal during this critical window of opportunity is to create the fastest, most efficient, and highest-capacity brain, setting the stage for future success. Much as we all strive for the fastest computer with the most storage capacity, you can achieve the same results with your child's brain. Again, the goal is not to overwhelm your child's brain with as many facts as possible before she starts kindergarten, but rather to create a brain that stores facts efficiently and, most importantly, is able to retrieve them easily. Essentially, the goal should not be *what* she learns, but *how* she learns.

During the first five years of life, when the brain is undergoing rapid development, children should spend most of their waking hours engaged in brain-building endeavors. Unfortunately, children are devoting too much time to activities that dull their brains, deaden their senses, and put their future academic careers at risk. Watching television or DVDs—even educational programs—for hours on end, as many children do, is not good for a growing brain. Nor is playing video games for hours at a time. But don't get me wrong—I'm not suggesting small children shouldn't have any fun or that they should be subjected to a rigorous academic setting. That would be a terrible mistake. Children learn best when they are happy, relaxed, and stimulated. That's one of the reasons why play is one of the best activities for young children.

It may surprise you to learn that physical activity is also a terrific brain builder. It boosts levels of the growth hormone in the brain that makes better brain cells. But perhaps the most brain-enhancing activity of all is imaginative play, the kind of play that comes naturally to children when they have the time and space to pursue it.

A SMART BRAIN IS A CREATIVE BRAIN

In recent years, there has been an emphasis on beginning academic training for children at younger and younger ages. We live in a very competitive world, and parents are afraid that if they don't push their children to learn how to read or how to do simple arithmetic at very early ages, they will fall behind and not do well in elementary school. Nothing could be further from the truth. The choice of early academic intervention, especially the kind of "drill and test" activities that are so popular today in many preschools, is the wrong approach. Instead of building great brains, we are merely creating tape recorders that can regurgitate information but cannot synthesize it to come up with new ideas. At a time when a child should be encouraged to be creative, which is the foundation for advanced thinking, many children are being loaded down with facts. More and more preschools are adopting a curriculum that pushes children into early academics. More and more elementary schools are eliminating creative outlets such as recess and music and placing more emphasis on academics, or more specifically, "teaching for test." I have nothing against academics, and I certainly believe that children need to be taught the basics, but, ultimately, this trend is going to result in poor performance at school in upper grades where critical thinking is essential. There is no scientific evidence that the push to engage preschool-age children in early academics actually works, and in point of fact, there is some evidence that they may turn out to be more stressed and less creative.

Any child can memorize his ABCs or learn to count if he is drilled long and hard enough, but these are not highly effective brain-building activities. It's far more important for the developing brain to learn the symbolic nature of letters and words than how to spell, as well as to fully understand what numbers mean and how to identify different shapes. You want your child to understand what these letters *represent*—that they are symbols and that they are made of shapes, and that numbers are also symbols made from shapes, and each of these symbols means something different.

Creativity is at the core of all problem solving, whether you are solving a math problem, writing an essay, or designing a science project. For example, if your child is confronted with a new challenge, such as a difficult math problem or a challenging essay question, what does he need to succeed? First, he must be comfortable with being in a novel and challenging situation. This comfort level is fostered during the first five years by allowing children to explore challenging situations, engage in creative play, and learn that failure *is* an option. In other words, it's okay to take intellectual risks. Next, his brain connections need to function at peak performance, allowing him to draw upon a variety of types of stored information from past experiences to find solutions to the new problem at hand. It could be solving a math problem, writing a song, reading a poem with understanding . . . it all requires creativity.

PREVENTING PROBLEMS DOWN THE ROAD

This book is not only about learning to develop your child's full intellectual potential—I also believe the techniques described here can help prevent many of the learning and behavior problems that are so prevalent today. Once rare, conditions such as attention deficit disorder (ADD) and attention deficit hyperactivity disorder (ADHD) are becoming epidemic, affecting 10 to 12 percent of all school-age children. Many children are brought to me by their desperate parents after they have been diagnosed with learning or behavior disorders that make it difficult if not impossible for them to do well in school and in life. I see a lot of unhappy kids who are disruptive, easily distracted, and frustrated with their lives. They don't have the discipline to sit still in a classroom or to learn how to read, or the social skills to maintain friendships. By age 5, they feel like failures, and very often, so do their parents. Their parents feel that they have no choice but to put their children on strong psychoactive drugs and are often coerced into doing so by teachers. I show these parents a better way to treat their children's problems than drugging them into submission. Simple changes in diet, different approaches to discipline, and improved nutrient intake through supplements can make a huge difference in these children's lives. I only wish that I could have gotten to these parents earlier, long before their children began having these problems in the first place, because, as you will soon read, problems such as ADHD are almost uniformly preventable and manageable without drugs.

THE ROLE OF PARENTS

Your job over the first five years of your child's life is to help her develop the best brain possible. There are countless opportunities throughout the day that can help make her smarter, happier, and better prepared for the world. Even if you don't have a lot of time, you can still find a few minutes every day to play a brain-stimulating game with your child, read to your child, and sing to your child. You can support her efforts to be creative by providing a rich home environment in which she can engage in imaginative play. You can make sure that your child lives and plays in as toxin-free and safe an environment as possible, and that she is getting enough brain-building nutrients.

Don't let your child miss out on this once-in-a-lifetime opportunity.

HOW TO USE THIS BOOK

How to Raise a Smarter Child by Kindergarten is divided into six parts.

Part I, "A Brief Window of Opportunity," describes the latest scientific breakthroughs in brain development and explains how you can use this information to help your child.

Part II, "Sharpening Your Child's Mind from Crib to Classroom," provides specific activities designed to build a better brain as well as offering guidelines for television, video games, and computers.

Part III, "Nutrition for a Smarter Brain," tells you everything you need to know about what to feed your child's developing brain to make it smarter.

Part IV, "Creating a Brain-Enhancing Environment for Your Child," alerts you to common toxins found in homes, schools, and playgrounds that can harm a developing brain, and tells you how to keep your children as toxin free as possible.

Part V, "The Brain–Body Connection," covers common medical procedures and conditions that can harm your child's brain. It includes chapters on asthma, ear infections, gluten sensitivity, snoring and sleep problems, head injuries, and vaccinations.

Part VI, "Fighting ADHD by Building a Better Brain," shows how to identify the risk factors for ADHD early, how to contain small problems before they become big ones, and what alternatives are available to the strong prescription medicine typically prescribed for this problem.

CHAPTER TWO

The First Thousand Days of Life

A Window of Opportunity for Your Child's Brain Development

Natalie's parents brought their 3½-year-old daughter to see me because they noticed that her mental development lagged behind that of her 5-year-old sister and 8-year-old brother. "By the time our other children were Natalie's age, they seemed to be more talkative and had better language skills," observed her mother. What particularly worried her was the fact that Natalie seemed less interested in reading and doing simple activities such as coloring or playing board games than her siblings.

Natalie's parents were terrified that I would detect a brain disorder or developmental delay in their daughter. And yet, upon examination, Natalie seemed quite normal. Her vision, hearing, physical coordination, and other functions of her brain were fine. So what, if anything, was holding Natalie back? When I asked Natalie a question, her answer—or lack of one—was quite revealing.

I asked Natalie, "What's your favorite book?" I was surprised when I got no response, only a blank stare. Upon further conversation with her parents, I learned that they regarded Natalie as a much "easier" child than their other two because she didn't need to be entertained. Natalie was content to spend much of her day watching TV or playing her siblings' video games.

No sooner had this information come to light than Natalie's mother added, "You know, when our other children were small, we used to read to them often, one on one. We've been so busy, we haven't done that for Natalie." I also learned that unlike her two siblings, who had been breast-fed for almost six months, Natalie was only breast-fed for 5 weeks, which meant she could be missing some important brain-building nutrients. I prescribed a nutritional supplement for Natalie to help enhance her brain development and compensate for her short time breast feeding. But nutrition alone could not solve Natalie's problem—Natalie's brain was craving positive stimulation from her parents. I told her parents about the importance of reading to children and engaging them in brain-building activities, particularly during the first five years of life. I recommended several books that were appropriate for Natalie and gave them a list of games to play with their daughter and other activities. Most importantly, I urged Natalie's parents to strictly limit her time watching TV and playing video games, which would force her to develop new interests.

Six months later, when I saw Natalie for a follow-up visit, the positive changes in this now 4-year-old were obvious. Her parents were overjoyed that her language skills had advanced considerably. What was even more exciting was her new interest in reading and in exploring books, and in activities such as coloring and finger painting. As her mother remarked, "Natalie's got an incredible imagination, but we never knew it."

Natalie's story underscores the importance of both nourishing and *nurturing* your child's brain during the first few years of life when the brain experiences its explosive growth spurt. How your child's brain develops during these early years will set the stage for all that transpires for the rest of his or her life.

The newborn brain must create the vast communication networks that enable the 100 billion neurons (brain cells) to talk to each other. Neurons communicate by forming connections called *synapses.* They send messages to each other by releasing chemicals called neurotransmitters that flow from one neuron to the next across their synaptic connection. Every activity that engages your brain involves the participation of millions of neurons chatting away with millions of other neurons via their synaptic connections.

Each neuron forms small branches called dendrites that allow for more surface area for synapse formation. The vast majority of dendrites—about 80 percent—are produced after birth. During the first three years the brain goes into overdrive, actually growing significantly more synapses than it will ever need. By the time your child is 3, his brain could have more than 100 trillion synapses. This is good because these connections are vital for future learning. Without enough synapses, neurons can't communicate quickly or effectively and mental activities that you take for granted, such as retrieving memories and processing new information, could not take place.

There is a downside to the excess production of synapses—it slows the brain down. Every bit of information that passes through a toddler's brain has to navigate through trillions of extra connections. Toddlers are notoriously slow to respond to verbal commands, such as "Pick up your toy," or "Get your jacket, we're going to the park." It's not that they're being contrary (at least not all the time!)—the reality is, their brains are bogged down by all those excess synapses. If you watch a 2-year-old's face, you can actually see him "thinking," trying to process information before he reacts.

PRUNING THE OVERGROWTH

If all those synapses were allowed to remain intact, the brain couldn't do its work well or efficiently. How do you create a highly functioning, streamlined, efficient brain out of this mass of synapses? How do you preserve the synapses that are important—the pathways to success—and dispose of the synapses that are just slowing the brain down?

When your garden is overgrown, you prune it, trimming back the excess foliage and weeds so that the other plants can thrive. At the same time, you have to fertilize and water the surviving plants or they will wither and die. Your child's brain is undergoing a similar process. As the brain is creating new synapses, it is simultaneously ridding itself of synapses it doesn't use in a process known as *synaptic pruning.* Synaptic pruning begins in the womb but rapidly accelerates after birth until age 2, slows down somewhat until age 6, and then picks up again until age 12. It continues, albeit at a slower pace, through the teen years. Synapses that are regularly used are nurtured and thrive, while the synapses that are underutilized wither away.

Synaptic pruning is critically important for brain development. It is not as much about losing synapses as it is about strengthening and building upon the ones that you already have. If a specific pathway is used a great deal, for example, if a child is stimulated by being exposed to new and interesting pictures, shapes, or words, or is engaged in conversation or listens to music, she will develop more synaptic connections to accommodate this information so she can retrieve it later.

Smarter Child Tip Repeated exposure to a particular experience is required to create a permanent connection. If early experiences are not reinforced, the pathways will weaken and the synapses will disappear. I know that many parents, myself included, have grown weary of reading the same book to their child over and over again and wonder why their child asks to hear it again and again. The answer is simple. Young children actually crave repetition because that's how they learn and that's how they strengthen their synaptic pathways.

PARENTS CAN MAKE A BETTER BRAIN

Parents can have a profound influence on the actual physical structure of their child's brain and, in turn, its functionality. Which synapses live and which synapses die is determined solely by experience and activity, and that can be in large part controlled by parents and caregivers. *As a parent, you have tremendous control over the activities and experiences to which your child is exposed, and therefore, you have considerable control over the process of synaptic pruning.* Although synaptic pruning will occur whether or not you participate in the process, without your help, the end result will be a less functional brain.

Children who are well nurtured and nourished and are given the appropriate mental and physical stimulation will develop strong neural connections that form the building blocks for higher learning. As you will learn, when you do the right things for your child's brain, you are actually turning on the genes that strengthen these precious neurons and the synaptic connections. You are literally turning on your child's smart genes. A wide array of sensory experiences will influence the development of these brain connections, including smell, sound, taste, sight, and touch. When you hug your child, talk to your child, read to your child, serve your child a tasty meal, sing to your child, play a memory game with your child, teach your child how to recognize different shapes and colors, or take your child to the playground, you are building pathways for success. The use of the synapse strengthens the synapse and allows it to survive.

If a child is stressed out, unhappy, understimulated, poorly nourished, or exposed to brain toxins in the environment, important neural connections will die, his brain will be less efficient, and simply stated, he will not be as smart.

WHAT MAKES A FASTER BRAIN

At the same time that the brain is forming vital neural pathways, it is undergoing another important process that can greatly enhance brain power—*myelination.* Myelin is a fatty substance that covers all the nerve cells in our body, including those in the brain, and functions like insulation wrapped around a wire. Myelin speeds up the transmission of electrical impulses through neurons. It makes for a faster, smarter, more responsive brain. And the lack of myelin is another reason why young children process information more slowly than older children and adults.

Myelination, like dendrite formation and synaptic pruning, begins in the womb but on a very limited basis. The brain stem (the lower portion of the brain that controls automatic functions such as breathing, swallowing, and the beating of the heart) and the spinal cord are both well developed by birth. If this didn't happen, the infant couldn't survive outside the womb. Over the next two years, myelin forms rapidly throughout the rest of the brain, first in the sensory part of the cortex that allows the newborn to respond to his or her environment and later in the more sophisticated areas of the cortex, the frontal lobes—also called the association areas—where information from various parts of the brain is analyzed in more complex ways. It is the later development of the association areas that ultimately allows us to be humans in terms of highly sophisticated mental activity. The thicker the frontal lobes, the smarter the brain.

Myelination also fine-tunes the nervous system, allowing for more sophisticated motor activity, from walking to running to being able to place your fingers in the right position to hold a crayon.

THE POWER OF A HUG

Two factors affect how fast and how well the brain lays down myelin: nurturing and nutrition. Research has shown that children who are hugged, kissed, and loved will actually make more myelin and that translates into a higher IQ. In one study, there was a remarkable enhancement of memory and early discrimination skills (the ability to recognize the differences between shapes and objects) in a full-term 4-month-old following an eight-minute massage. What is so intriguing about this finding is that early memory and sensory discrimination skills directly predict later IQ.

The best myelin is built from the best fat, and the best fat for this process is DHA (docosahexaenoic acid), which is found in the placenta and breast milk and is now added to most infant formula. DHA is an omega-3 long-chain polyunsaturated fat that represents up to 25 percent of the fat found in the brain. DHA is densely concentrated in the retina as well and is requisite for normal development of the brain and eyes. Several studies have linked DHA intake in babies to higher IQs and it is so important for brain development that I talk about it in more detail in Chapter 7, "Feeding the Newborn Brain for Optimal Performance." DHA is especially abundant in the cortex, which is responsible for higher functions such as learning, reasoning, and memory. By ensuring that their babies get an optimal amount of DHA, parents can enhance myelination and vastly improve the quality of their baby's brain.

YOUR BABY'S BRAIN

Newborns do things because they are programmed to do them, not because they are making thoughtful choices. Make a loud noise and a newborn will turn to see where the noise is coming from. Move an object directly in front of a newborn's eyes, and her eyes will follow the object. These are reflex activities. The infant is functioning on brain stem, or primitive brain, level because the more sophisticated parts of the brain are not yet plugged in for function.

The brain develops from the bottom up, meaning the lower, more primitive portions of the brain (the brain stem) develop earlier than the higher, more sophisticated brain areas such as the frontal lobe. Frontal lobe activity—the sophisticated, critical thinking and fine motor skills that are unique to humans—kicks in much later and continues to develop well into adolescence.

The regions of the brain that regulate higher brain activity in newborns are still undergoing basic development, including dendrite formation, synaptic pruning, and myelination. In contrast, the brain stem, located at the base of the brain, at the top of the spinal cord, is well developed at birth. The brain stem controls the autonomic nervous system, which includes essential functions such as breathing and heart beat regulation. It is also involved, along with another part of the brain (the limbic system), in regulating how the body responds to stress. The cerebellum, which lies on top of the brain stem, coordinates the body's movements. The cerebrum, above the cerebellum, is the largest part of the brain and consists of two structures or hemispheres, the right hemisphere and the left hemisphere. Each hemisphere is divided into frontal, parietal, occipital, and temporal lobes, and each is responsible for different aspects of mental and physical function.

EMOTIONS FIRST

The limbic area of the temporal lobes, known as the emotional center of the brain, is one of the first areas of the brain to develop. The limbic center triggers the release of stress hormones into the bloodstream when we are upset or perceive we are in danger. The ability to react quickly to danger is vital for survival. Our human ancestors couldn't have lasted very long if they weren't able to escape predators—but that same response can interfere with brain development.

The hippocampus, the memory center of the brain, so vital to learning, is also located in the limbic center. Once again, this makes sense for survival. It was necessary for our human ancestors to remember dangerous situations so they could avoid them. That's why memories are more deeply ingrained if accompanied by emotion, positive emotion being the most effective. If the brain is dealing with intense stress, it reverts back to the lower brain stem "fight or flight" response and cannot focus its energy on higher learning. You'll remember the feeling of fear and what made you scared, but you are in no frame of mind to focus on academic pursuits. That's why children who feel safe, happy, and well nurtured retain information better and do better at school than children who are under stress. And that's why it's so important for small children to perceive learning as an enjoyable experience filled with positive emotion.

The temporal lobes also house the hearing centers of the brain, which develop very early and are actually functional even before birth. That's why fetuses can hear sounds within the womb and are born with the ability to recognize their mother's voice. The occipital lobes are the vision centers of the brain; they interpret the images sent from the eyes via the optic nerve and develop rapidly after birth. The parietal lobes interpret sensory input and allow us to perceive pain and touch.

Much of childhood is devoted to growing the frontal lobes, which continue to mature and to be fine-tuned well into adulthood. By age 2, a child will have a basic understanding of symbols—that a written number may represent the number of candies in his hand. It will take years for the frontal lobes to mature to the point that a child can write a coherent essay drawing on information and experiences stored away in different parts of the brain, and perhaps decades before she can write a great novel.

THE BRAIN–BODY CONNECTION

We tend to think of the brain as the site of learning, intellect, and reason and forget the fact that it also controls all of our motor activities. Not surprisingly, there is a direct link between the physical and mental functions, especially when it comes to intelligence. At any age, physical activity improves brain power. In both children and adults, exercise directly turns on the smart genes that produce BDNF (brain-derived neurotrophic factor), the growth factor in the human brain that strengthens and enhances brain function and is involved in the formation of dendrites and synapses and in synaptic pruning. That's right, exercise not only strengthens your child's body, but her brain as well. So when you let your child crawl on the floor (in a childproof safe area) or take your toddler to the park and let her run around or push the merry-go-around, you are actually improving her mental skills. Allowing your child to constantly engage in sedentary activities, such as watching TV or playing video games, is going to impede her mental growth. It's up to parents to make sure that their young children get enough physical activity during this formative time.

The newborn is very limited in terms of motor activity, which develops slowly in comparison to other animals. Many animals can walk within a few hours of birth—not so humans. At birth, infant motor function is essentially reflex activity that is controlled by the primitive brain stem. When you stroke an infant's cheek, she will respond by turning her head and opening her mouth, known as the rooting reflex, which prepares her for a feeding. When there is a slight drop in an infant's head (which should always be supported) the infant responds with the Moro reflex, characterized by extension of the legs and outward flinging of the arms. This reflex likely serves to protect the infant should she be dropped.

The myelination of the motor pathways both to the motor cortex and to the more sophisticated areas of the brain that involve motor activity is not completed for several years. Myelination not only allows for more refined activity, but also speeds up transmission of signals between neurons, which explains why a baby's movements are typically slow throughout the first year of life.

If you watch your infant in the crib, you will see that much of his waking time is spent flailing around with his arms and legs. These are actually very important activities through which the infant is learning how to control his extremities. When these early flailing motor activities are integrated with vision as well as sensation, the infant learns, with practice, that he can control the placement of his hand into his mouth. Once the infant has mastered this feat of hand–eye coordination, he is ready to experiment with easy-to-reach (and child-safe) toys.

REACHING OUT

By about 4 months, an infant will be able to reach for an object and grab it, a major developmental milestone. That simple achievement teaches a baby that he has some control over his physical environment, another important life lesson. Activity boxes on the crib are a terrific way for an infant to integrate sensory stimulation (feeling the object) with auditory and visual stimulation.

As motor development is enhanced with time, at around 9 months to a year old, the child develops the pincer grasp, in which he can hold an object between his thumb and fingers. This, too, is a tremendous step that paves the way for fine motor activities such as writing, holding a fork, or manipulating a mouse. Fine motor activities develop slowly, and even at age 5, some kids may still struggle doing things such as tying their shoelaces or holding a pencil. There are games parents can play with their children that can help them develop these skills (see Chapter 3), but keep in mind that it may take some children longer than others, and that this is not a sign of lack of intelligence.

During the first year, major muscle groups in the trunk, arms, and legs undergo rapid development. By 6 months a child can usually sit up on her own; within 9 months or so she may begin to crawl, and by around a year or so she may stand up and take a few steps. Similar to adults, babies must exercise their muscles to achieve and maintain strength. When a baby is lying on her stomach and tries to push herself up, she is actually developing her arm muscles while at the same time strengthening her neck muscles as she moves her head from side to side. Unfortunately, infants spend very little time on their stomachs these days because sleeping in that position increases the risk of sudden infant death syndrome (SIDS.) Therefore, most parents are advised even before they leave the hospital not to allow their babies to sleep on their stomachs. Yet, depriving an infant of time lying on his stomach can delay his motor development. In a recent study in the *Journal of Pediatrics,* researchers found that specific motor milestones such as sitting, crawling, and pulling themselves up to a standing position were significantly delayed in infants who slept on their backs versus those who slept on their stomachs. Even though these babies eventually catch up, to me it's a sign that babies need to spend at least some waking time on their stomachs. That is why I recommend allowing your child to spend some time playing in the prone position. (See Chapter 3.)

Motor skills continue to develop throughout early childhood. By age 2, kids are typically able to run, climb onto and off of furniture, kick a ball, and walk up and down stairs with support.

By age 3, most kids can master riding a tricycle, bend over without falling, turn the pages of a book one at a time, and effectively hold a pencil.

By age 4, motor development has reached the stage where kids should be able to throw a ball overhand, hop on one foot, and even use a children's scissor. But again, all of these milestones are reached through experience and a rich nurturing environment.

BUILDING MEMORY

Memory is a fundamental component of all learning skills. Much like a computer, your child's brain must have the storage capacity to file experiences away so that he can draw upon them when needed, whether it is recognizing a face, remembering a word, or linking several sophisticated thoughts together to write a great essay for the SATs. Interestingly, research shows that a good memory during infancy is a powerful predictor of IQ at age 6. You may wonder how it is possible to measure memory in an infant. One interesting way to evaluate infant memory involves an assessment of what is termed "novelty preference," which measures the time it takes for an infant to become bored looking at a specific picture or object. In a laboratory setting, scientists show an infant a picture. After a minute or two, they place a second picture alongside the original one and measure the time it takes for the infant to focus on the second picture. The rationale behind the test is that an infant who has a good memory will quickly process the old picture and be ready to learn something new (the second picture) as opposed to the infant who isn't learning as quickly and still finds the original picture interesting. Studies have shown that infants with the best memory skills ultimately have the highest IQs. That's why I encourage parents to start memory-enhancing activities early on. (See Chapter 3.)

Infants need age-appropriate memory challenges to exercise their memory pathways. Subtle changes in their environment help enhance memory, forcing them to compare past memories to present memories. Every few days, change something else in your baby's room. Hang a new picture on the wall, or move a chair to a different position in the room. All of this helps to enhance infant memory.

At birth, infants have very basic memory skills. They can recognize that something is familiar when they see it, but to the best of our knowledge, they can't conjure up an image of a person or an object on their own. They'll recognize Mommy when she comes into the room, but we don't think that infants have the ability to wonder, "Where is Mommy?" We call this kind of transient memory *recognition memory.* Infants do not yet have long-term memory, which is why we as adults can't consciously remember experiences from infancy later in life. Psychoanalyst Sigmund Freud believed that we repress our memories of infancy, but recent breakthroughs in our knowledge of brain development have shown that the long-term memory pathways are not pruned or myelinated until around age 3½. In other words, until after age 3, we have no way to store memories.

MEMORY BREAKTHROUGH

At around 8 months, babies experience a major breakthrough in memory. They develop recall memory, that is, they can remember objects and people even when they're not there. That's why many babies at this age begin to show signs of separation anxiety when a parent leaves the room. For the first time, they are capable of remembering people even when they are not presently with them.

As the frontal cortex undergoes pruning and myelination, memory becomes more sophisticated. Exercises and activities that draw upon memory function will refine the efficiency and speed of those specific pathways. I'm not talking about mindless activities that require rote memorization and no thinking, but rather activities that require a child to make connections between one concept and another. (Many of the games that I describe in Chapter 3 will help enhance memory skills.)

At around 6 months, speak to your child about things that may have happened in the recent past, even though he does not have the language skills to respond to you. Ask questions such as "Where is your blanket?" and answer, "Your blanket is on the couch." By 1 year, challenge memory in a more complex way. Even though it may seem that you are having a one-way conversation, it is still very important to talk more extensively about the past, allowing the toddler to bring back mental images of previous events. "Remember yesterday when we were in the park and we saw the big dog?" "He was a big dog and what color was the big dog?" This interaction with your toddler requires that he recall a far more detailed account of his experience, being able to play back that memory in his mind and analyze it to come up with the answers. By 18 months, your child should be able to remember events that occurred up to several weeks in the past. Ask your child, "Do you remember your birthday party? Who was there?" By doing this, you are giving the memory pathways a good workout and are also building verbal skills.

Playing simple memory games with your child will continue to build and strengthen his brain's ability to restore and retrieve information, functions that essentially define the term *memory.*

At age 5, when your child's brain has reached its adult size, the process of synaptic pruning has slowed significantly. This is not to say that the brain is fully formed—far from it. The young brain still has a long way to go in terms of acquiring knowledge, as well as refining the way various brain areas communicate with each other. Your efforts during the first thousand days will help your child complete the task of creating a brain that is efficient, high capacity, and able to process information quickly, attributes that will give your child a meaningful advantage for the rest of his or her life.

PART II

SHARPENING YOUR CHILD'S MIND FROM CRIB TO CLASSROOM

CHAPTER THREE

Easy and Fun Activities to Build a Smarter Brain

I have designed some simple, yet highly effective brain-building activities for you to do with your children. Each activity will sharpen skills that are required for later academic achievement and ultimately create a smarter, faster brain. My goal is not to fill your child's head with a lot of facts—it is to expand her brain power and capacity. At this stage of your child's life, it is much more important that she learn *how* to think rather than *what* to think.

Although I recommend activities for different age groups, each child is an individual. If your child is not conforming precisely to my age recommendations, don't worry about it. Some children may move ahead faster on some activities, but need more time on others. Always let your child be your guide.

Many of these activities can be upgraded to grow with your child. For example, a simple card game you can start playing with your child at 18 months can be enhanced so that it is challenging enough for her when she is 5 years old and beyond. Children love the security of familiar surroundings and activities: They enjoy playing the same games over and over again through the years, which gets me to another point. Bigger, flashier, more expensive toys are not necessarily the best choices for your child's brain. The best toys are those that give your child an opportunity to initiate and create. Old-fashioned wooden blocks, jigsaw puzzles, and time-honored favorites such as board games and Tinkertoys provide more stimulation for a young brain than many of these high-tech, high-priced gimmicky toys. I may recommend that you purchase a specific toy that I think is exceptional; however, in most cases, you can use inexpensive materials and toys that you probably already have around the house. (For more information on my favorite toys for kids, see Appendix C, "Dr. Perlmutter's Picks.")

- These activities require parental interaction and *supervision.* In some cases, you will be using materials that your child should not have access to without an adult close by.
- Do these activities when your child is alert and rested, not when he is tired, hungry, or cranky.
- Turn off the TV and the radio. Background noise is very distracting to young children and interferes with their ability to focus on the task at hand.
- Your child will find most any new activity interesting, but will quickly become bored once he has mastered it. If he looks away or becomes fussy, it may be a sign that it's time to give him a new challenge. If you regain his interest with the new activity, you should continue to do it. If he is still looking bored, it's his way of telling you he's had enough for now. Give it a rest.
- Enjoy yourself. These activities are meant to be fun. Don't put pressure on yourself or your child. If your child appears not to be enjoying an activity, pick another one.
- It's great if you can work with your child every day for about a half an hour or so. If you miss a day or two, it's fine.
- Use your imagination. Feel free to embellish these activities or create some of your own with your child.

Where's Mommy? Where's Daddy?

Suggested Age Range: **Newborn to 6 months**
Goal: **Sharpens auditory discrimination skills**

Objective: Inside the protective world of the womb, the sounds of the outside world were muffled as the infant floated in the protective amniotic fluid that buffered loud or disturbing noises and kept background noise to a minimum. Now outside the womb, your infant is barraged with a world of intense sound coming from all directions. If the newborn could actually hear everything in his environment, his brain would be overwhelmed by all the stimulation. It's just not ready to take it all in. Your infant can only respond to loud noises, which means much of the background noise is selectively shut out. Over the next few months, the auditory centers of the brain undergo rapid synaptic pruning, which will fine-tune hearing. Your baby is not only able to hear more sounds, but is also better able to screen out background noise and can be more selective about what he consciously listens to. Newborns are most sensitive to low-pitched sounds, but by 3 months they are able to respond to higher-pitched sounds. Interestingly, even a newborn is able to locate where a sound is coming from and turn his head toward a sound stimulus. This ability dramatically improves during the first six months of life as the higher brain takes over and the baby integrates hearing with visual activity. For example, an infant hearing a barking dog will turn reflexively to where the sound is coming from. Eventually, he will learn that dogs make a barking sound, so when he hears barking, he will mentally visualize the image of a dog. At around 6 months, as his brain becomes more sophisticated, he will begin to think, "Gee, where is my dog?" and look for the dog even *before* the dog barks.

It's very difficult for a baby to pick out specific relevant sounds against background noise that is less important; therefore, speaking to your child and reading to your child should be carried out in an environment free of distracting background noise. It's great if a family eats dinner together, but if the TV is blaring, the child misses out on all the benefit of conversation and close family contact.

The auditory system needs the right kind of stimulation for optimal development. During the first year, it's important to provide a rich environment with respect to auditory stimulation by taking your baby out to see new things and hear new sounds.

Identify specific sounds for your child; point out the sound of birds chirping at the park, or the bell on the ice-cream truck, or even the annoying sound of a car horn. Let your child play with an activity box on his crib or playpen that gives off different sounds when he pushes the right buttons. Helping your child identify specific sounds helps improve his auditory discrimination skills, which sharpens his ability to discern the difference between sounds.

Activity: Even infants as young as 1 day old can recognize their mother's voice. It may take a bit longer for a baby to recognize his father's voice, but this is a great way to teach him.

Place your baby in her crib lying on her back. Stand at the side of her crib and keep calling her name. Your baby will soon "localize," which means she will turn her head and body in the direction of where you are standing.

After your baby has directed her attention to the side of the crib where you are standing, stop calling her name. Move to the other side of the crib. Begin calling her name again until she turns her attention toward you once again.

Don't overtire your baby! Repeat this game one or two times per side. Most babies will respond within a minute or two to hearing their names called unless they are very sleepy. (If you do this game over the course of several days and your baby doesn't appear to hear your voice, it could be an early sign of a hearing problem.)

Peek-a-Boo

***Suggested Age Range:* 3 to 6 months**
***Goal:* Strengthens memory, enhances auditory discrimination skills, teaches cause and effect**

Objective: Every culture has its version of "peek-a-boo," a game that not only delights your baby but challenges and strengthens her memory. This is a particularly good activity for infants, since they normally focus on faces.

This simple exercise helps refine your infant's ability to discern specific sounds and voices from background noise that can be ignored. It helps your baby focus on the specific sounds (phonemes) of her native language, which will sharpen her hearing and, later, improve her understanding of spoken language and enhance her verbal skills.

Activity: Stand next to your baby's crib. Smile at your baby and get her attention. When she is looking at your face, cover your face with a brightly colored pillow or cloth. Wait a few seconds and then uncover your face and say "peek-a-boo" in an animated, high-pitched voice. Your baby will smile when she sees your face.

As your baby begins to enjoy this activity, try asking, "Where's

Mommy?" (or "Where's Daddy?") when your face is covered and then "Here's Mommy!" when your face is uncovered. Enhance this game by moving the pillow or cloth from side to side and up and down when you reveal your face. Periodically change your position, moving to a different side of the crib. Play this game for a few minutes at a time and stop when your baby seems to lose interest.

Go to the Next Level

Activity: By 6 to 9 months, your baby will have the motor skills to actively participate in this game. With your baby sitting in his high chair, hold a cloth in front of your face within his reach. Again, ask the question, "Where's Mommy?" or "Where's Daddy?" This time, don't pull the cloth away yourself; wait for your child to do it for you. When he reaches for the cloth and can see you, say "Here's Mommy." From this simple and fun activity, you are teaching your baby the principles of cause and effect. He is learning that "If I pull the cloth away, I will see Mommy and she will say, 'Here's mommy.' " From that lesson he is also learning that he is capable of manipulating his environment. It is through these activities that your child begins to understand the physical world. It's his first lesson in physics. This will also serve him well in behavioral areas. He will soon understand that if he behaves a certain way, people will do specific things, such as pick him up if he cries or smile back if he coos.

Mobile Play

Suggested Age Range: **Newborn to 6 months**
Goal: **Improves visual discrimination skills, early introduction to colors and shapes**

Objective: We hang mobiles over a baby's crib for all the right reasons: Mobiles are, by definition, "mobile." They are constantly in motion, which is wonderful for the development of visual-motor skills. When a baby looks at a mobile, she is learning how to control where she directs her gaze to focus on objects of interest. She is learning how to visually pursue objects as they move as well as how to keep her gaze fixed upon a particular object even though her head may be moving. She is also honing her visual discrimination skills, learning how to appreciate differences in physical characteristics such as shape, size, and color. The many shapes that comprise a mobile also enhance your baby's perceptions of comparing and contrasting, two skills that are essential for nearly every mental exercise, including the ability to recognize the subtle differences between words, colors, sounds, and faces.

Activity: The best mobiles consist of several brightly colored objects of varying shapes and sizes, with each object hanging freely. You can greatly enhance the benefit of the mobile by gently blowing on it, moving it with your hand, or turning off all the lights in the room and shining a flashlight on it. Babies find these activities to be very exciting, as not only do they see the mobile in a new "light," but they are also fascinated by the shadows that are created on the ceiling, especially if the light is directed from underneath the mobile. Some mobiles have built-in music boxes, which not only adds to their entertainment value but also stimulates auditory pathways.

Activity: Here's another simple activity that turns a mobile into a powerful learning tool, giving your baby her first experiences with actually manipulating her environment. Take a piece of ribbon (around thirty to thirty-six inches long) and tie one end gently around your baby's ankle or wrist. Tie the other end to an object on your baby's mobile, or perhaps to a bell or chime hanging over the mobile. Be careful that the ribbon doesn't restrict your baby's arms or wrist movements and is not tied too tightly. And always keep a careful eye on your child while you are playing this game. When your child moves her arm or leg, she will cause the mobile to move. If the ribbon is attached to a chime or bell, she will also hear a sound. Your baby will be fascinated by this activity and will soon learn that the movement of the arm or leg activates the mobile. This is fundamentally important in that your child is learning about cause and effect and the manipulation of her environment. When your child shows signs of boredom (she stops playing with the mobile), remove the ribbon and let her rest or move on to another activity.

When you play this game again, tie the ribbon on the same wrist or leg for the next three or four days. As your baby learns to manipulate the mobile and seems to lose interest, it's time to switch to the other side or other extremity.

Caution: Never leave your child unattended with the ribbon attachment.

Activity: Wrist or ankle rattles (soft bands that can be attached to the wrist or ankle with velcro closures) are great toys for this age group and can be purchased at most toy stores. By wearing the rattle on her wrist or leg, your baby quickly learns that shaking her arm or leg can produce a sound, and again she is learning an important lesson about manipulating her environment. Start by putting the rattle on her wrist and then after a few days, switch to the other wrist. When your baby appears to lose interest in the wrist rattle, move the rattle to her ankle and then alternate legs every few days.

Encouraging Manipulative Play

***Suggested Age Range:* 3 to 6 months**
***Goal:* Improves hand–eye coordination**

Objective: At around 3 months, your baby will have developed sufficient motor skills to actually play with objects. By now he is well attuned to the concept of manipulating his environment, having learned how to create sounds with his wrist or feet by wearing rattles or manipulating his mobile. Your baby is now ready to actively manipulate toys of various sizes and textures. When your child plays with these objects, feeling them, rolling them around, and learning how they behave based upon how he treats them, these actions are called *manipulative activities.* It is through manipulative activities that your child gains his early knowledge of the physical aspects of the world through interaction with such simple things as blocks, balls, and variously shaped objects. These activities provide early experience understanding physical relationships, paving the way to understanding concepts like size comparison, a fundamental building block for math skills.

Activity: Place your baby on the floor on his stomach and allow him to "explore" the toys, reaching for them as he scoots around the floor. Place three or four soft toys on the floor, such as a soft ball, a few soft blocks, or small stuffed animals. Use soft, cushiony toys that are small and light enough to be held in your baby's hands and can be easily gripped. Be sure that the toys do not have any sharp edges or small pieces that your baby could choke on. Don't hand him the toys! Allow him to reach for them himself—this helps enhance both balance and hand–eye coordination. As noted in Chapter 2, parents are instructed to have their babies sleep on their backs to prevent SIDS. Yet studies show that babies who don't spend any time lying on their stomachs may show delays in crawling or walking. Do allow your child to have some supervised play time on his stomach to promote good motor development. If your baby should fall asleep on his stomach, immediately turn him over onto his back.

After giving him ten or fifteen minutes of play time on his stomach, turn your child over so that he is lying on his back. Your 3- to 6-month-old will especially enjoy lying on his back, where he can actually pick up the toys and observe them from various angles.

Smarter Child Tip When your child has had enough time playing on his own, sit on the floor and support your baby, allowing him to sit up and reach for the toys. Your baby will be mastering the skill of transferring an object from one hand to another, which helps develop dexterity and coordination. You can help this along by taking his empty hand and putting it on the object held in the other hand. Your baby will eventually get the message that this is a good thing to do and will practice it on his own.

Tracking an Object

Suggested Age Range: **3 to 6 months**
Goal: **Helps build and reinforce the neural pathways involved in memory, develops early number skills, improves discrimination skills**

Objective: When an infant first opens her eyes, her view of the world is quite different from what it will be by her first birthday. At birth, infants have difficulty focusing on objects and see things best if they are held eight to twelve inches away from their faces. It is difficult for them to discern shapes or borders, while at the same time they are attracted to oval shapes such as the human face. For the most part, they can only see bright, primary colors and their peripheral vision is more developed than their central vision. Infants can perceive moving objects better than objects at rest, which is why they enjoy looking at their mobiles—to them it's the best view in the house. During the first year, the world comes into focus very quickly as vision skills mature rapidly.

Vision develops at a very rapid rate following birth; by the end of the first year, most of the important aspects of vision are in place. Refinement of vision, like any other brain function, depends upon the process of synaptic pruning. If the neural pathways for vision (located in the occipital cortex area of the brain) are not stimulated early and often, vision cannot develop normally even if there is nothing structurally wrong with the eye or optic nerve. Although it's rare, children can be born with cataracts, a condition we normally associate with aging. Cataracts, an opaque covering that forms on the lens of one or both eyes, can interfere with vision, especially in a baby whose vision is just developing. At one time, it was standard procedure to wait until these children were 2 years old to surgically remove the cataracts, but now the operation is performed as early as possible, usually within the first few months. The delay in restoring normal visual stimulation resulted in severe and permanent vision problems down the road. And when you lose vision, you lose much more than the ability to see. So much of early learning experience happens through our eyes. Vision is critical for reading and math skills, hand–eye coordination, spatial orientation, and depth perception.

At about 6 months of age, the control of eye movements shifts from a brain-stem reflex activity to a more sophisticated type of control coming from higher brain centers. From that point on, the infant gains volitional control over where he looks as opposed to having the eyes move simply as a reflex. What is important about this change is that it signals a major leap in memory function. The eyes are now under direct control to scan an object of interest, and that visual information is then compared to memories of previous visual experiences. This is how we make new memories as well as reinforce old memories, beginning the lifelong process of comparing and contrasting, the fundamental activity involved in learning.

Until around 6 months, your baby is unable to imagine an object and then seek it out. Basically, at 3 months, it's "out of sight, out of mind." The baby mind is incapable of thinking, "Where is my teddy bear? My teddy bear is always on the bookshelf, so if I look at the bookshelf I'll see my teddy bear." Although this seems ridiculously simple to the adult mind, the task of locating the teddy bear requires a fairly sophisticated thought process: (1) Your baby must remember that the object exists in the first place. This means that she needs to have the memory of the teddy bear stored away in her mind where she can retrieve it at will; (2) she needs to remember where the teddy bear is located and she must be able to retrieve that information as well; (3) she must coordinate all this information to carry out the purposeful act of directing her eyes to where she expects to find her teddy bear. This seemingly simple task is really quite sophisticated!

This simple exercise teaches infants how to direct their vision when appropriately stimulated.

Activity: For this game, you will need three brightly colored blocks and balls around three inches in size. (Remember that your infant can see primary colors the best, such as red, yellow, and blue.)

Place your face about two feet away from your baby's face. Smile! Babies are programmed to understand human expressions. Your smile (and relaxed attitude) will signal to your baby that this "face time" together will be fun.

Hold one ball or block in the middle of your baby's field of vision, around ten inches away from his face. Let your baby focus on the object for a few seconds. Then, slowly move the object about six inches down and to the left. Your baby will notice that the object is no longer where it was before and will look around until he finds it again.

After your baby finds the object in its new location, give him a few seconds to focus on it and then move it about six inches down and to the right and wait for him to find it again. Once your baby has relocated the object, let him focus on it and then move it up six inches to the upper left side. The point is to continue moving the object to the left, right, up, and down, each time allowing your baby to find it in its new location.

Go to the Next Level

Activity: Initially, this game is going to be fun for your baby, but after she masters it, she will quickly become bored and start looking away. To keep her interest, vary the object (switch from a ball to a block) or use a different-colored object. Once your baby shows signs of boredom, introduce two of the same objects into her field of vision, such as two blocks or two balls of the same color. Having to track two objects will be a greater challenge, and therefore more interesting for your baby. Eventually, when she gets bored you can vary the exercise by choosing two of the same objects but of different colors (for example, one red ball and one yellow ball). When she gets bored with that you can use two different shapes in the same color (like a red square and a red ball), and for an even greater challenge, switch to a ball and a square of two different colors.

Smarter Child Tip Every time you make a subtle change in the exercise above, you are enhancing your baby's discrimination skills, the fundamental building blocks for intelligence. These skills are needed to differentiate shapes and sizes of objects, letters, and numbers.

Puzzles

***Suggested Age Range:* 12 months to 3 years**
***Goal:* Develops hand–eye coordination**

Objective: Puzzles are a terrific teaching tool, helping children better understand spatial relationships, improve hand–eye coordination, enhance fine motor skills, and help develop basic math skills. Although children can do puzzles independently and should be encouraged to do so, the experience can be vastly enhanced under the direction of an adult.

Activity: Start your child out with a few simple, wooden jigsaw puzzles designed for ages 12 to 18 months. Puzzles for beginners should be easy to do and fairly obvious. Stick to puzzles that have no more than four pieces and have simple designs of familiar objects, such as food, animals, cars, or airplanes. As your child becomes more proficient at putting together simple puzzles, gradually move him up to more intricate puzzles with more pieces. Once again, follow your child's cue. Don't push him forward if he's not ready and don't make him do a puzzle that he finds boring. Some puzzles also include sound effects. For example, if the puzzle piece is a picture of a cow, when the piece is inserted back into its correct position, it makes a mooing sound. The integration of sound in puzzles is a great way to maintain a child's interest as well as stimulate the auditory areas of the brain to enhance learning. As your child gets older, puzzles containing more abstract concepts such as numbers and letters will create the ideal foundation for early math and literacy skills.

Don't expect your child to instinctively know what to do with a bunch of puzzle pieces. Start by showing him the intact puzzle. If it's a picture puzzle, ask him, "What is this puzzle supposed to be?" At 12 months, he's not going to be able to answer verbally, so you can answer for him. "It's a picture of a cow." Then ask him, "How many pieces are in this puzzle?" Take out all the pieces, show each piece to your child, tell him the correct number ("This puzzle has four pieces"), and put them back where they belong. Now remove one piece from the puzzle. Hand him the piece and let him figure out how to put it back. You can assist him by moving the piece near to where it belongs and letting him figure out the rest. If your child is having difficulty, patiently show him how to put the piece back and then let him try it again. Let your child master each puzzle piece individually before you take the puzzle completely apart for him to put back together.

Activity: Once your child has mastered putting the four pieces together, increase the challenge by turning the puzzle upside down. This early geometry lesson will help your child better understand how the different shapes fit together.

Activity: As your child becomes more skillful and is thoroughly familiar with two puzzles, mix it up, literally. Remove the pieces from two different puzzles (use puzzles with no more than four pieces), mix them up, and let your child try to sort through the pieces and put both puzzles together. Be sure to choose two puzzles that have very different shapes and pictures so that your child can clearly see the difference between the two.

Smarter Child Tip Numerical puzzles with pieces shaped as numbers are a useful tool for teaching counting. Puzzles containing the numbers 1 to 10 provide a wonderful way for children to experience the "feel" qualities of numbers, further ingraining the picture of the number into their minds. You can further enhance this experience by showing your child what a particular number represents. For example, when your child puts the number 2 back into the puzzle, hand him two small balls and say, "Two." Every time your child puts back another puzzle piece, add another ball to his collection until he has put in the last piece and completed the puzzle. This activity paves the way for early recognition of the symbolic nature of numbers and is far superior to simply teaching a child to memorize how to count from one to ten.

Go to the Next Level

Activity: 2½- to 3-year-olds are ready for more complicated puzzles with interesting pictures. To add to the creative challenge, encourage your child to make up a story about what is happening in the puzzle picture that she is putting together. Get your child started by asking something about the puzzle, such as, "Why is the little girl tasting the porridge?" or "Why are all those animals in the boat?" Having your child participate in making up a story is a terrific way to encourage the imaginative play that starts about this age and is so critical for developing the portions of the brain involved in more sophisticated functions.

Card Game

***Suggested Age Range:* 12 to 18 Months**
***Goal:* Teaches colors and shapes**

Objective: In working with children over the past twenty years, I have found that this simple card game is an effective and enjoyable way to strengthen a child's memory while at the same time enhancing the discrimination skills so fundamental for recognizing numbers and letters. What's nice about this exercise is that it doesn't require any expensive toys or software. Your only investment is a pack of file cards and some nontoxic markers.

Activity: For this activity, you will need one pack of unlined three-by-five file cards and six brightly colored nontoxic markers. Take three file cards. On one file card, make a red circle. On the second file card, make a yellow circle, and on the third card, a blue circle.

With your child seated in his high chair, show him the red card and then say, "Red." Then show him the yellow card and say, "Yellow." Then put both cards upside down on his high chair, covering the pictures. Ask him, "Where is the red circle?" and then turn over the card with the red circle, show it to him and say with enthusiasm, "Here's the red circle!" Ask him, "Where is the yellow circle?" and then turn over the card with the yellow circle, show it to him and say with enthusiasm, "Here is the yellow circle!"

Continue with the game until it appears that your child is indicating with his hands which card you should turn over. It is critically important that you avoid repeating this to the point of boredom. Stop the game while your child is still showing interest—a few minutes is more than enough time for most children. This way, your child will look forward to the next time you take out the cards, not dread it as a stressful time.

After your child is familiar with the red and yellow circles, substitute the card with the blue circle for either the red card or the yellow card so that your child must now learn a new color but is still playing with one familiar card. Start the new game with the blue card. Show your child the blue card and say, "Blue." Put the blue card face down on the high chair. Then repeat the exercise exactly as you did it before with either the yellow or red card. Even though your child may know what the yellow or red card looks like, you still need to identify it as "Red" or "Yellow" before you turn it face down. Once your child has learned to identify and point out the blue card, mix it up again. Keep the blue card in play, substitute the remaining card for the card with the different-color circle. Keep mixing up the three cards until your child has learned this game.

If he doesn't get it right away, be patient, he will eventually ace this card game. But there's a more valuable lesson to learn. You must let your child know early on that it's okay to make a mistake. Kids who are afraid to make mistakes will not develop into creative thinkers who take intellectual risks and will avoid rather than embrace challenging situations.

Smarter Child Tip The card game can grow with your child, helping to improve early mathematical and literacy skills. As your child becomes familiar with colors and shapes, you can gradually introduce cards with numbers and letters. For example, once your child can discern the difference between a circle and a triangle, he will notice that the letters *C* and *V* have different shapes, as do the numbers 3 and 4. This is a much stronger way to reinforce basic skills than simply having your child memorize his ABCs, or how to count to ten.

Go to the Next Level

Activity: Once your child has mastered the three cards with different-colored circles, you can vary this game by introducing new cards with different shapes and colors. Take three blank file cards; on the first card, draw a red square, on the second card a blue square, and on the third a yellow square. Take three more blank file cards and on the first card, draw a red triangle, on the second card a blue triangle, and on the third a yellow triangle. Add these cards to your three circle cards. You now have nine cards in play.

Select two cards of the *same color,* but *different shapes*—one circle and one square. Show your child the card with the circle and say, "Circle," before putting it face up on the high chair so that the picture is visible. Then show your child the card with the square and say, "Square," before putting it face up on the high chair so that the picture is visible. With both cards facing your child, ask him, "Where is the circle?" If he gets it right, praise him by saying, "Yes! That's the circle!" If he guesses wrong, say, "No, that's the *square.*" Once again, point out the circle card and the square card and ask him again to find the square. After another try or two, he'll get it.

As your child improves his performance, this game can be modified by adding a triangle card. But don't add the new shape with two other shapes on the table—three shapes are too much for your child to keep track of right now. It's best to introduce the triangle with a square of the same color since the square is a similar shape. Although your child won't understand on a mathematical level that a triangle has one less side than a square, he none the less will recognize the difference in the shapes and this will hone his discrimination skills. And one day, when it's time to learn geometry, these neural connections created during his early years will kick in and your child will be well prepared for the challenge.

Grab Bag

Suggested Age Range: **18 months to 4 years**
Goal: **Enhances sense of touch, teaches the brain to think in 3-D**

Objective: Children learn best when they can engage all their senses: vision, hearing, smell, taste, and especially touch. Unfortunately, most formal learning activities involve hearing and sight but ignore the other senses, especially touch. This activity challenges children to use their sense of touch, which stimulates new neural pathways in the brain and teaches them to appreciate the physical differences among objects. The point of this exercise is to teach children to identify a shape, number, or letter by touch alone. When asked to find an object solely by touch, the child first conjures the image of the object. Then, she asks herself, "What would the object feel like?" This strengthens and facilitates the brain pathways connecting visual memory areas with those areas involved in interpreting touch sensation.

Activity: For the "grab bag" exercise, use a soft, small fabric bag or small pillowcase. The first step is to teach your child the rules of the game. Show your child a small rubber ball and put it in the bag. Then ask your child to put her hand in the bag and tell you what she is feeling. Don't let her look inside the bag. Depending on how verbal your child is, she will either say, "Ball" or make a sound similar to *ball.* You can help out and say, "Do you feel the ball?" After your child has retrieved the ball, put the ball back in the bag. Show your child one of her building blocks and let her see you put it in the bag along with the ball. Then ask your child to put her hand in the bag and ask her what she is feeling. She will try to say, "Block," but if she's not yet verbal, you can help her by saying it for her. Now ask your child to find the specific object: "Where's the ball?" Repeat the exercise several times until your child fully understands the game. When your child understands how to play the game, you can increase the challenge by adding different objects to the bag with different shapes, sizes, or even textures. For example, you can put a hard rubber ball in the bag along with a soft ball and ask your child to retrieve the soft ball. Or you can put a big plastic cup in the bag along with a smaller cup and ask your child to retrieve the bigger cup, or you can put a triangle and a square in the bag and ask her to pick out one of the shapes.

Go to the Next Level

Activity: Once your child starts to play with wooden numbers and letters, you can put them in the bag as well. First, make it easy by having two objects that are markedly different from each other. For example, put a ball and a wooden number 2 in the bag and ask your child to find the number. Once your child is able to feel the difference between the number and the ball, further refine the exercise by putting one number and one letter in the bag and asking her to retrieve the number. When your child becomes adept at distinguishing the numbers from the letters, increase the challenge by putting two letters or two numbers in the bag and asking her to pick a particular number or letter.

Go to the Next Level

Activity: At around age 2½ or 3, instead of just asking your child to find a particular letter, ask her to find the first letter of a particular word, for example, ask her to pull the letter that the word "bear" starts with. You can remind her of the "buh" sound in the word "bear." If you have been working with your child on phonics while you are reading together, your child should be able to recognize that the "buh" sound belongs to the letter *B* and pull the *B* out of the bag. As your child's literacy skills get stronger, you can put up to seven letters in the bag and ask her to spell and find the letters for entire words, such as "cat," "bat," and other simple words with which she is familiar.

Memory Builder

Suggested Age Range: **18 months to 5 years**
Goal: **Sharpens memory and concentration**

Objective: This is a great way to enhance memory skills and to teach children how to stay focused on a task. You can start playing a simplified version of this game with a child as young as 18 months and continue playing a more sophisticated variety throughout grade school.

When your child is young, you can play this game with the file cards from the previous card game. By age 4, you may be able to switch to a real deck of cards.

Activity: Go through your deck of file cards and pull out six squares, two of each color, for a total of three matching pairs. Place all the cards face down (with the blank side up) on your child's play table or high chair. Ask your child to turn over one of the cards so you can both see the colored square and place it back in its original spot among the other cards. Be sure to identify the color and the shape. For example, if your child turns over a blue square, be sure to say, "That's a blue square." Then ask your child to find another blue square among the remaining cards. Your child will pick another card out and turn it over. If it's a blue square, get excited and tell him, "Good job." Let him keep the cards. If the colors don't match, identify the color of the card that he picked ("No, that's green") and let him pick again until he finds the blue card. Once he understands how to play the game, turn the cards face down after each use. This will force him to remember which card is which and where they are located.

By age 4½ or 5, you can introduce a real deck of cards and your child can play the memory game matching cards by number.

Smarter Child Tip The game becomes a much more powerful teaching tool if it is interactive. When your child fully understands the game, it's more fun if you take a turn and then let him take a turn. You can add to the challenge by adding more cards, mixing up shapes (using cards with circles, squares, and triangles), and eventually adding pairs of cards with numbers and letters.

Stacking and Sorting Games

***Suggested Age Range:* 9 months to 2 years**
***Goal:* Enhances hand–eye coordination, reinforces the concepts of "bigger than" and "smaller than," teaches child about visual-spatial relationships**

Objective: At 9 months, your baby is ready for simple stacking games, which form the foundation for understanding spatial relationships, counting, and geometry. Begin with very easy stacking games so your child can learn the basics: how to stack one object on or into another. By the time your child is 3, she may be making intricate designs with building blocks or Legos.

You can play these games with an assortment of stacking toys suitable for your child's age (such as rings and a peg) and other materials you have around the house including plastic measuring cups, attached measuring spoons, and a set of plastic "nesting" cooking bowls. Children 12 to 15 months old are ready to play with wooden or plastic building block sets, such as Lego's Duplo building blocks, Lego baby blocks, and Small World Toys building blocks, which are designed to be safe for this age group.

Activity: At 9 months, children enjoy playing with the same classic stacking toy that you probably played with yourself: plastic rings that fit on a peg. The rings are typically different sizes and are supposed to be stacked from largest to smallest, but in reality, they can fit on the peg in any order. I know that this may look really simple to an adult, but don't expect your child to know how to do this on her own. It's not intuitive. Initially, you will have to show your child how to stack the rings one on top of the other. At the same time, reinforce the concept of big and small by saying "Big" when you're holding the big ring and "Small" when you're holding the small ring. When your child does this herself, she may not stack the rings correctly, but it doesn't matter. When she's finished, tell her she's done a great job anyway. Make sure that she feels you approve of what she's doing. You can then show her another way to stack the rings, this time in the right order, and point out the small and large rings. Some kids will catch on at this point, others won't. But don't make a big deal out of it. You don't want to make your child so fearful of trying something new that she loses her adventurous spirit. In the long run, taking intellectual risks is what makes someone smart and a great student. When your child loses interest in stacking the rings, put the toy away and let her do something else.

Activity: This is a great high chair activity; your child can do it while you're in the kitchen so you can keep an eye on her while you prepare a meal. By 12 to 14 months, your child will be ready for playing with "nesting cups" in which a series of smaller cups are put into one large cup. Working with nesting cups represents a big leap from simply stacking rings because the rings can fit over the peg in any order, but the cups have to be stacked in precisely the right order or they won't fit together. When using nesting cups, start with just two or three so your child learns the basic concept that the small cups go into the big cup. Nesting cups usually come in different colors, which provides a wonderful opportunity to teach your child how to identify colors in the real world, not just in picture books. If you are showing your child the small yellow cup, be sure to identify it for her, as "small" and "yellow." When your child has mastered using two cups, add a third and so on until you have given her the entire set to work with. When your child has completed the entire set of nesting cups and is showing signs of boredom, change the exercise by giving her a set of colorful plastic cooking bowls that can be stacked according to size or a set of plastic measuring cups or measuring spoons. This will give her an opportunity to try her new skills out on different objects.

Go to the Next Level

Activity: Building blocks take stacking exercises to a whole new level. The sky's the limit—literally. By around age 12 to 18 months, children should be encouraged to play with simple blocks, learning how to stack one on top of the other. Be sure that the blocks are easy to hold and small enough to fit into a toddler's small hands. (But not so small that they can be swallowed!) As children naturally have a tendency to put everything in their mouths, it goes without saying that you must keep a careful eye on children at this age. Most kids at this point are somewhat clumsy and uncoordinated: it's difficult for them to stack the blocks neatly enough so that they don't fall down. Lego baby blocks (which snap together) are great because they are easy to manipulate and designed specifically for ages 1 and up. Duplo blocks also snap together and are good for kids 18 months and older. Old-fashioned wooden or plastic building blocks are also good for kids, but are somewhat harder to use for toddlers because they require more manual dexterity and coordination to keep them in place. Just because they are more challenging doesn't mean that children shouldn't use them, especially if they enjoy playing with them. Encourage your child to keep going and not get discouraged if he doesn't get it right away. This activity is a wonderful way to build hand–eye coordination and fine motor skills. Use block building as an opportunity to reinforce numbers. Every time your child completes a block tower, count up the number of blocks in his stack. Ask him if it's more than or less than the number of blocks he stacked last time. Once again, the process of actually *feeling* the number of blocks helps reinforce the concept of numbers as symbols. It also helps to send a message that math is fun.

Mix It Up

***Suggested Age Range:* 2 to 5 years**
***Goal:* Strengthens memory and counting skills**

Objective: This simple exercise helps hone memory and counting skills. It also trains your child to recognize letters, shapes, and numbers. For this activity, you will need random pieces from puzzles—all shapes, all sizes. Don't throw a puzzle out just because it's missing a few pieces. Put the remaining pieces in a designated "puzzle box" and save them for this game.

Activity: Begin the game by placing two or three pieces from the puzzle box on your child's play table. Be sure that each piece is a clearly identifiable object, letter, or number (such as a flower, the letter *A*, or the number "3"). The pieces don't have to be from the same puzzle. Let your child look at them and ask him, "How many pieces are there?" Then you say, "There are two pieces," and show your child the puzzle pieces, identifying each one clearly. "This is a red flower," "This is the letter *A*," and so on. Cover the pieces with a "magic cloth"—you can use a brightly colored piece of fabric to add interest to the game, but you can also use a dish towel. When you cover the puzzle pieces, discreetly remove one of them. Then, with great fanfare, uncover the puzzle pieces and ask your child, "How many pieces do we have now?" If your child answers correctly, say, "Yes, you're right"; if not, tell him the right answer. Then say, "What do we have here now?" and point to the remaining object(s) and identify them once again. Then ask your child, "What piece is missing?" and if he guesses it, you can show it to him.

When your child has mastered two objects, you can add a third and then a fourth. Older kids (those over 4) may be able to track five or even six objects. By varying the number and type of puzzle pieces, you can enhance the learning experience and keep it interesting for your child.

Go to the Next Level

Activity: When your child becomes proficient at counting up the pieces and identifying the objects, he's ready for a new challenge. Instead of removing a puzzle piece and asking your child to identify what's missing, as you cover the pieces with the cloth, discreetly *add a new piece* to the other puzzle pieces. When you remove the cloth, ask your child, "What's new?" and when he identifies the new piece, ask him, "How many do we have now?"

Through the years, you can adapt this game to accommodate your child's new skills and interests. Mix some interesting items with the puzzle pieces, including a photograph of your child or other family members, or even real-life objects like pieces of fruit or a small toy. By the time your child turns 5, you can add word cards to the puzzle box, reinforcing words that he has already learned to read.

Crafts Projects

***Suggested Age Range:* 12 months to 3 years**

***Goal:* Exercises fine motor skills, improves manual dexterity and understanding of visual-spatial relationships**

Objective: The areas of the brain that control fine motor movements are among the slowest to develop, which is why toddlers have difficulty doing simple tasks that require manual dexterity such as holding a fork, writing with a pencil, tying a shoelace, or trying to use a telephone keypad. The problem is, toddlers have very few opportunities to practice their fine motor skills. Vigilant parents keep very small items out of their children's reach for fear that their children might swallow them—which is absolutely the right thing to do but has consequences in terms of physical development. Moreover, many of the basic "hands on" activities such as old-fashioned games like stringing beads or playing marbles have been overshadowed by high-tech electronic handheld toys or computer games that offer little in terms of developing fine motor skills. Many children are no longer creating art projects with crayons and paint. They are following computer programs, using a mouse instead of a paintbrush. I wonder how many parents give their children these toys not only to keep them entertained, but also because they don't have to worry about their children choking on them or making a mess! So what's a parent to do? There are safe, easy ways to encourage your child to practice the skills that stimulate development of the fine motor pathways in the brain.

Activity: While your 9-month-old is sitting at her high chair, here's a great way to help improve her manual dexterity as well as hone her counting skills. The best part is, if she eats the game, that's fine too. Put a bunch of cooked peas and sliced carrots (diced small enough for her to put in her mouth without choking) on the top of her high chair. Be sure that the peas and carrots are cooked until they are tender. Show your toddler how to separate the peas from the carrots by picking up each pea and carrot separately. Count with her as she moves each pea and carrot. This activity will not be easy for your toddler and she will be working hard to keep her fingers in the correct position.

Activity: By 1 year, children should be given an opportunity to manipulate small objects under parental supervision. You must watch your child carefully while doing this activity. Gather up about ten or so colorful objects such as medium- and large-sized buttons and keep them in a closed container away from your child. (You don't want her doing this herself.) Try to pick colorful, interesting-looking buttons. When you're ready to play with your child, get the container and empty it onto her play table. Ask her to pick up each object individually and put it back in the bowl as you count up the total number of buttons. This is not only a good exercise for manual dexterity but helps teach counting skills. Again, keep in mind that this is a supervised activity, as buttons and other small objects (smaller than 1¾ inches) represent choking hazards.

Smarter Child Tip At around a year old, many children will be ready to hold a crayon and at least scrawl with it if not color. Please encourage your child to do this! This is an opportunity for her to practice the fine motor skills she will need for writing letters.

Go to the Next Level

Activity: At around 18 to 24 months children are ready to do basic craft projects that require fine motor skills. At this point, your child is able to grasp objects between his thumb and forefinger (known as the pincer grasp, which usually develops by 12 to 16 months). Stringing beads is great because it not only promotes manual dexterity but requires staying on task to complete the job. When you purchase a craft kit, be sure it is designed for the appropriate age group. Stringing beads is a great way to develop hand–eye coordination, but beads should be large enough so the child can handle them (around 1¾ to 2 inches in diameter). Supervise your child when handling small objects such as beads, especially if he has a tendency to put things in his mouth.

Go to the Next Level

Activity: Age 2½ to 3 is a great time to introduce your child to Play-Doh, which not only stimulates fine motor skills but encourages children to use their imagination. There are so many ways to have fun with Play-Doh. Children can create objects by manipulating the Play-Doh with their hands or they can incorporate tools such as flat wooden sticks to cut the Play-Doh, as well as rolling pins to roll it out and molds to make special designs such as animal shapes, letters, or numbers. Play-Doh is also a terrific tool for teaching colors: combining two colors, such as red and blue to make purple, or blue and yellow to make green, is a fascinating experience for your small child.

Go to the Next Level

Activity: By age 3, your child's hand–eye coordination and manipulative skills should have advanced to the point that she is ready to create more intricate building designs. There is no better activity for this stage of development than the old-fashioned Tinkertoy construction set, which consists of wooden dowels and connectors with plastic pieces that can be put together to make different objects. Tinkertoys are a wonderful way to enhance a child's visual-spatial skills as well as further hone fine motor movements. Challenge your child to use her imagination when playing with Tinkertoys by asking her to create familiar objects such as a house or airplane, as well as structures with moving parts such as a windmill or wagon.

Imaginative Play

***Suggested Age Range:* 2½ to 5 years**
***Goal:* Teaches concept of symbolism**

Objective: Activities that encourage imaginative play teach children the concept of symbolism, which is at the foundation of reading, spoken language, mathematics, and virtually every higher intellectual function. When a child picks up an object and pretends it is something else, or pretends *he* is *someone* else, he is paving the way for abstract thinking, which is essential for advanced brain development. It takes a leap of imagination for a child to understand that numbers and letters are actually symbols for other things. Before a child can read, he has to comprehend that the shape of the letter *P* translates into a particular sound, that groups of letters form words, and that words have meaning beyond the letters. Before a child can do simple arithmetic, he needs to know that the number 5 is not a "thing," but represents a certain amount of quantity, and then when numbers are combined, they represent different things. The very same skills, albeit at a more sophisticated level, come into play when a high school student is asked to write an essay analyzing the motivation of a character in a book. Once again, he has to understand the concept of symbolism and the meaning behind the words. Not surprisingly, studies show that children who engaged in the most imaginary play during their preschool years developed into the strongest students.

The earliest signs of imaginative play begin at around 18 to 20 months, when a child may mimic your activities by talking on a play telephone or pretend her doll is a real baby. At around 2½ or 3, when children begin to interact with other children, they become more involved in making up games with story lines and pretending to be characters in their own mini-dramas. During these play scenarios children learn important lessons in cooperation that will last them a lifetime. Play activity gives children rich experiences with language and strengthens the internal mental processes that provide the support for future literacy skills. Many modern childhood activities discourage imaginary play. TV, videos, and video games spoon-feed intricate plots and story lines to kids, robbing them of the need to dream things up for themselves. Early on, parents need to stimulate their children to exercise their creativity.

As early as 3 months, parents should show children how simple objects can be brought to life through creative play. With your child watching you, take a plain sock and using nontoxic marker, draw a face on it. Put the sock on your hand and make it talk to your child or act out a short play for your child. Animate your child's toys. Tell your child a story using his favorite stuffed animal as a character as you play with the stuffed animal. Your child will be delighted with these games, but more importantly, you are introducing him to an important new concept.

Activity: By the time your child is 3, your home should be stocked with toys that enhance symbolic play such as toy houses, toy people, toy furniture, toy food, and toy utensils. When your child is playing independently or with a friend, encourage dramatic play by setting up a scenario such as "Let's imagine we're going to the store to buy food for dinner," or "Let's pretend that you're Peter at the pizza shop and you have to feed lunch to a lot of hungry children." Watching children create a pretend drama is a breathtaking experience when you recognize how powerful this activity is in terms of enhancing future brain power. You can periodically interject a plot line that makes the story more interesting and calls upon your child to use problem-solving skills. For example, tell your child that the grocery store is out of milk and he needs to buy something else for the family to drink. Playing in an imaginary store is also a terrific way to teach simple addition and subtraction.

By age 4, children should be encouraged to play "dress up" and should have access to old clothes, jewelry, and other items from which they can create costumes.

Smarter Child Tip Try to incorporate a creative component in some of your child's day-to-day activities. For example, bath time can be used as a vehicle to tell a story, perhaps using some of your child's favorite bath toys. When your child is sitting in her car seat in the car, point out the sights along the road and tell a story.

The "Google" Game

Suggested Age Range: **3 to 5 years**
Goal: **Hones computer skills, enhances discrimination skills**

Objective: This game accomplishes two tasks: It provides you with a fun way to teach your child basic computer skills while at the same time offering him an opportunity to enhance his all-important discrimination skills. From this activity, your child can learn a fundamental lesson on how things are different (in terms of category, shape, size, color, etc.) and how things are the same.

Activity: This activity involves creating a large picture library for your child by downloading images of objects, people, plants, and animals from your computer and pasting them onto large file cards that are sorted and stored in file card boxes. To begin, have your child sit down next to you by the computer. Go to Google and click on the "Images" link in the opening screen. (Be sure that your filters are turned on "High.") Decide ahead of time with your child what kinds of images you are searching for that particular day. For example, if you type in "things that fly" you will be shown numerous images of airplanes, insects, birds, kites, and even balloons. You can then decide which of these objects you want to download. Once you select ten or so pictures, print them out and paste each one on a separate file card. Then ask your child to sort the cards into various categories. For example, "Separate out the living things from the nonliving things," or "Separate out the things that have wings from the things that don't." When you are finished, put the cards in the file box. Every few days do another search for a different category. For example, you can type in the word "plants" or "dogs" or "cats" and download pictures of different species.

As your picture library expands, you can ask your child to sort the pictures by whatever parameters you choose. For example, one day, you can ask your child to pick out the animals from the flowers, or the dogs from the cats. As your child becomes more sophisticated at differentiating between similar things, you can ask him to sort out the different plants in terms of trees or flowers, or breeds of cats by color or even size.

Go to the Next Level

Activity: Challenge your child's discrimination skills. Put seemingly unrelated images together in a group and ask your child, "Why are they alike?" Start with images that have obvious similarities such as a bird, a butterfly, and a helicopter and work your way up to images that have more subtle differences, such as a house and a bird's nest, or a kite and a fishing pole (both have string). A more challenging and, therefore, even more brain-enhancing twist to the game is to choose two or three unrelated images and ask your child how or why they are similar. This adds a much higher level of creativity to the response and you will be surprised and delighted by your child's responses.

As you work with these images, find one that is "special" to your child and talk about why. Put that image on the refrigerator door or on a bulletin board in your child's bedroom. Periodically, select a new "special" picture.

Initially, you will probably do most of the work on the computer yourself, but as your child learns how to use the mouse and click on the correct icons, let him take over as you watch.

Math Games

Suggested Age Range: **1 to 5 years**
Goal: **Builds early number skills**

Objective: These simple exercises not only provide a fundamental understanding of "more than" and "less than," as well as addition and subtraction, but provide your child with a basic understanding of the number line concept, which will be fundamental to your child's understanding of mathematics when she enters kindergarten.

Children are born with an innate sense of mathematics. Comparing numbers of objects or the relative sizes of objects is part of the human experience, as demonstrated by the fact that virtually every culture on the planet has its form of counting. You may be surprised to learn that even a 5-month-old baby has a basic, albeit primitive, understanding of addition and subtraction. Professor Karen Wynn at Yale University performed a simple experiment with 5-month-old babies utilizing a small stage and Mickey Mouse dolls. First, each baby was given an opportunity to look at one Mickey Mouse doll on the stage. When the babies showed signs of boredom, which meant that they had become familiar with the doll, the researchers covered the stage with a screen, blocking the doll from view. The researchers then allowed the babies to observe them placing a second Mickey Mouse doll behind the screen. Unbeknownst to the babies, however, the researchers then secretly removed one of the Mickey Mouse dolls. When they raised the screen, allowing the babies to see the stage, the researchers reported that all the babies looked very surprised when they saw only one mouse doll and not two. The babies were surprised to see that the reality did not measure up to what they had previously counted and therefore expected to see. This led the researchers to conclude that babies had an instinctual number sense, understanding the concept that two is more than one. In the second part of the study, the researchers began by showing the babies two dolls and then raising the screen. The researchers then made it appear as if they were removing one of the dolls when in fact they did not. When they raised the screen, once again, the babies looked surprised when they saw that there were two dolls, which led the researchers to conclude that 5-month-olds have a rudimentary understanding of subtraction.

If math is such a natural part of our makeup, why do so many kids have such difficulty with math in school? In my opinion, one problem is how we introduce math to preschool-age children. We mistakenly believe that teaching children to count from one to ten or having them memorize their multiplication tables is somehow enhancing their knowledge of mathematics. This emphasizes *what* our children learn rather than *how* our children learn. In reality, it's far more important for a child to first be taught the underlying concepts of what numbers mean and given a true understanding of the cornerstones of mathematical literacy: What does "more than" mean? What does "less than" mean? What does "bigger than" look like? What does "smaller than" look like? Of course children need to know how to count and how to read numbers, but they also need to know the true meaning of numbers. It's critical to build on the innate interest in numbers demonstrated in infancy and not let it disappear or be annihilated by a rote repetitive approach to math.

Activity: At 12 months old, encourage your baby to maintain her innate interest in math by naturally incorporating counting into your everyday conversation. Show her how numbers relate to her life. Ask simple questions and provide the answers. "How many shoes is Mommy wearing? Mommy is wearing two shoes, just like you, one on each foot." "How many dolls are in the carriage? There is one doll in the carriage." "How many balls are in the basket? There are three balls in the basket." At this stage, don't try to teach your child any math and don't expect her to follow even the simplest addition problems. It's not important. Your goal should be to enhance her understanding of what the numbers *represent.* Challenge your child with simple tasks that stimulate her to make size comparisons. While your child is sitting in her high chair let her play with two different size plastic measuring cups. After she grows bored with that, give her two yellow cups of the same size and one red one of a different size. Keep changing the color and size of the cups. This simple activity will help her understand the concept of "bigger than" and "smaller than" and enhance visual-spatial skills.

Go to the Next Level

Activity: At 18 months, add file cards with the numbers 1 to 10 to your card exercises. This will help your child begin to recognize numbers and learn their names. Age 2 is a good time to start playing counting games with your child. Two-year-olds don't understand abstract concepts; therefore, simply counting numbers without any visual reinforcement is not very effective. Your child will be more receptive if you are counting real things that she cares about, such as toys, cookies, or items of clothing. Start with three objects (they don't have to be all alike) and count them from left to right, saying, "One, two, three" and then ending with "we now have three things." Count up the objects left to right a few more times, allowing your child to become familiar with the activity. Then make a change. Recount the same objects from right to left. Do that a few times and finish by counting the middle object first. Over time, this will teach your child that the order is irrelevant when you are counting objects, a concept that most children will not fully grasp until they are 3 or over. Try to vary the objects that you use in this activity. It's important for your child to understand that the number 5 has the same meaning whether you are describing 5 cookies or 5 dominos or 5 balls or 3 cookies and 2 dominos.

Go to the Next Level

Activity: By age 2, look for opportunities in everyday life to reinforce the concepts "bigger than" and "smaller than." When you go to the playground, point out "Jane is bigger than her little brother Adam." When you come into the house and you both take off your shoes, pick up your shoes and your son's shoes and show him, "Daddy's shoes are bigger than Josh's shoes." Take two of your child's toys of differing sizes and ask, "Is the truck bigger than the ball?" Start off comparing toys in which the difference in size is very obvious, and as your child develops an understanding of bigger than and smaller than, challenge his skills with objects in which the size difference is more subtle.

Go to the Next Level

Activity: By 2½ most children will be able to identify numbers 1 through 10 and are beginning to more fully develop an appreciation of "more than" and "less than." You can play a simple counting game with your child that will foster the ideas of more than and less than as well as pave the way for an understanding of addition and subtraction. For example, put five blocks on the floor and ask your 2½-year-old to count them. When he completes the task, say to him, "Yes, you have five blocks," and then hand him another block and ask, "How many blocks do you have now?" Most children between the ages of 2½ and 3 will have to recount all the blocks before coming to the conclusion that now there are six blocks. Some children, however, will remember that the last number they counted was 5 and will simply say, "Six." While seemingly a subtle difference, this is actually a very sophisticated leap ahead in intelligence, since it is at the core of mathematics: when you add two numbers together you end up with a different number.

You can steer your child to reach this developmental milestone by doing the following: When your child has counted five blocks, you then say "Five" and immediately hand him another block, and if your child doesn't say "Six" (and most won't) say it for him. After you repeat this exercise a few times with you prompting your child, he will eventually get the hang of the game. Once he does, the next time you play, have him count out the five blocks and as you hand him the sixth, say "Five and one makes six." Repeat the exercise using other simple sums such as 2+1, 3+1, etc. Once he is playing along with you and is doing the simple arithmetic, the next step is to take away one of the blocks and ask your child, "How many are left?" Similarly, your child may need to recount the blocks once one has been removed. Follow a strategy similar to what you did previously, call out the number of blocks that you start with before removing one. For example, if you start with four blocks, say, "We have four blocks," then take one away and say, "How many do we have now?" If your child doesn't answer, coax him along by saying "Three." Repeat the game and soon he will get the hang of it.

Go to the Next Level

Activity: At 3, children have made incredible gains in their knowledge of basic mathematics and understanding of one-to-one relationships, laying the groundwork for the study of ratios. Take advantage of the many opportunities in everyday life to enhance your child's understanding of this mathematical principle. When your child helps you set the table, emphasize the fact that each setting gets one cup, one plate, and so on. When you help your child put on his shoes, point out that he has two feet so he needs two socks and two shoes. These real-life math lessons will serve your child well down the road when he is introduced to these concepts in school.

Go to the Next Level

Activity: By age 3½ you should be providing your child with mental math challenges that require memory and visualization as opposed to just number exercises that involve things he can presently see and touch. For example, when your child is helping you set the table for six people and there are only four plates on the table, ask him how many more plates are needed to make six. Ask him a follow-up question: "How many places were set for dinner last night? How many people did we have for dinner last night?" Let him think about it. This is not only a terrific exercise for developing early mathematical skills but also strengthens memory in relation to math skills, paving the way for higher achievement.

Go to the Next Level

Activity: Challenge your child with questions that force him to think "out of the box." When you are setting the table for dinner, set seven place settings when there are supposed to be six and ask him how many need to be taken away. But again, make it fun. If you are setting the table for four people, you can put two plates in front of Daddy's place. Ask your child, "Why do we have five plates instead of four?" Let him think about it and see if he comes up with an answer. If not, you answer, "Because Daddy is very hungry tonight."

Go to the Next Level

Activity: By age 4, your child is able to comprehend the more abstract concepts of symbolism and value, primarily through imaginative play. Playing "make believe" store with your child is a wonderful way to teach her about money as well as hone her math skills. Use fake dollar bills or monopoly money (so you don't end up losing money), and you can use real coins as long as your child doesn't put small objects in her mouth. Otherwise, use poker chips, which are larger and easier for you to watch. White poker chips could represent a penny, red poker chips a nickel, blue poker chips a dime, and green poker chips a quarter. Set up a make-believe store at home, putting price tags on your child's favorite toys. Start with easy numbers, such as 5 or 10 cents so that your child understands the concept of using a chip to pay for a toy. Then you can move on to more complicated calculations such as charging her 7 cents, which means she will either have to use a nickel chip and two penny chips or give you a dime chip and get back change.

You can play a variation on this game when you take your child shopping at a real grocery store, which will make the time go by a lot faster as well as teach an invaluable math lesson. Tell your 4-year-old, "Let's pretend that we only have $20 to spend on groceries today." Then, as you pull objects off the shelf and fill up your cart, add them up to the nearest dollar. When you are ready to add another item, remind your child where you were before (if she forgets) and ask how much you will have if the new object costs $2. Say, "We were at $12. If we add the peanut butter that costs $2, then how much will that make?" When you reach a number such as $15 or $18, ask your child, "How much more can we spend?" When you reach $20, add a few extra items to your grocery cart and exceed your $20 limit. Then ask your child what you should take away to get back down to $20. This is a powerful lesson in subtraction and one that will be far more meaningful to your child than a repetitive math game on a screen.

Easy and Fun Activities to Build a Better Brain

Suggested Age Range: Newborn to 1 year

Activity: Where's Mommy? Where's Daddy?

Goal: Sharpens auditory discrimination skills

Activity: Peek-a-Boo

Goal: Strengthens memory, enhances auditory discrimination skills, and teaches "cause and effect"

Activity: Mobile Play

Goal: Improves visual discrimination skills, early introduction to colors and shapes

---

Activity: Encouraging Manipulative Play

Goal: Improves hand–eye coordination

Activity: Tracking an Object

Goal: Helps develop memory, early number skills, and discrimination skills

---

Activity: Stacking and Sorting Games

Goal: Enhances hand–eye coordination, reinforces the concept of bigger than and smaller than and teaches visual-spatial relationships

---

Suggested Age Range: 1 to 2 years

Activity: Stacking and Sorting Games

Goal: Enhances hand–eye coordination, reinforces the concept of bigger than and smaller than and teaches visual-spatial relationships

---

Activity: Puzzles

Goal: Develops hand–eye coordination

Activity: Card Game
Goal: Teaches colors and shapes

Activity: Grab Bag
Goal: Enhances sense of touch, teaches the brain to think in 3-D

Activity: Memory Builder
Goal: Sharpens memory and concentration

Activity: Math Games
Goal: Builds early number skills

Suggested Age Range: 2 to 3 years

Activity: Mix It Up
Goal: Strengthens memory and counting skills

Activity: Crafts Projects
Goal: Exercises fine motor skills, improves manual dexterity and understanding of visual–spatial relationships

Activity: Card Games
Goal: Teaches colors and shapes

Activity: Imaginative Play
Goal: Teaches concept of symbolism

Activity: Grab Bag
Goal: Enhances sense of touch, teaches the brain to think in 3-D

Activity: Math Games
Goal: Builds early number skills

Suggested Age Range: 3 to 4 years

Activity: Crafts Projects
Goal: Exercises fine motor skills, improves manual dexterity and understanding of visual-spatial relationships

Activity: Grab Bag
Goal: Enhances sense of touch, teaches the brain to think in 3-D

Activity: Imaginative Play
Goal: Teaches concept of symbolism

Activity: The "Google" Game
Goal: Hones computer skills, enhances discrimination skills

Activity: Math Games
Goal: Builds early number skills

Activity: Card Game
Goal: Teaches colors and shapes

Activity: Mix It Up
Goal: Strengthens memory and counting skills

Suggested Age Range: 4 to 5 years

Activity: Card Game
Goal: Teaches colors and shapes

Activity: Math Games
Goal: Builds early number skills

Activity: Imaginative Play
Goal: Teaches concept of symbolism

Activity: Crafts Projects
Goal: Exercises fine motor skills, improves manual dexterity and understanding of visual spatial relationships

---

Activity: Mix It Up
Goal: Strengthens memory and counting skills

Activity: The "Google" Game
Goal: Hones computer skills, enhances discrimination skills

CHAPTER FOUR

Enhancing Your Child's Verbal and Reading Skills

The first three years of life are critical for the development of verbal and reading skills. During this intense period of synaptic pruning and myelination, the foundations for both reading and speech are being embedded in the brain, providing parents with a unique opportunity to help their children become strong readers with exceptional verbal skills.

Language and literacy are closely linked and develop in a similar fashion. The brain may be wired for speech earlier than it is wired for reading (which is why children can talk before they can read), but both skills build upon each other and involve the same basic principles. Whether you are learning to speak or read, you must have a basic understanding of sounds and symbolism and how the two are intertwined.

Mastering an oral language requires a child to become familiar with the basic sounds—the phonemes—that are used to make words. Although there are only twenty-six letters in the English language, there are forty phonemes because some letters have more than one sound. For example, the letter *c* has a hard sound in the word *cat,* but a softer sound in the word *space.* The study of phonemes is phonics. Once a child begins to pick up the basic sounds involved in speech, she must then recognize that those sounds become words that represent things such as objects and people, and concepts such as large and small. A child must then learn how to put these words together to make simple sentences, which most children can do by around age 2 or 2½.

The process of learning to read follows a similar logic. While a child is learning to speak, she is simultaneously becoming aware that there is a written form of language that consists of twenty-six letters, that each letter symbolizes a different sound (or sounds), and that letters form words and words form sentences. Although a child may not be able to actually read words until she is 4 or 5, or write simple sentences until she is in grade school, the basic fundamentals of literacy are established in her brain much earlier.

Two Languages Are Better Than One

Can babies learn to speak two languages simultaneously? Absolutely! If a child is raised in a bilingual household, he will readily pick up a second language. Up until around the age of 8, a child can learn to speak a second language (or even a third) without any difficulty whatsoever. Being exposed to multiple languages is nothing but good for your child's brain development. If your child spends time with a relative or babysitter who is not fluent in English, ask that person to converse with your child in her native language. This helps prune synapses in your child's brain, paving the way for that brain to be more receptive and able to appreciate more diverse phonemes in the future. If a child is learning to speak more than one language at a time, it may result in a slight lag in speech, but once the child begins talking, he will speak fluently in both languages.

The precise mechanism of learning a language may vary from language to language. For example, a child whose native language is Mandarin, whose alphabet system, unlike English, is based on numerous symbols or pictograms, will have a somewhat different experience than a child learning English. Nonetheless, the basic task of putting words together to make simple sentences is the same whether you are speaking Mandarin or English. What's interesting is the fact that the human brain is capable of learning any type of language, whether it consists of letters, pictograms, or even hieroglyphics.

In the womb, the developing baby is becoming familiar with the basic sounds of his native language. During the last three months of gestation, a baby can hear muffled sounds and is born recognizing his mother's voice. Infants are especially primed to tune into human speech. From the first moment you look into your newborn's eyes and begin talking to him, you are providing him with the early tools for speech and literacy.

NOUNS FIRST, VERBS LATER

There are two important areas of the brain involved in speech production: Wernicke's area and Broca's area. Wernicke's area, which develops first, sits atop the left temporal lobe just behind the area where auditory information is processed. Wernicke's area is credited with our understanding of the meaning of words. Interestingly, it is situated right next to the areas in the brain involved in interpreting visual experiences (like reading), which reinforces the close link between literacy and language. Wernicke's area is connected by a large nerve pathway to Broca's area, another critically important area for language, which sits in the back of the frontal lobe. Broca's area deals with more sophisticated concepts of speech, such as grammar—specifically, how nouns relate to verbs, and how nouns and verbs are modified by adjectives and adverbs. When you conjure up the mental image of a noun—for example, when you think of a car—you are in Wernicke's area. But when you describe the basic characteristics of the car using adjectives ("a fast red car"), you have moved into Broca's area. Broca's area is myelinated later than Wernicke's area and therefore is not activated until a child is about 18 months old. That's why a child's earliest words are always nouns.

During the first year of life, your child will begin to grasp the concept that words represent objects—that when Mommy says "bottle," she is referring to something the child can touch, feel, and even taste. This is the beginning of a rudimentary understanding of symbolism, a critical turning point in brain development.

Face Time

***Suggested Age Range:* 4 to 12 months**
***Goal:* Enhancing verbal skills**

Objective: By 4 months old, many children will recognize several spoken words including their name. By the end of the first year, most children recognize around seventy spoken words and may even be able to speak a word or two. There is no magic to learning how to speak: Babies learn to speak by being spoken to and hearing others speak. There is no substitute for human-to-human contact. In particular, babies need "face time" with a caring adult. By observing the mouth movements of parents and caregivers, babies learn how to form words with their own mouths and how to associate the right sounds with the appropriate mouth movements. Young children—even babies—should be included in family meals. Even though an infant can't participate in the conversation, she is getting a great deal out of listening to other family members talk. And do try to include your baby in the conversation. Look at her when you talk, even ask her questions—make her feel part of the activity.

Activity: Learning to speak requires a basic understanding that (1) the sounds that you hear come out of someone's mouth and (2) you are capable of making those same sounds yourself. Babies need to "feel" speech as well as hear it. Your baby will naturally try to touch your mouth when you are talking. Encourage this! While speaking, singing, or reading to your baby, place her hand over your lips. Let her feel how your mouth moves while you are speaking. This "hands on" learning reinforces a baby's visual observation of how speech is formed.

READING TO YOUR CHILD

Start reading to your baby within the first days of life. Reading to your baby while he lies in his crib enhances bonding and develops language skills.

When your baby is around 3 to 4 months and can hold up his head on his own, it will become more comfortable for you to sit in a chair as you can hold your baby in one arm and hold the book in the other as you read to him. By around 4 months, your baby will show an interest in handling the book. By all means, encourage your child to grab the book and play with it. The baby who smells, holds, and even tastes a book will understand on a very basic level that books are an important part of life. In addition, stimulating more of his senses during reading builds a smarter brain by challenging it to integrate multiple types of sensory experience at the same time. This is an early exposure to "multitasking," training the brain to process different types of information simultaneously and quickly, a fundamental characteristic of a smart brain.

YOUR HOME LIBRARY

There are two types of books designed for babies and toddlers: picture books and storybooks. Picture books typically have one or two pictures on a page—usually of familiar objects—and a one-word caption identifying the object. Storybooks, which are also illustrated, have simple plotlines. Children should have both types of books in their home library. Don't be reluctant to read a storybook to your baby because you are afraid that she may not understand what you are saying. It doesn't matter if she doesn't follow the story. And don't assume that you have to stick to the easiest books. It's never too early to read a classic such as *The Cat in the Hat* or *Sam I Am* to your child. Rhyming books are great because they help teach phonics (the use of phonemes) and can encourage the development of both language and reading skills. Your baby will gain a great deal simply by listening to your voice, hearing the fluctuations in speech and the rhythm of the words. You read the words, she looks at the pictures. She hears you use the phonemes of the specific language you are reading in and her ears become attuned to variation in sounds. Eventually it begins to sink in that the pictures actually represent the words and the words are a story.

Books with large pictures are best at around 4 to 6 months because your child is still unable to discern much visual detail. Each page should contain one or two pictures at most and the illustrations should be quite simple and realistic. Babies respond well to books with large photographs, especially those with familiar objects such as animals, cars, people, fruit, vegetables, utensils, and even letters and numbers. Stick to books that are illustrated with bright primary colors, particularly for children up to 8 to 10 months old because they are less responsive to pastels.

POINT OUT THE PICTURES

When you read to your child, it's important to point to a specific picture and identify it for him. If it's a picture of a house, say, "This is a house," if it's a picture of Elmo, say, "This is Elmo." Do it every time you read the story. This will help your child develop the ability to visualize a picture or an object in his head when he hears the right name or word. The ability to conjure up a mental picture of a person or object based on auditory stimulation is a major developmental leap for a child. This is a much more sophisticated association activity, one in which a stimulus, in this case sound, can stimulate another part of the brain, in this case the part of the brain that enables us to create mental images.

Smarter Child Tip Read with a lot of feeling—memories are ingrained more deeply when they are accompanied by emotion. Be dramatic, get excited, laugh, and have a good time when you read to your child. It should be an enjoyable experience for both of you.

SMALL TALK

By 6 months, most children begin "babbling," which is an early attempt to imitate the language that they have been hearing. It's a great time for parents to jump right in and reinforce this activity by imitating the sounds that your child is making. Most parents do this instinctually. Your baby will be fascinated by this activity and will soon understand this "communication" that you have established with him. But even more important than your baby recognizing that making sounds is somehow an important thing that people do, babbling allows your child to learn early on how specific movements of his tongue, cheeks, lips, and diaphragm can be modified to create unique sounds, a fundamental skill he will need when he actually begins to form words.

When your baby first utters his first precious word, which is usually *Mama,* turn to him and repeat, "Mama." This encourages him to continue this activity, which provides a powerful building block for the development of language skills. You can build upon this activity by changing either the consonant or the vowel sound. For example, after your child has said "Mama" for several days and seems to have mastered that sound, you can encourage him to try something new. The next time your child says "Mama," repeat "Mama" but then say "Moo Moo," or "Papa." Your child will compare the new sound with his memory of the previous sound, and of the motor activity of his mouth and tongue that it took to create that sound. Over the next several months the child will learn to change the sound and follow your lead. At the end of the first year, most children can say a word or two, but language skills really pick up in the second year as hearing becomes more refined and children are able to discern subtle differences in sound.

At age 1, your child's brain is primed to learn nouns, that is, he begins to understand that certain sounds represent certain objects. He will understand about seventy words, usually describing things in his everyday life, such as bottle, blanket, or cat.

Find It!

***Suggested Age Range:* 6 to 9 months and up**
***Goal:* Teaches symbolism (objects in books represent real objects)**

Objective: This simple exercise with your child will help show her that pictures of objects represent real objects.

Activity: When your baby is able to sit unassisted, at around 6 to 9 months, sit her next to you on a couch, freeing both your hands to hold the book. When you are reading about a specific object for which there is a picture, ask her to find the object. Your baby does not have the fine motor skills yet to point to the object in the book, but she will be able to slap the picture with the palm of her hand. When she does, reinforce her answer by saying, "Yes. You're right. That's a car." If you see a picture of a banana and an apple side by side, point to the banana and say "banana" and then move on to the next page and say "apple." Feel free to embellish by saying things such as "We like apples," or "Apples are red." Try, however, to emphasize the word *apple* at the beginning and end of your discussion of that page. After reading the book several times, open the page that has, for example, a banana and an apple and ask your baby, "Where is the banana?" Allow her to slap at the book. If she guesses wrong, say, "No, that's the apple" as she is slapping the book. Move the book so that her slap strikes the banana and say, "Yes, that's the banana."

Within a short time, your baby will respond instantly to your questions. Once she becomes used to the game, mix it up a bit. Your natural tendency will be to ask her to locate things that are on the left side of the book and then move to the right (because we read from left to right). For variety, ask her to locate an object on the right side of the page and then move to the objects on the left side. This will teach your child to observe in all directions, not just left to right but up and down as well. This helps a child develop the visual skills needed to most effectively scan objects to learn about their spatial orientation.

Go to the Next Level

When your baby masters a particular book, retire that book, but only temporarily. Starting at around 7 or 8 months, introduce books that have up to four objects per page. Once you have introduced a new book and have read from it for several days, bring back an old favorite that will be delightful for your child. This reinforces his previous learning and memory.

Once your child is able to identify an object in a book, you can show him how the picture in the book is actually a three-dimensional, real-life object. When you are reading to your child, try to gather up as many of the objects in your child's book as possible. For example, if your child is pointing out the banana and apple in his book, he will be delighted when, after he slaps the banana on the page, you produce an actual banana for him to hold, smell, and taste. This takes the picture book experience to a much higher level of learning, as your child soon recognizes that the picture "symbolizes" the banana while there is no actual banana in the book. This is a fundamental leap in the child's understanding of symbolism, paving the way for reading and math skills, which are predicated on symbolism as letters symbolize certain sounds and numbers symbolize specific values in quantity and size.

Surprise Your Child

Suggested Age Range: **1 year and up**
Goal: **Reinforces literacy pathways, stimulates memory**

Objective: By age one year, reading with a parent or caregiver should be a regular part of your child's life. I recommend selecting three or four books that your child enjoys and reading them over and over again to your child as opposed to reading a new book every day. Repetition reinforces learning by exercising the literacy pathways in the brain that are being formed for future use. It also stimulates memory, which is also critical for language development. But sometimes, an unexpected change in the story can be a powerful learning tool.

Activity: When a child is familiar with a story, he learns to anticipate what comes next. In fact, after hearing a story several times, many children can commit it to memory and "read" along with you. This doesn't mean that children don't learn by being thrown an occasional curveball. After your child has become very familiar with a story, change the story around every so often when you read it to him. Your child may not have the vocabulary to register his surprise, but you will notice the surprised look on his face when you veer away from the real story. This is another simple way to challenge and enhance your child's memory skills. Your child will be forced to contrast his previous understanding of the story against the current story, which will stimulate his brain to work harder and strengthen the formation of neural pathways. As your child gets more familiar with the book, make subtler and subtler changes. For example, if the character in the book was given a big red ball, your child will certainly recognize the dramatic "mistake" you make when you change it to a bicycle. If you change the "big red ball," to a "big blue ball," or a "small red ball," you are making a more subtle change that can help enhance discrimination abilities. With each small change in the story, you are helping your child further refine his memory and discrimination skills. As your child's reading and verbal skills improve, introduce a new book to him and retire the old book that your child has outgrown. But don't throw it out! Your child will love to look at his old favorites for years to come.

"Feeling" Letters

Suggested Age Range: **1 year**
Goal: **Using touch to reinforce learning**

Objective: By around his first birthday, your child's vision will be developed enough so that he can actually see the different letters on a page, but of course, he won't know what they are. This doesn't mean that it's time to start drilling the alphabet into your child. Forcing your child to memorize the ABCs is not going to help him become more literate and is a real waste of time. It's more important for your child to understand the concepts of literacy—that is, that the squiggles on a page are letters, that letters represent sounds, and these sounds come together to represent a person or a thing.

Activity: One year of age is an ideal time to introduce your child to the "sound" and "feel" of letters. When my children were around this age, I went to the hardware store and bought a set of large wooden block letters that I kept in a basket near the children's books. Every time I read a book to them, I would hand them a letter to hold, and they would identify that letter in the book and make the sound of the letter. For example, if I was reading *The Cat in the Hat,* a great rhyming book, I would hand Austin the letter *C,* identify the letter *C* on the page, make the hard "c" sound, and then point out the cat. I made it into a game and we had fun. Having a child physically hold a letter, see a letter as it is used in a book, and hear the letter being sounded out by a parent is a far more powerful learning experience than memorizing the ABCs.

DEVELOPING PROFICIENCY IN PHONICS IS KEY

As noted earlier, there are twenty-six letters in the English language but there are forty phonemes. Some letters have multiple sounds, such as the letter *T,* which sounds different in the word *tack* than it does in the word *cloth.* Children must become thoroughly comfortable with phonics to master both language and literacy. Nursery rhymes and rhyming books are an especially good way to train your child's ear to discern the different sounds of words and letters, particularly during the first year. Rhyming pictures should be placed around the room to reinforce learning. A picture of a moon next to a spoon, a tree next to a bee, a bat next to a cat, and so on will help enhance the child's verbal understanding of word sounds (phonemes).

Between 12 and 18 months, your child's vocabulary expands rapidly, with toddlers learning to speak two to three new words every day, but actually understanding the meaning of many more. By 18 months, there is a huge leap in brain development characterized by a change in how your toddler speaks. Suddenly, she is stringing together two or three words to make simple sentences. And as Broca's area kicks in, she is now able to find the words to modify the nouns. Out of the blue, your toddler will say things such as "red ball," or "car go," and by the age 2 her sentences become more complex. Interestingly, girls seem to acquire language skills about one to two months earlier than boys, but boys eventually catch up by around age 4 or 5.

THE CREATIVITY CONNECTION

The process of learning to read first involves the recognition of letters on a page and the sounds they symbolize. That is why creative play is so important for the development of literacy, as it teaches the child the concept of symbolism. Imagine a child looking at a book with the word *dog* on the page. The word is broken down into its phonemes of "duh," "ah," and "guh." The word is then "sounded out" mentally until it is appropriately identified. It is then associated with a mental picture reflecting the child's past experience with the word *dog,* either your pet dog, a dog he may have seen at the park, or a dog on TV. Once the word is identified and the specific meaning is attached to it, the information is further projected to the emotion centers of the brain so that the child has not only a simple picture of what the word means, but an emotional feeling for the word as well. Eventually, your child must commit the forty phonemes of language to memory so that he is able to skip the mental "sounding out" phase and effortlessly jump to visualizing the whole word as he reads. Thus, good, fast, efficient readers don't actually have to sound the word out in their mind to gain its meaning. On the other hand, poor readers typically get stuck in the sounding-out phase because, for various reasons, they have not adequately learned their phonemes.

It is critical for parents to make sure that their children know their phonics! Research clearly demonstrates that children with a strong foundation in phonics do read faster and more efficiently and gain more meaning out of what they read. Reading with your child will help him begin to associate letters with sounds, and so will playing the card games I recommend in Chapter 3. Some children will easily grasp this concept and almost miraculously start to read. Other children, however, may require a bit more help. There are some excellent software packages and educational toys available to assist you in teaching your child phonics. I particularly like the Reader Rabbit Early Learning System, a computer program that I used when my own children were small that is good for children ages 3 to 5. I also recommend the Letter Factory, an interactive video by Leapster for children ages 4 to 6 that is especially good for teaching phonics. As good as these high-tech toys may be, I offer one caveat. The synthesized computer voice used in many of these games is far from a real human voice, and therefore, I don't believe it is anywhere nearly as effective as the real thing. These educational toys can help parents teach their children early reading skills, but they are no substitute for parental involvement. The best way for children to learn language and ultimately phonics is to listen to real, live, breathing human beings who speak with love and emotion. And that's YOU!

HOW TO READ TO YOUR CHILD

When my children Reisha and Austin were young, we would curl up on the couch every night before bedtime and read a story. I have no doubt that our evening ritual contributed to the fact that my children, who are now in their teens, are both avid readers. I encouraged my children to interrupt me at any time to ask questions or make comments—even silly comments. I would stop and ask them questions about the story or relate an incident or character in the story to something that had happened during the day. I didn't know it at the time, but by reading *with* them and not *to* them—by engaging them in the activity of reading with me—I was giving them a far richer experience. In fact, I was helping to better hone their early literacy skills.

Unbeknownst to me, I was practicing a technique called *dialogic reading* that was developed by Grover J. Whitehurst, Ph.D., director of the Institute of Education Sciences of the U.S. Department of Education. Dialogic reading is a powerful learning tool. In one study conducted by Dr. Whitehurst, at the end of a four-week period, preschool-age children whose parents routinely interacted with them while reading were six to eight and a half months ahead on standardized language skill tests compared to children whose parents simply read to them. In other words, *how* you read to your child can make a real difference in how well your child learns to read.

What's the best way to read to your child? Every page or so, or whenever appropriate, ask your child a question about the story. For example, if you're reading *Goodnight Moon* to your child, ask, "Do you really think that there's a man on the moon?" or "Why is it getting dark when the light is turned off?" or "Can the lamp talk?" If your child is too young to talk, answer the questions yourself. As your child gets more verbal, he will know the drill and begin asking you questions when you read his favorite stories.

Why does interactive reading produce children with superior verbal skills? When you ask a child a question about the plot or a character, he is being challenged to think in a way he would not if he were simply listening to the story. When you read interactively, you are challenging your child to associate what's going on in the book with previous experiences and memories. This enhances his brain's ability to make comparisons and come up with solutions. More importantly, it activates the association areas in your child's frontal lobes, the most advanced and sophisticated part of the brain. When you ask your child, "If the dish really ran away with the spoon, who do you think would be the faster runner?" you are providing an extremely powerful stimulus for his brain to make comparisons based on previous experiences to come up with the answer.

Of course, there are times when you should snuggle up with your child and read to him without asking questions. Take your cue from your child. Although most kids will love being asked for their input, a tired, cranky child may want to simply relax and be read to. That's fine, too. When your child is rested and in a better mood, he may be more interested in sharing the reading experience.

Enhancing Your Child's Verbal and Reading Skills

Suggested Age Range: 4 to 12 months

Activity: Face Time
Goal: Enhancing verbal skills

Suggested Age Range: 6 to 9 months and up

Activity: Find It in the Book
Goal: Teaching symbolism

Suggested Age Range: 1 year and up

Activity: Surprise Your Child

Goal: Reinforce literacy pathways in the brain, stimulate memory

Suggested Age Range: 1 year

Activity: "Feeling" Letters

Goal: Using tactile stimulation to reinforce learning

Suggested Age Range: 1 month and up

Activity: Reading to and with Your Child

Goal: Foster love of reading, enhance verbal and writing skills

CHAPTER FIVE

Give Your Child the Music Advantage

Parents often ask me whether the so-called "Mozart effect" is real—that is, whether playing Mozart for babies will actually make them smarter. My answer is a qualified yes. Exposing your child to music—especially Mozart—is going to have a beneficial impact on brain development. But there's a much bigger story about music and the brain that parents should know to ensure that their children achieve the full music advantage.

The Mozart effect is based on a study showing that listening to specific Mozart sonatas can improve spatial-temporal reasoning abilities, which provide the foundation for understanding advanced mathematical and scientific concepts. People with the highest degree of spatial-temporal reasoning excel in the study of math and science and make great engineers, architects, surgeons, and graphic designers. There's a significant difference, however, between *passively* listening to music and *actively* making music. The Mozart effect is temporary—the benefits seem to wear off within an hour. The benefits of actually playing a musical instrument appear to be permanent.

The proof is in the brain scan: MRIs of the brain show that musical training in early childhood leaves an indelible—and positive—mark on the brain. Learning an instrument can actually enhance the growth of areas of the brain involved in analytical thinking, math, problem-solving skills, memory, and fine motor skills. More importantly, learning a musical instrument early in life can *permanently* change the structure of the brain.

Why does music exert such a powerful influence on the brain? Babies are born with a fairly acute sense of hearing that allows them to detect subtle variations in human voices, such as differences in pitch, tempo, and loudness that prepare them to learn the specific nuances of language. Similar to language, music is sound made up of various patterns of tones, inflections, and rhythms. Just as infants are primed to absorb as much information as they can about the various qualities of human speech, including rhythms and pitch, they are also genetically prewired to respond to these same qualities in music. Interestingly, parents seem to know intuitively how to talk to their infants in a manner to which they are most likely to respond. Infants are more able to appreciate high frequencies during the first few months of life. The high-pitched, singsong, variable speech that we acquire when talking to infants (dubbed "parentese" by researchers) is precisely the type of speech most likely to be heard by an infant. Music and language development are so closely linked that the areas of the brain that represent language and music exist side by side and develop essentially along the same timeline. Enhancing your infant's musical experiences will strengthen those parts of the brain that can vastly improve early language skills.

MUSIC CAN RAISE IQ

Renowned neuroscientists Gordon L. Shaw and Francis Rausher are credited with recognizing the so-called Mozart effect in college students at the University of California at Irvine. In an article published in *Nature* in 1993, they reported that if college students listened to a Mozart sonata for ten minutes before taking an exam, they scored higher on tests designed to evaluate their spatial IQs. Further research suggests that the Mozart effect is temporary and the benefits may wear off fairly quickly, in about an hour. As noted earlier, the real "Mozart effect" may have less to do with *listening* to music than with actually playing a musical instrument. Shaw and Rausher later conducted a study involving seventy-eight children enrolled in preschool. Thirty-four children received private piano lessons, twenty received private computer lessons, and twenty-four received either voice lessons or no special training. After six months, both groups of children were tested on their spatial-temporal reasoning. The test results were striking and dramatic. The group receiving the piano lessons scored almost 34 percent higher on the various tests of spatial-temporal reasoning. These researchers also found that the amount of improvement in spatial-temporal reasoning function was 800 percent higher in 3-year-olds given keyboard and singing lessons for an eight-month period than in children not exposed to musical training. When a child takes on a proactive role and is actively involved in the learning process, it makes a huge impression on his brain, whether the activity is reading, learning numbers, or exploring music.

Here's more proof that musical training can raise IQ. In another study carried out at the University of Toronto, Dr. E. Glen Schellenberg showed that children receiving thirty-six weeks of musical training ultimately had a full-scale IQ advantage of 5.4 points over children of a similar age not receiving music lessons. Dr. Schellenberg calls our attention to the important role of music education in enhancing not so much *what* the brain learns, but *how* the brain learns, by stating, "formal education is promoted not only for gaining literacy and numeric skills, as well as specific knowledge in various domains, but also for developing the *capacity* for reasoning and critical thinking. Extracurricular experiences such as music lessons appear to play a role in this process."*

THE BRIDGE BETWEEN THE RIGHT AND LEFT BRAIN

Scientists tend to compartmentalize the various functions of the brain, designating one a music center, another a language center, and yet another one a visual center and so on. While this is true to some degree, what really characterizes intelligence is the ability of various brain areas to share in a specific type of experience. For example, when we see an object, it may activate the visual center of the brain, but it also challenges the memory center to compare and contrast the current visual experience with previous experiences. Other areas of the brain are then activated, notably the limbic system, to determine the emotional significance of that event—is it pleasurable or threatening? Although music is represented in only a small area of the temporal lobe, it has vast ef-

*Schellenberg, E. Glenn, "Music Lessons Enhance I.Q.," *Psychological Science* 14(8): 511–14.

fects in terms of activating multiple areas. Music is one activity that may bridge the gap between the creative right brain and the more down-to-earth left brain. We tend to think of music as being a right-brain activity, but new research demonstrates that *both* hemispheres are actively involved in the musical experience. The corpus callosum is a large, white-matter tract that connects the left and right hemispheres. Adults who began musical training as young children have a significantly larger corpus callosum than those who did not. Enhanced growth of the corpus callosum allows better communication between the hemispheres, making for a smarter, more efficient brain. This greatly enhances brain power by allowing someone to utilize both the "right brain" qualities such as creativity, intuition, and subjectivity, and the "left brain" qualities such as organization, logic, rationality, and objectivity. It enhances the number of tools or approaches available for problem solving, especially in novel situations.

So how can you give your child the music advantage?

SING TO YOUR CHILD

Forget about cornering the market on Mozart CDs: The most powerful musical influence in your child's development is your singing voice. Even if you don't have a great voice, it's still music to your child's ears. As discussed earlier, experiences associated with emotion make a profound impression on the brain. This also extends to your baby's earliest auditory experiences: Those that are associated with emotional experience will have a more dramatic effect upon the developing brain. A mother holding her infant in her arms, looking into his eyes, singing to him, and making him feel loved is powerful medicine, dramatically strengthening those synapses vital for language development, mathematical understanding, and abstract thinking. Even at this early stage, your child is learning to produce sounds as a prelude to speech. Simple songs repeated during your child's first year of life may actually inspire her to sing her very first words. In the first few days of life, involve your baby as a participant in the musical experience. As you sing upbeat, active nursery rhymes and simple songs to him, gently tap your child to the beat of the song and grasp her arms, teaching her to clap to the beat.

Infants are more able to appreciate high frequencies during the first few months of life. Therefore, your infant will respond best to high-pitched sounds such as the harmonica, music boxes, and lullabies sung in a high-pitched voice.

Singing songs with your child that involve physical play allows her to integrate different senses including touch, sight, and hearing, which is how infants learn best. Games such as "Patty Cake," in which you sing a simple song to your child while clapping her hands, or "This Little Piggy Went to Market," in which you sing and count her fingers and toes, are wonderful ways to play with your baby while allowing her brain to absorb the different sounds of language and musical rhythms.

Smarter Child Tip You can sing the same songs to your infant over and over again, but do make subtle variations in the pitch and tempo—this will help your child develop an ear for language. It also helps sharpen his memory because it will force him to compare the old song with the new version.

Expose your child to a variety of sounds, but keep in mind that his hearing is very sensitive. An unusual sound, such as a bell, a whistle, or a rattle, can be very exciting to a baby, as long as it is played softly and does not overstimulate the hearing pathways.

Where's the Rattle?

Suggested Age Range: **1 to 3 months**
Goal: **Develops audio localization skills**

Objective: Infants have difficulty localizing sound, that is, figuring out where a particular sound is coming from. This exercise will help develop your child's localization skills.

Activity: Gently (and I do mean gently) shake a rattle about twelve inches from your baby's face and then move the rattle slowly around his head, stopping long enough for his eyes to focus on the rattle before moving it to a new location.

INTRODUCE YOUR CHILD TO DIFFERENT TYPES OF MUSIC

In the same way that your child learns early on to appreciate the various specific sounds, or phonemes, of his native language, he learns to enjoy the qualities of music appropriate for his culture, much as we learn to enjoy the food of our native cuisine. Music is enjoyed by every culture on the planet, but the type of music varies from culture to culture. Middle Eastern music has a different rhythm and tone from Asian music, as African music has a beat and sound that are quite unlike Western music. Yet all of these musical experiences can be used to boost brain power. It's important to expose your child early on to a variety of music styles, even from other countries. Children will find the differences in musical styles to be very stimulating and they can further enhance discrimination skills and memory. Furthermore, what better way to instill in your child a world view that is so necessary for today's shrinking globe than to have him develop an appreciation of cultural differences. Indeed, even lullabies sung in a foreign language are good for your child, as they help to create an expanded array of brain pathways that will remain with him for the rest of his life.

Making Noise

Suggested Age Range: **4 to 5 months**
Goal: **Improves hand–eye coordination, teaches cause and effect, stimulates musical pathways in the brain**

Objective: At around 4 or 5 months, when your baby begins to gain the ability to manipulate objects, it's a perfect time to give her all kinds of noise-making devices including rattles and music boxes. Encourage your child to experiment with sound.

Activity: At around 9 months, your child will love "playing the drums" using a lightweight metal cooking pot and spoon. Leave a toy piano around on the floor so your child can play with it when she crawls around her room. Although these activities may get on your nerves, these early musical experiences actually teach your baby critical lessons in the physical laws of cause and effect at the same time that she is learning about rhythm. Experiencing and creating rhythm makes for a smarter child as it builds the framework for recognizing not only rhythms in music, but the rhythmic qualities of human speech as well.

Fill in the Word

Suggested Age Range: **1 year plus**
Goal: **Enhances verbal skills, improves memory**

Objective: At around a year, when you sing a familiar song to your child, add to the mental challenge by singing a few phrases and then leaving out a word, pausing a few seconds, and then waiting for your child to react. Even before your child can verbally fill in the word, his brain will be making the correction, forcing him to draw upon his memory to create the word internally. Eventually, sometime between his first and second birthday when he can speak, he may very well sing the word with you. It will also motivate your child to learn how to speak the words that he is thinking, which will vastly enhance his verbal skills.

Activity: At around 18 months, you can further engage your child intellectually by singing a familiar song but dropping in a wrong word or phrase when he least expects it. For example, "Twinkle twinkle little star" becomes "Twinkle twinkle little boat." Let your child jump in and say, "No, star!" Not only is this a great memory exercise for your child, but it also teaches him the importance of actually listening to what someone says, an important classroom skill.

By age 2, you should be actively singing *with* your child. Singing songs either together or accompanied by prerecorded music should be a natural daily activity that brings joy to you both and strengthens the parent–child bond. At this stage, your child is starting to master his first "musical instrument," his voice. Just as research has demonstrated that children 3 years and older who have had formal instruction in a musical instrument excel in a variety of cognitive areas, the same holds true for children who have received simple voice training. The point is, there is a huge difference between simply listening to music (although profoundly beneficial) and actually *creating* music.

FORMAL MUSICAL TRAINING BY AGE 4

By the time your child is 4, she has finally developed the necessary manual dexterity and memory capacity to begin learning how to play a musical instrument. Now is the prime time to start your child on some form of formal musical training as long as it is conducted in an age-appropriate fashion. In other words, find a teacher who knows how to keep it fun. The music lesson should be a maximum of forty-five minutes per week, and if your child gets bored or restless before then, tell the music teacher to end early or allow your child free time to practice. Parents should encourage their child to practice the instrument for about twenty minutes per day and work with the child to keep her engaged. Good choices of instruments include a small keyboard, xylophone, or even a violin. Research shows that the most important criterion predicting how much a child will gain from music instruction is not so much the instrument chosen, nor the specific technique of instruction, but the degree of parental involvement. As with any other activity your child explores, your interest and input is the most important predictor of success.

How do you find the right music teacher or school? If possible, try to get a recommendation from the parents of other children who have had a successful experience with an instructor or music school. Once you've got a few referrals, check them out for yourself. If you are looking for private music instruction, be sure that the teacher is experienced in dealing with small children, who don't have the same attention span as older children. Ask the music teacher specific questions such as "How do you keep small children interested and engaged when you are teaching?" and "If a child begins to get restless, how do you handle the situation?" Watch how the teacher interacts with your child to be sure that he or she actually likes teaching small children. A warm, enthusiastic music teacher can go a long way in igniting your child's love of music, and an overly demanding, rigid teacher can have just the opposite effect.

There are many music programs available today for small children. You can often get a referral to a music program from a music store, preschool, or local "Y."

The Music Teachers National Association (MTNA), a nonprofit group dedicated to promoting musical education, can help you find a music teacher who has been certified by the group. For more information visit their website at www.mtna.org.

Give Your Child the Music Advantage

Suggested Age Range: Throughout infancy and childhood

Activity: Listening to Music

Goal: Develops early skills for recognizing differences in tone and tempo, fundamentals for language skills

---

Suggested Age Range: 1 to 3 months

Activity: Where's the Rattle?

Goal: Develops audio localization skills

Suggested Age Range: 4 to 5 months

Activity: Making Noise

Goal: Improves hand-eye coordination, teaches cause and effect, stimulates musical pathways in the brain

---

Suggested Age Range: 1 year plus

Activity: Fill in the Word

Goal: Enhances verbal skills, improves memory

Suggested Age Range: 4 years plus

Activity: Formal Musical Training

Goal: Develops musical pathways in the brain, enhances understanding of mathematical concepts, primes the brain for reading

---

CHAPTER SIX

A Smart Approach to TV, Computers, and Video Games

Preschool-age children are spending more time than ever before in front of a screen—TV, video game console, or computer. We live in a wired world and there's no turning back. My two children grew up watching TV, playing video games, and using computers at young ages and they are both strong students. That's not all they did: They participated in lots of other activities during the course of a day, including reading, playing outdoors, and enjoying card and board games. Electronic entertainment and computers were just another part of their active, full lives.

Many well-meaning parents may try to shelter their children from these activities on the theory that they are bad for their child's development. I believe that this "turn back the clock" approach is unrealistic and possibly even harmful. A child who lacks basic computer skills when she enters kindergarten is not as well prepared for school as a child who has been using a computer since her toddler years. There are also social consequences to being raised outside of the popular culture. A child whose parents completely shelter her from TV or video games may feel left out when other kids are talking about their favorite shows or games. I'm all for raising real kids in a real world. But that doesn't mean that it's okay to hand your child the TV remote or joystick and give her free reign to do whatever she wants. It's critical for parents to (1) understand how best to use the electronic media so that it works *for* your child and not against her and (2) tightly control the time a child spends in front of the screen because when it comes to the electronic media, children have absolutely no willpower.

For better or for worse, electronic activities are usurping the traditional tried-and-true activities that we know can enhance brain development—free play, participation in music, reading, manipulating objects, and spending time with responsive adults who monitor behavior and social interactions. The question is, can these new "electronic relationships" provide the brain with the appropriate stimulation during its growth spurt, or will they only stunt brain growth?

Each form of electronic media is different in terms of its impact on children. Therefore, I have divided the following discussion into three parts, covering (1) TV, with DVDs and videotapes included as well; (2) computers, and (3) video games.

YOUR CHILD'S BRAIN ON TV

There's a school of thought that believes TV is a vast wasteland and the best policy for TV is no TV at all. I don't agree. If they use it appropriately, savvy parents can turn TV into a positive experience for their children. There are some wonderful programs, especially those on public TV stations, such as *Sesame Street, Reading Rainbow,* and *Teletubbies,* that can teach children positive lessons. Furthermore, there's nothing wrong with a child enjoying a program simply for its entertainment value. Everyone needs some downtime, including small children, and especially their parents. There's no denying that TV provides parents with much-needed respite from the rigors of child rearing. The problem is, in many cases television is replacing the day-to-day social interaction that is absolutely essential for a developing brain.

Watching television has become the number one recreational activity in America. The average U.S. household has at least two TVs, with nearly two-thirds of all homes having three or more. In a typical American home, there is a TV set on somewhere in the house for an average of seven hours a day.

- Children under 3 spend on average between one and three hours a day watching TV, a huge chunk of their day considering that they may nap for an hour or two daily.

- Children between the ages of 2 and 5 spend about three hours a day watching TV, or as much as 25 percent of their waking hours.

At a time in their lives when children are primed to achieve significant milestones, from learning language to honing critical thinking skills to developing creativity to building strong bodies, they are riveted to the TV. And those hours watching TV don't include the amount of time children spend on video games or on computers. Children spend more time each year in front of the TV than they do in school.

So what's wrong with children spending time watching TV, especially if you confine your child's viewing to high-quality shows on public TV or age-appropriate DVDs or videos such as *Baby Mozart.* There are three major problems associated with TV viewing.

- Early exposure to TV or DVDs can have a potent and negative effect on the wiring of a developing brain, resulting in learning and behavior problems down the road.
- The content of many TV shows and commercials is inappropriate for young children—it's too violent and too sexy—and contributes to mood, learning, and behavior problems. As far as I'm concerned, *all* commercials geared to young children are inappropriate, preying upon them at a time when they still lack the discrimination skills needed to evaluate advertising claims and develop sales resistance.
- Time is spent watching TV or DVDs (even the best DVDs) at the expense of other activities that are beneficial to a developing brain, including reading, physical activity, and developing interpersonal skills.

NO TV FOR KIDS UNDER 2

TV can be harmful for children under 2, particularly in terms of their verbal skills. Despite the fact that there are TV programs and media products (DVDs, tapes, video games, and computer games) directed to this age group, they have the potential to cause more harm than good. The years from birth to age 2 are absolutely critical for language development—if it doesn't happen then it's not going to happen. Children's brains are wired to pick up speech from caring, attentive adults and from interaction with other children, not from a one-sided conversation emanating from a TV screen. To learn the appropriate use of language, a child must receive the right responses from those around him when he attempts to talk. When a child begins to babble or says, "Mama," he needs a human being to respond to his speech, correct any errors in his speech if necessary, and use words in sentences. This kind of give and take with loving adults is what makes a child literate, and this is what builds the pathways for verbal and literacy skills in the brain. Television does not provide this important feedback. It's far better for a child to sit in her high chair or booster seat and observe adults in conversation than to be kept entertained by watching television.

It's not that children over 2 don't need as much adult interaction as younger children—clearly they do—but it's unrealistic to assume that you can keep a child away from TV forever. TV is too deeply ingrained in our society. Starting at around age 2, it's preferable to show a child the right way to watch TV, that is, you select a favorite show or tape for a limited period of time and you turn off the set when you're finished.

TV TEACHES BAD BEHAVIOR

TV watching can also interfere with the development of social skills that are fundamental to success in life. The behavior of TV characters—especially on shows not geared for children—is often outrageous, and small children will take away the wrong lessons from these negative role models. The American Academy of Pediatrics Committee on Public Education recently issued a comprehensive statement regarding television and children. The group noted, "More than 1,000 scientific studies and reviews conclude that significant exposure to media violence increases the risk of aggressive behavior in certain children and adolescents, desensitizes them to violence and makes them believe that the world is a 'meaner and scarier' place than it is."

Moreover, when a child is watching TV, he is not interacting with other adults or children, and is getting no feedback in terms of his own behavior. Children learn by both observing adults and other children and being gently reprimanded by adults when they do wrong. When a child constantly sees behavior on TV that is not allowed at home or at preschool, he is likely to think it is normal unless someone is telling him otherwise. This paves the way for behavior problems down the road. For example, a study published in the April 2005 issue of *Archives of Pediatrics and Academic Medicine* found a strong correlation between the amount of time a child spent watching television at age 4 and the likelihood he would become a bully later on in school. As the study explains, bullying behavior is a sign of lack of empathy and poor social skills, which can make a child disliked by others, including his teachers.

TV IS SEDUCTIVE

If a child is given the choice between reading a book and watching a TV show, chances are she'll gravitate to the TV almost every time. Television is very seductive to small children. The developing brain is designed to seek out stimulating environments the way a thirsty person seeks out water. The combination of fast-moving images on the screen and a lively sound track is irresistible to a young brain. There is some evidence that watching TV at a very young age may overstimulate the brain, causing it to "short circuit" or shut down, which could affect basic brain wiring during the critical period of synaptic formation and pruning. During the formative years when your child's brain is undergoing its major growth spurt, the right kind of stimulation and feedback can help build the neural pathways that provide the foundation for future learning. The flip side of this axiom is that the wrong kind of stimulation and lack of feedback can have a detrimental effect on a child's brain. Simply stated, it can stunt the growth of your child's brain.

EXCESS TV INCREASES THE RISK FOR ADHD

A groundbreaking study published in *Pediatrics,* a leading medical journal, revealed that children who watched the most TV between the ages of 1 and 3 were most likely to develop attention problems by age 7. For every hour of TV watched daily during the critical years of brain development, there was a 10 percent increase in the likelihood of having an attention problem. This doesn't mean that these kids were destined to have ADHD, but it suggests that they would clearly have difficulty sitting still in a classroom or staying on task, two very important skills for academic success. Small children by nature tend to have short attention spans, a fact that is well known to TV programmers. TV programs and videos geared to toddlers typically feature short, quick takes that move the viewer rapidly from scene to scene, like an MTV video. Although this type of programming is designed to keep toddlers and preschool children engaged, it may train their brains to expect information in short, quick spurts, which can interfere with children's ability to concentrate on more detailed topics when they are older. A child accustomed to watching a succession of the three-minute vignettes typical of most children's television programming is going to be challenged when she is expected to stay seated for a thirty-minute lesson on reading or math.

Smarter Child Tip Turn off the evening news. It's not just violence in television programming that can have a negative impact on small children. The American Academy of Pediatrics Committee cautions that the constant bombardment of violence on the news—from bombings to murders to natural disasters—can be very frightening to small children. I don't think that children under the age of 7 or 8 should watch the evening news, and even then only with a parent who can explain what is happening on the screen. Children who constantly feel threatened and scared revert back to lower brain activity—the fight-or-flight response—and are not receptive to learning or to engaging in activities that develop their higher brain.

SMALL CHILDREN CAN'T DISCERN REALITY FROM FANTASY

Children under the age of 4 or 5 have difficulty differentiating between reality and fantasy. What appears to be obviously fake and over the top to an adult can seem very real to a child. If a child constantly sees conflicts resolved with some sort of violent outburst, even done in a humorous context, she may not get the joke and think this is appropriate behavior. If she repeats the same behavior in preschool, she risks being labeled a disruptive child. Even worse, a child may think that accepting physical or verbal abuse is also part of the norm. Moreover, children may be frightened of what they are seeing on TV but are not able to express their concerns to their parents. As discussed earlier, if a child's brain is constantly locked in "fight-or-flight mode" she will be less receptive to learning.

I would like to make a distinction between the serious, gory violence typical of many TV shows today and the silly, slapstick violence typical of cartoons. I don't believe that mildly violent cartoons are necessarily bad for children as long as they can tell the difference between fantasy and reality. These shows are fine for kids over the age of 4, but I wouldn't allow younger kids to watch them. I also think it's advisable for parents to periodically do reality checks with their children and say, "Gee, it's funny when Johnny hits Matt on TV, but if someone really did that you really wouldn't like it."

THE HOUSE RULES ON TV

It's incumbent upon to parents to take the lead and establish their own "house rules" on TV, video games, and computers in their household. Write down your house rules and post them in your house in a place where everyone can see them. Kids respond well to consistent and reasonable guidelines; as early as possible, let your child know the house rules regarding television. The younger the child, the easier it is to control TV viewing—older children can be more persistent and feel more pressured to keep up with the shows that are watched by their peers. In many cases, parents may feel compelled to give in to the wishes of older children as long as they are doing well in school and meeting their responsibilities. During the first five years of life, however, parents can help their children establish sensible television viewing habits that will lead to better decisions about TV viewing later in life. Here are some things to keep in mind:

Limit the Time Your Child Spends in Front of the TV Screen

TV (including videos and DVDs) are time wasters for children under 2. On most days, children over 2 should be allowed to watch up to one hour a day of TV, DVDs, or videos *combined.* There may be times, such as on a Saturday morning or when she's sick, that you allow your child some extra TV. But try not to make a habit of it.

Turn TV into an Interactive Experience

My primary problem with TV and other electronic entertainment is that it is so one-sided—the TV screen does the talking and the child does the listening. You can change this dynamic by watching a program along with your child and offering him an opportunity for dialogue. During the TV program, ask your child questions such as "What's Ernie doing?" "Why is Big Bird acting so silly?" "What color is Mary wearing today?" If your child lacks the verbal skills to answer the question, answer it for him. You can stimulate creativity in your 3- or 4-year-old by asking, "What's another way that the story could have ended? Could Ariel and Sarah become friends? Which ending do you like better?" "Who's your favorite character on Full House and why do you like her?" "Did Jennifer do something mean to Lauren?" This is a great opportunity for parents or caregivers to sit down, get off their feet, cuddle with their children, and have some relaxing interaction.

Use TV Commercials as a Tool to Teach Critical Thinking

Although I would prefer that children under 5 not be exposed to TV commercials, I know that they will be. Parents should let children know early on that commercials are designed to sell and are not always truthful. Point out, "Doesn't it seem wrong for this commercial to try to make you think that eating candy is good for you?"

Don't Use TV as a Reward or Punishment

Dangling TV time as a carrot to get your child to do something that you want him to do is sending the wrong message. It's making children think that TV is extra special and that they should want to watch TV instead of doing other things. You wouldn't tell your child, "If you don't pick up your blocks you can't read today." Nor should you say, "If you hit your sister one more time, no TV." The best approach is to treat TV like you treat any other activity.

Let Your Child See You Reading

Do you turn on the TV every spare minute? Don't set a bad example for your child. Let her see you reading the newspaper, thumbing through a magazine, or reading a book for pleasure. She will quickly understand that reading is a desirable activity, not a chore.

Turn Off the TV When No One Is Watching

In many homes, TV has become "background noise": it's on but no one is really watching it. This can be especially damaging to small children, whose brains aren't yet equipped to distinguish between important talk and background chatter. How is a child supposed to develop proper verbal skills if she can't understand what she's hearing in her own home?

No TV During Family Meals

Small children who are included during family meals develop a greater vocabulary than children who are not—as long as someone is speaking to them. There's no point in eating together if the TV is doing all the talking. What's even more worrisome is that during meals, parents may try to catch up with the evening news, or watch shows they like that may be inappropriate for small children. The solution is simple: Keep the TV off during family meals.

No TV in Your Child's Room

With so many American households having multiple TVs, many are ending up in children's bedrooms. This is a big mistake. As soon as children are able to manipulate the remote control (around age 3–4) you lose control over their TV viewing.

Commercial Free Is Best

Try to keep your child away from TV commercials for as long as possible. Commercials make kids want to load up on sugary, high-fat junk food, which is very bad for their brains. I prefer that children watch commercial-free programs on public TV or commercial-free DVDs or videos.

Use the V-Chip

All television sets thirteen inches or larger manufactured after 2000 must have V-chip technology that enables parents to block programming that is inappropriate for their children based on a rating system known as "TV Parental Guidelines." I urge all parents to take advantage of this technology. The shows are rated according to language, violence, and sexual content and whether or not the plotlines would frighten small children. The ratings are as follows:

TV-Y This rating indicates that a program is designed to be appropriate for children of all ages, including those from 2 to 6.

TV-Y7 This rating indicates that a program is designed for children age 7 and above and may include some fantasy or violence that could be disturbing to younger children.

TV-G This rating indicates that although a program is not *designed* for children, it is appropriate for children of all ages.

TV-PG (Parental Guidance Suggested) This rating indicates that the program contains language or themes that may not be appropriate for small children. Most sitcoms—many of which have highly sexually suggestive content—fall under this category as do some nighttime dramas, which may also include violence. Children under 5 should definitely not be watching TV-PG programs. Use your V-chip to block these programs during the hours that your child is watching TV.

TV-14 (Parents Strongly Cautioned) This rating indicates that a program contains material that may be unsuitable for children under 14 due to language, violence, or sexual content. Use your V-chip to block these programs during the hours that your child is watching TV.

TV-MA (Mature Audience Only) This rating indicates that a program is specifically designed for adult viewing and may unsuitable for children under 17. Use your V-chip to block these programs during the hours that your child is watching TV.

TEACHING YOUR CHILD EARLY COMPUTER SKILLS

Although I don't advocate prohibiting kids from watching TV or playing video games, you could argue that it's possible for a child to succeed in school without ever doing either. You can't make the same argument about using a computer. The fact is, sometime early in his school career—perhaps even in kindergarten—your child will be interacting with a computer. Throughout his school years, he will be using a computer to do research, write papers, and even access library books. It's critical for a child to feel comfortable following directions from a computer screen, typing on a keyboard, and manipulating a mouse.

EARLY COMPUTER USE RAISES IQ

The question is, when is the right time for a child to learn these important skills? There is compelling evidence that children who enter kindergarten with a basic knowledge of computers are poised to do better in school than those who have had little or no exposure to computers at home. In a recent study that appeared in the *Journal of Pediatrics*, researchers from the University of Ohio evaluated 122 children ages 3 to 5 to determine if there was any advantage in a child using a computer before starting school. The results were remarkable. According to the researchers, children who used computers three to four times a week either at home or at a friend's or relative's house scored on average 7 to 10 points higher on tests designed to estimate IQ, as well as significantly higher on school readiness tests (which assess children's understanding of basic concepts such as size, direction, position, time, quantity, and classification), as compared to those who did not have access to computers. Interestingly, exposure to video games did not provide toddlers with the same benefits. (See the section on video games later in this chapter.)

Please note that when I refer to computer programs, I am not talking about electronic educational toys or "smart toys" that do not teach children basic computer skills. Children learn how to operate the keypad in a way that is specific to the game, but it's not the same as a computer set up. Therefore, when I talk about computers, I'm talking about the traditional computer setup; screen, keyboard, and mouse.

At around age 3, most children have the attention span and manual dexterity to work on a computer keyboard and manipulate a mouse. This is not to say that they are going to do it as well as an adult, but they can begin to learn the basic motions. This is a good time to introduce your child to a computer and to work with her so that she becomes truly comfortable with this technology. I would not recommend having your child use a computer any younger than age 3, as I don't think that d get much out of it. If you happen to be on your computer r 18-month-old comes over to see what you're doing, by all ›ick her up, put her in your lap, and let her see what's going on. If she wants, you can even let her play with the mouse. But I would not make it an everyday occurrence. It's just not going to be a meaningful experience and your child can make better use of her time.

Computer training can help prepare a child for school but it can also be isolating. Therefore, I recommend that when using a computer, children work with an adult who can provide positive human interaction, which is the way children learn best.

Here are some tips on how to make sure your child gets the most out of his computer experience:

Use Age-Appropriate Software

Software for children should be developmentally appropriate, that is, specific for a particular age range. Be sure to buy programs that are designed for children 3 years and over. For ages 3–5, the goal should be to teach children basic computer skills, such as how to follow directions, how to navigate through a computer menu, and how to use the mouse or keyboard to make something happen on the screen. The instructions should be simple. Even if you have a very smart child, don't assume she can use a program that is designed for older kids. It will only frustrate her and turn her off to the experience. It's far better for a child to gain confidence using a computer than to feel continually challenged by it. One of my favorite programs is Shelly's My First Computer Game, produced by ABT Interactive, which is geared for ages 3–6. The program is simple enough for a 3-year-old child to understand and navigate on her own (although I still prefer that she work with an adult). As the child masters different skills, she can move up to different levels and do more sophisticated activities. I also like Reader Rabbit, which I used with my own kids. It not only taught them computer skills but strengthened their reading skills as well.

Avoid "Drill and Practice" Software

Small children should not be using so-called drill-and-practice programs that test toddlers on the alphabet or counting, which is typical of many programs for elementary school children. These programs are as boring and repetitive as they sound and take the fun out of learning. It's more important that children use programs that familiarize them with the computer and how it works rather than pursue the mastery of a specific subject. Ironically, many child psychologists believe that overuse of this type of software can destroy a child's creativity, which is so essential for academic success. (In my opinion, many of these programs are just an electronic version of what's bad in the classroom—drill and practice instead of interaction and input.) A good program will enhance listening skills, help a child learn how to follow directions, and reinforce reading and math readiness without holding a child captive to a series of repetitive exercises.

Limit Computer Time

Children under 3 should not be using a computer. Children between the ages of 3 and 5 can be allowed to use a computer for about thirty minutes daily. As important as computers are to our lives, kids should be spending most of their time doing other things, such as reading or playing outdoors.

Follow Your Child's Cues

Some children have short attention spans and may get bored quickly sitting at a desk. If your child would rather be moving around and playing, let him. There's lots of time for him to become computer literate. If your child seems uninterested in the computer, it could also be that the particular program is too stimulating and your child is shutting down. Some programs may be too fast paced and involved for small children. There's simply too much happening on the screen for the child to take in. If you think that this could be the case with your child, try a calmer program even if it's for a younger child. This could reengage your child's interest in computers, getting him ready for more advanced programs.

Surf the Net Together

If your child is interested in going to specific Web sites for children, do it together. No child should be allowed to surf the Internet on her own. For a list of my favorite websites for children, see Appendix C, "Dr. Perlmutter's Picks."

Computers Are Not Substitutes for Books

Computers are a wonderful adjunct to basic learning tools but are no substitute for books. Reading from the written page is still the preferred method for learning. We may become a completely wired world as this century progresses, but children need to experience early on the uniqueness of each individual book in their collection, how the content remains constant every time it is opened while the interpretation and understanding can vary.

Be Aware of the Ratings

Video games (and computer games) are rated by the Entertainment Software Rating Board. The ratings are as follows:

Early Childhood (EC) These games are suitable for children age 3 and over.

Everyone (E) These games are suitable for children age 6 and over. They may contain some mild cartoon or fantasy violence and/or occasional mild (as opposed to strong) language.

Everyone 10+ (E10+) These games are suitable for children over the age of 10 but may have mild violence and "minimal suggestive themes."

Teen (T) These games are suitable for teens over 13 and may contain violence, strong language, and/or suggestive themes.

Mature (M) These games are not suitable for people under the age of 17 due to mature themes, sexual content, or intense violence.

Adults Only (AO) These games are not suitable for people under the age of 18 and may contain graphic depictions of sex or violence.

I urge parents to click onto the ESRB website, which enables you to check out the ratings of individual games and provides additional information on game content.

VIDEO GAMES: A LITTLE GOES A LONG WAY

Video games are usually played on video game consoles (such as Xbox or Playstation 2) and require a joystick to maneuver through the game, but they can also be played on computers with the appropriate hardware or with handheld devices. Video games have been around for more than three decades, yet they seem to become more controversial with each passing year. There is no shortage of critics who say that these games are corrupting our youth—it's harder to find anyone who has anything positive to say about them. Video games are an easy target. For one thing, many of the most popular games are incredibly violent and contain sexual content that is definitely not for children, although the games may fall into their hands. There are hundreds of games that are not violent and are age appropriate, but they don't get the same kind of publicity. Perhaps because it is a newer medium, there are far fewer studies exploring the impact of video games on children than that of television, and the few studies that have been done show a link between aggressive behavior and playing video games with violent content. Parents are understandably concerned about the long-term impact of video games on their kids. Like television, video games are seductive to young minds because they also are very stimulating to the sensory portions of the brain. If given a choice, many kids, especially boys, would spend every free moment gaming. According to the National Institute on Media and the Family, the average child plays video games around nine hours a week, and that's not counting the twenty-five or so hours spent watching TV, or time on the computer. Video games appear to have a greater allure for males than females—about 70 percent of the players of the most popular console-type games are male, but that could be due to the fact that the games are typically very male oriented.

Furthermore, many parents of school-age children tell me that when their children play video games, they undergo a personality transformation and appear to be in an almost trancelike state. When the parent tries to get her child to stop playing, she hears the universal cry, "Just let me get to the next level," and the child will keep going unless the joystick is physically taken away from her. This poses a real problem for parents who find that video games are sapping the time their child should be devoting to doing homework or other activities. As a result, grades often suffer.

THE CASE FOR VIDEO GAMES

Why would I allow children to play video games at all? There are positive aspects to playing video games that their critics don't mention. First, video games are a user-friendly introduction to electronic media and can help demystify technology for children. A child growing up today is going to be interacting with electronic equipment—from ATMs to PDAs to computers—for the rest of her life. It's important to feel comfortable and not intimidated by technology (which is also why I feel it's absolutely essential for every child over 3 to develop computer skills). Second, video games may help develop hand–eye coordination, which is useful for playing ball, using a computer mouse, driving, and other activities. I use the word *may* because although one would expect video games to improve hand–eye coordination, simply because of how the games are played, there have not been any studies to indicate that this is true. Nevertheless, it takes a certain amount of skill to manipulate a joystick, and I would bet that many of today's pilots, engineers, and surgeons played video games as kids. Third, video games can enhance mathematical skills. In a typical game, you reach a certain number and you move on to the next level. Even the most math-resistant kid will eagerly count up his points so he can move ahead in the game. Finally, if a child plays the game with a partner, he learns to be a team player, another valuable skill. For boys in particular, video games provide a way of social bonding, and the kid who doesn't play is going to be the odd boy out.

So what's an appropriate strategy for video games in your home?

Set Strict Age Limits

Video games are not appropriate for children under the age of 3. First, they don't have the manual dexterity to manipulate a joystick. Second, they should be doing other things with their time. Third, they can hurt themselves. Their hands and arms are not developed enough to sustain the strain of video game playing. The repetitive motion of manipulating the joystick can damage tendons in the arm and hand. Even older children need to be careful about developing repetitive stress syndrome from overplaying video games, but younger children are especially vulnerable.

Choose Age-Appropriate Games

By around age 3, some children may be ready to play age-appropriate games, preferably ones that are designed for a preschool-aged child and are not violent. If you have older children at home, be vigilant that younger children do not use their games. Games designed for school-age children can be surprisingly violent.

Some manufacturers of educational toys offer interactive products that resemble video games, but unlike standard action video games, these games promote reading and math skills. These include products produced by LeapFrog, Fisher-Price, and the V.Smile TV learning system. I include some of these games in Dr. Perlmutter's Picks because they are useful in terms of reinforcing literacy and math skills and children seem to enjoy them, but it's a rare child who will be happy to play these games exclusively once he sees the real thing.

Set Strict Time Limits

As with TV, excess playing of video games can prevent a child from getting enough physical activity, which can lead to obesity. Moreover, if children play video games by themselves for hours on end, they may not learn appropriate social skills necessary for success in school and in life. Don't allow your child to play video games for more than thirty minutes daily. Period.

The two real problems with video games are (1) the amount of time spent playing them and (2) content. Parents have control over both of these factors:

Smarter Child Tip Prescreen a video game before allowing your child to play it. Make sure that you feel it is suitable for your child. When you select a video game for your child, make sure it is age appropriate.

TV AND THE RISK OF EARLY PUBERTY

Children who spend the most amount of time in front of an electronic screen may also be at risk of premature sexual development. Even if not actually entering puberty, they mature sexually at earlier ages than peers who don't watch as much TV. This relationship is stronger for girls than for boys. The average age of puberty, or first menstruation, is around 12.8 years for Caucasian girls and up to a year younger for African-American girls. Many girls these days are showing signs of precocious sexual development, including well-developed breasts and pubic hair growth, well before these ages. Early physical development can be especially devastating for girls; it is linked to poor academic performance, low self-esteem, depression, and even substance abuse.

Although no one knows for sure why watching TV would cause premature sexual development, there are several explanations. First, as discussed earlier, excess TV viewing is associated with childhood obesity, which can boost levels of the female hormone estrogen, which, in turn, can hasten sexual development. Second, TV viewing as well as prolonged exposure to artificial light suppresses the production of a hormone called melatonin that helps regulate sexual development in both boys and girls. As children enter early adolescence, melatonin levels fall naturally, signaling the start of bodily changes that culminate in puberty. Artificially suppressing melatonin, however, could cause a child to go into puberty prematurely.

In a recent study conducted at the University of Florence, researchers studied seventy-four children between the ages of 6 and 12 years old who normally watched around three hours of television every evening. For a seven-day period, the children were not allowed to watch any TV or to use sources of artificial light such as computers or video games. At the end of the week, the children's melatonin levels had risen by an average of 30 percent, with the youngest children showing the greatest increase. Excess TV watching is disrupting normal hormone cycling in children, which, at least indirectly, can affect both their health and academic performance.

The intense sexual content of many television programs could rev up hormone production in children who are not meant to be exposed to this type of stimulation at so young an age. Adults often forget that even though very young children can't talk, they can listen and observe. Their brains soak up everything in their environment. You may think that a 1- or 2-year-old is not observing sexy soap opera scenes or the casual sex on a sitcom, but she is. And by the time a child is 4 or 5 and beginning to develop a sense of her sexual self, she is definitely picking up the suggestive themes on TV. It's very important for parents and caregivers to keep kids away from shows that are not appropriate for their age.

A Smart Approach to TV, Computers, and Video Games

Smarter Child Guidelines for TV		
No TV for children under 2	Limit TV/DVD watching to no more than 1 hour daily	Turn TV into an interactive experience
Use TV commercials as a tool to teach	Don't use TV as a reward or punishment	Let your child see you reading
Turn off the TV when no one is listening	No TV during family meals	No TV in your child's room
Commercial free is best	Use the V-chip	Be aware of TV ratings

Smarter Child Guidelines for Computers		
Use age-appropriate software	Avoid "drill and practice" software	Limit computer time to 30 minutes for preschool children
Follow your child's cues	Surf the net together	Computers are not substitutes for books
Be aware of the ratings		

Smarter Child Guidelines for Video Games		
No video games for children under 3	Choose age-appropriate games	No more than 30 minutes of video games daily

PART III

NUTRITION FOR A SMARTER BRAIN

CHAPTER SEVEN

Feeding the Newborn Brain for Optimal Performance

The best brains are made from the right stuff. And beyond just providing the raw materials for building the optimal brain, good nutrition plays an even more active role in brain development than was once believed. New research reveals that specific nutrients actually turn on the genes responsible for enhancing and refining brain development. Parents must be vigilant that their infants are getting enough of these critical nutrients during this critical growth period.

For the sake of your child's brain, I urge you to breast-feed your child for a full year. Breast milk is the ultimate brain food. Countless studies have shown that children who are breast-fed have as much as an 8-point IQ advantage compared to children who are formula fed. New infant formulas enhanced with DHA (docahexaenic acid—the "good fat") more closely resemble breast milk and may help to close the IQ gap. Nevertheless, breast milk is still the best choice not only for your baby's brain, but for his general health as well. In addition to being a treasure trove of vitamins, minerals, proteins, and essential fats, breast milk also supplies a child with things that no formula can ever duplicate. These include growth factors necessary for proper development as well as antibodies and other immune factors that strengthen your baby's natural defenses against disease.

Unfortunately, few women actually do breast-feed for even up to six months. Although close to two-thirds of all new mothers breast-feed for the first few weeks after birth, by six months that number falls to under 30 percent. By 2 months old, most American babies are given formula for at least some of their feedings. I understand that breast-feeding can be difficult for mothers who work outside the home or mothers at home with other children who demand attention. Nevertheless, breast-feeding is well worth the extra effort. Many women stop breast-feeding simply because they never get the hang of it. It's a myth that breast-feeding comes naturally to women or that it is easy. But there are places to go for help with breast-feeding—some hospitals have lactation specialists on staff to help new mothers learn the right technique for breast-feeding, and groups such as the La Leche League can also provide assistance.

BREAST MILK IS ONLY AS GOOD AS A MOTHER'S DIET

Having sung the praises of breast milk, I want to add one caveat. Breast milk is only as good as a mother's diet. Although breast milk is still the best source of nutrition for infants, it may not be as good as it can be unless the mother is eating an optimal diet. If you are breast-feeding your child, please read the section "Breast Milk to Build a Better Brain" later in this chapter.

MOST BABIES ARE FORMULA FED

I'm a realist and I understand that many of you will be using commercial formula to either augment breast-feeding or for complete nutrition when you stop breast-feeding. Although it will never be as good as breast milk, commercial formula has gotten a lot better in recent years. Not all formula is equally good for your child's brain. If you choose to give your child formula, I urge you to read about how to choose the best formula for your child at the end of this chapter.

For the first four months of life, breast milk (or formula) should be your infant's only source of nourishment. In this chapter I discuss how to optimize breast milk and formula to make sure that your child is getting the right nutrients to grow a bigger and smarter brain. In Chapter 8, I show how to introduce solid food to your baby for maximum brain development, as well as how to feed your toddler's growing brain.

NUTRIENTS TO GROW A BETTER BRAIN

During the formative first years of life, a surprising number of children do not receive adequate amounts of required nutrients. I'm not talking about the kind of overt malnutrition that will produce obvious health results such as stunted growth or disease—I'm talking about subtle deficiencies that are all too common in America today. Countless numbers of children are being shortchanged when it comes to getting enough good fat (DHA) and minerals such as iron and iodine. Even a minor shortfall of these important, brain-building nutrients can interfere with brain development.

DHA: IS YOUR CHILD GETTING ENOUGH OF THE SMART FAT?

Is your infant getting enough DHA? Maybe not. And you may not be getting enough of this brain-boosting fat, either. Recent studies show that the amount of DHA in the breast milk of American women is among the lowest in the world. Considering how important DHA is for brain development, this is cause for alarm.

DHA is an omega-3 long-chain polyunsaturated fatty acid that makes up fully 25 percent of the total fat found in the brain. DHA is not produced by the body to any significant degree and therefore must be obtained through food or supplements. DHA is found in fatty fish (such as tuna, mackerel, salmon, halibut, and sardines) and is present in breast milk. It has only recently been added to infant formula. There are high concentrations of DHA in the brain's cortex, the gray matter in the outer layer of the brain that is responsible for higher functions such as learning, reasoning, and memory. It's also an important component of myelin, the protective covering around nerve cells that speeds up transmission in the neurons, making for a faster brain. DHA is also vital for the development of the retina and critical for visual function. This has obvious implications for early literacy. But perhaps the most exciting role of DHA in brain development is its newly discovered function in turning on the production of genes responsible for a critical brain growth hormone, brain-derived neurotrophic factor (BDNF). In this role, DHA turns on the smart genes, boosting levels of BDNF, which is

rmation of synapses, dendrites, and other important cells
rain development.

DHA MAKES BABIES SMARTER

Medical research demonstrates time and again that infants whose diets are rich in DHA perform better on tests of mental function. And a recent study revealed that the infants breast-fed by mothers who took DHA supplements had improved hand–eye coordination at 2½ years old compared to babies whose mothers did not take DHA. The DHA-supplemented mothers had 75 percent more DHA in their breast milk than the nonsupplemented mothers and their babies had 35 percent higher DHA blood levels. On the other hand, low levels of DHA in children have been linked to an increased risk of ADHD, vision problems, violent behavior, and depression. DHA is so important to brain health that it is added to 75 percent of the infant formula now sold in the United States, although some brands of formula have more optimal levels of DHA than others.

Breast milk and DHA-fortified formula are the best sources of DHA for the first four months of life. Nursing mothers should take a DHA supplement to make sure that their DHA levels are optimal. Once whole foods are introduced into the diet, toddlers should be encouraged to eat DHA-fortified foods including DHA-enriched eggs, whole-grain products, and cereals.

Optimal Amounts of DHA

Nursing Mothers: Take a supplement containing 400 milligrams of DHA daily. I recommend Neuromins, Natrol DHA Omega-3, and Dr. Perlmutter's DHA.

Formula-Fed Infants: Look for formula containing around 19 milligrams of DHA per 5-ounce serving.

Children 2 and Over: From ages 6 months to 2 years: 100 mg daily; from ages 2–5: 200 milligrams daily.

Depending on your child's age, capsules may be swallowed or chewed, or punctured with a pin or needle and the contents mixed in with cereal or other food. I recommend NeuroMins for Kids (100- or 200-milligram capsules) and my own brand, Dr. Perlmutter's DHA for Kids (100-milligram capsules).

ARA (ARACHIDONIC ACID)

The other critically important fatty acid for brain development is ARA (arachidonic acid). ARA is the principal omega-6 fatty acid in the brain. Like DHA, ARA is essential for growth and development of the brain and visual system. In addition, ARA is the precursor to a group of hormone-like messenger chemicals in the body called *eicosanoids*, which play an important role in immune function, blood clotting, and other important functions. Breast milk is a rich source of ARA and many infant formulas are enriched with both ARA and DHA. However, DHA deficiency persists as a problem because it is not that common in the food supply.

Optimal Amounts of ARA

Nursing Mothers: Nursing mothers should get an adequate amount of ARA from their diet.

Formula-Fed Infants: Look for formula containing around 34 milligrams of ARA per 5-ounce serving.

Children 2 and Over: ARA is abundant in the food supply, found in meat, milk, and eggs, so neither mother nor baby need to take supplements. Once children begin eating solid food, they are rarely deficient in ARA.

IRON: THE BRAIN-BOOSTING MINERAL

When you think of iron deficiency you probably think of anemia; however, a shortage of this mineral in infants can slow down brain development. Why is iron important to the brain?

- Without adequate supplies of iron, fewer neural connections can be formed.
- Iron is required for the production of myelin. An interruption in the production of myelin results in both mental and motor impairments.
- Iron is required for the function and synthesis of dopamine, a neurotransmitter that plays a critical role in mental and physical health. Deficiencies in this mineral may impact dopamine activity and thus affect learning, memory, and attention.

Even subtle shortages of this crucial mineral can adversely affect intelligence and behavior—and correcting minor deficiencies with iron supplements is extremely beneficial. And if you don't think that your child could be iron deficient, think again. Iron deficiency in children is quite common in the United States. According to the Third National Health and Nutrition Examination Survey (NHANES III), a large government-sponsored study of nutritional trends, 9 percent of American children between the ages of 1 and 3 are iron deficient and 3 percent have iron-deficient anemia. My guess is that an equal number of children under 1 are also iron deficient, especially those 6 to 12 months old.

There are several reasons why so many children in this age group don't get enough iron. First is our surprisingly low rate of breastfeeding. Breast milk is an excellent source of iron for babies, even better than formula. Normally, it is difficult for your body to absorb the iron you get from food, but breast milk contains a specialized form of iron bound to a protein called lactoferrin that is 100 percent bioavailable to the infant. Unfortunately, as discussed earlier, only a small number of babies are actually breast-fed even until 6 months. Second, cow's milk, which is a poor source of iron, is introduced into many children's diets early. A child who fills up on cow's milk and isn't getting any additional iron supplements is at risk for iron deficiency. (I don't recommend giving cow's milk to children under the age of 1.)

If you give your child commercial formula, use only iron-fortified formula. Not all formula is iron fortified, and if your child is not getting iron-enriched formula, he or she is clearly at risk of running short of this essential mineral.

I also recommend that nursing babies receive iron supplements beginning at 4 to 6 months. There are two sources of iron in food: *heme* and *non-heme.* The most bioavailable is heme iron, which is found in foods from animal sources such as meat, poultry, and fish. Plants contain non-heme iron, which isn't as easily absorbed. Foods containing vitamin C (citrus fruits, berries, cruciferous vegetables) increase the absorption of iron and must be included in a toddler's diet.

Smarter Child Tip How do you know if your child is getting all the iron he needs? Normal blood tests performed on infants at 9 months of age evaluate hemoglobin (the iron-carrying protein found in red blood cells) to determine whether or not the child is anemic. While this test picks up obvious anemia, it is an extremely poor indicator of early iron deficiency. Instead, ask your pediatrician to test your child's ferritin levels. Ferritin is a protein that stores iron in the body and *serum ferritin* is an accurate indicator of the amount of iron stored. The lower the level, the more likely the child is to be iron deficient. (See the resource section for information on the ferritin test.)

If your child is prone to iron deficiency, be extra vigilant about making sure that her diet includes enough iron-rich foods and the vitamin C necessary to absorb them.

After six months, a breast-fed baby should be given iron supplements. The preferred form is ferrous sulfate or infant vitamin drops with iron, and the suggested dose is 6–8 milligrams of oral elemental iron daily. Low-weight and preterm infants may require higher doses of iron beginning in the first month. Like all drugs and nutritional supplements, iron preparations should be kept out of the reach of children. Between the ages of 1 and 3 years children require 8–10 milligrams of elemental iron supplement each day.

At around 4 to 6 months, you can add iron-enriched cereal to your child's diet. For the first year of life, iron-fortified cereals can help prevent iron deficiency.

Optimal Amounts of Iron

Nursing Mothers: Take a supplement containing 40–50 milligrams of iron per day. I recommend Thorne Basic Prenatal, Citracal Prenatal Plus DHA, and Dr. Perlmutter's Prenatal and Nursing Multivitamin.

Breast-Fed Babies over 6 Months: Infants 6 months and over should be given infant vitamin drops with iron. The suggested dose is 6–8 milligrams of oral elemental iron daily, and the preferred form is ferrous sulfate because it is better absorbed.

Formula-Fed Babies: Babies should be given only iron-enriched formula containing 1.8 milligrams of iron per 5-ounce serving.

For Children 1 and Over: Between the ages of 1 and 3 years children require 8–10 milligrams of elemental iron daily.

IODINE

Iodine deficiency, which is becoming a growing problem in the United States among nursing mothers and infants, can have a profound impact on your child's brain. Iodine is a crucial nutrient in the synthesis of thyroid hormones thyroxine (T4) and triiodothyronine (T3), which are primary regulators of metabolism, growth, and development. Thyroid hormones turn on the genes that are involved in the formation of myelin and dendrites (the branches that grow off neurons to accommodate new synapses) and can also boost levels of BDNF, the growth hormone that is a key factor in making a smarter brain.

Although rare in the Western world, severe iodine deficiency is a leading cause of preventable brain damage and retardation worldwide. The introduction of iodized salt in the United States in the 1920s significantly reduced severe iodine deficiencies in this country. What's alarming, however, is the fact that iodine levels in pregnant women are on the decline. According to the most recent National Health and Nutrition Examination Survey (NHANES 2000) urinary iodine levels, an accurate measure of iodine intake, are just *half* of what they were in the general population thirty years ago. Given the important relationship between iodine and thyroid function, this is a cause for alarm.

The primary source of iodine in the diet is iodized salt but half of the salt used in the United States is not iodized, including sea salt and kosher salt. The salt in processed salty snacks such as pretzels and nuts is not iodized either, nor is that used to make pickles, sauerkraut, and related foods. Moreover, many nursing mothers steer clear of salt because it causes bloating. Nursing mothers must be especially vigilant about their iodine intake. That is why I recommend that nursing women take 150 micrograms of supplemental iodine daily to ensure that their breast milk contains adequate levels of this essential mineral. Multivitamin and mineral supplements that contain 100 percent of the minimum daily requirement for iodine will supply 150 micrograms.

Here's one rare instance where formula may have an edge over breast milk: Formula is supplemented with iodine, so there should be little risk of an infant developing an iodine deficiency.

Several environmental toxins reduce iodine levels in breast milk. One of them is cigarette smoke, which is yet another reason why nursing mothers should not smoke. Another iodine-inhibiting chemical is *perchlorate,* a contaminant that comes from, believe it or not, rocket fuel. Ammonium perchlorate is an ingredient in solid propellants for rockets and missiles. Used since the 1940s by the defense department, massive amounts of perchlorate have been disposed of at military sites throughout the country over the years. It has found its way into our food and water—and, according to recent studies, is present in most samples of breast milk. Researchers from Texas Tech University recently analyzed breast milk from 36 women randomly selected from across the country, and samples from every single one of them had traces of perchlorate. There was also an inverse correlation between perchlorate concentration and the iodine content of breast milk. Women who had high concentrations of perchlorate had correspondingly low levels of iodine. This means that not only are nursing children getting reduced amounts of iodine in breast milk, but perchlorate may also interfere with their iodine absorption.

Perchlorate is so ubiquitous in the environment, you can't avoid it. But you can protect your baby from its bad effects by making sure that you are getting enough iodine. That's why it's so important to take an iodine supplement.

I also recommend that nursing mothers have their iodine levels tested. This is a simple test that involves collecting a urine sample for evaluation at a lab. If the urine iodine level is high, that's good. It means your body has plenty of iodine and is excreting what it doesn't need. If your test reveals that you have an iodine deficiency, you need to take immediate steps to correct it both to protect your own thyroid function and to ensure your nursing baby is receiving enough of this brain-saving nutrient.

Smarter Child Tip It's difficult for nursing mothers to get enough iodine from food alone, which is why I recommend taking a daily supplement as well as enhancing your diet with iodine-enriched food. Good dietary sources include sea vegetables (such as kelp, kombu, dulse, and nori), which you can find at most health food stores.

Optimal Levels of Iodine

Nursing Mothers: Take a multivitamin containing 150–200 micrograms of iodine. I recommend Thorne Basic Prenatal, Citracal Prenatal Plus DHA, and Dr. Perlmutter's Prenatal and Nursing Multivitamin available at www.YourSmartChild.com or (800) 530–1982.

Formula-Fed Babies: 5 ounces of formula should contain 9 micrograms of iodine.

Toddlers and Children: Toddlers and children rarely need to take iodine supplements.

BREAST MILK TO BUILD A BETTER BRAIN

Not all breast milk is equal: A well-nourished mother produces the best breast milk. For nursing mothers, the concept of eating for two doesn't end with pregnancy. Any deficiencies in your diet will be passed on to your child, so optimal nutrition is important.

Even though you may be anxious to get back to your pre-pregnancy weight, now is not the time to diet. Your energy needs are increased at this time—in fact, they are even greater during breast-feeding than during pregnancy. Nursing women need to consume an additional 400–500 calories per day to keep up with increased demands.

- Eat a healthy, nutrient-dense diet. Avoid junk food that provides empty calories but little in the way of nutrition.
- Stick to whole grains, lean protein (free-range chicken, turkey, hor-

mone- and antibiotic-free lean beef, organic low-fat dairy products), and lots of fresh fruits and vegetables.

- Try to eat organic, pesticide-free produce at least for the duration of breast-feeding. Pesticides are powerful neurotoxins that can be harmful both to you and your infant. Look for produce with the USDA organic seal. (Be sure to wash all produce carefully because organic produce may be prone to fungal growth.)
- Because your baby counts on you for essential vitamins and minerals, these needs also increase during this time. Nursing mothers should take a high-potency multivitamin and mineral supplement.
- Limit your intake of fish. High levels of mercury and pesticides make fish less-than-ideal food for lactating mothers. Although that may seem hard to swallow, the good news is that some fish, like wild salmon (not farm raised), are relatively low in mercury and pesticides and can be consumed once or twice a month. I would not recommend eating even these good fish more often than that because of the potential of toxin buildup in your body that could be passed on to your baby.
- Many public water supplies are contaminated with pollutants such as perchlorate, pesticides, and lead. I recommend that you drink chemical-free bottled water or install a water purification system in your home. (I prefer the reverse osmosis system. For more information see the resource section at the end of the book.)

Vegetarian Alert Women who are strict vegetarians take note: Your baby may be lacking an important B vitamin, B_{12}. B vitamins in general and B_{12} in particular are critical for the developing brain and nervous system. Breast-fed infants of vegetarians may have limited stores of vitamin B_{12}. Since a deficiency in this vitamin can lead to irreversible neurological damage, nursing mothers who are strict vegetarians or vegans should take a supplement. I recommend that you take a B-complex vitamin containing at least 400 micrograms of folic acid (800 micrograms is preferable), 500 milligrams of vitamin B_6, and 500 micrograms of vitamin B_{12}.

GET GOOD FATS INTO YOUR BABY'S BRAIN

Be vigilant about taking your DHA supplement and be sure to avoid all bad fats that can be passed on to your infant. Trans fats are particularly detrimental to a developing brain. Trans fats are created during the process of hydrogenation when polyunsaturated vegetable oils are chemically altered to extend their shelf life. Excess levels of trans fats in brain cells result in slower, less efficient brains. Furthermore, trans fats have none of the brain-boosting qualities associated with DHA. Even more devastating, trans fats also inhibit the enzymes that convert other fats into DHA, resulting in even lower levels of this protective and essential fatty acid. Fortunately, a savvy consumer can easily avoid trans fats. You don't have to eat them and you don't have to pass them on to your baby in your breast milk!

Your best defense is to read food labels. Trans fats are a common ingredient in processed foods such as chips, breads, crackers, and frozen foods. Read food labels. Fortunately, manufacturers are now required to list the trans fat content of processed food on their labels so it's much easier to avoid them than it used to be. Second, stay away from fried foods. Trans fats are also formed when vegetable oils are heated to very high temperatures—picture french fries in vats of bubbling oil. Fast food is the major source of trans fats in the U.S. diet, so steer clear of fast-food restaurants unless you can stick with the salads or broiled entrees.

AVOID UNNECESSARY MEDICATIONS

While you are nursing, check with your doctor before taking *any* medication, prescription or over the counter. A nursing mother's occasional use of over-the-counter drugs such as acetaminophen (Tylenol), aspirin, or ibuprofen will not harm her baby, nor will an occasional alcoholic beverage. Most drugs attach to proteins in the mother's blood and therefore only pass into breast milk in small amounts. Some drugs, however, may pass into breast milk and should be avoided.

What Supplements Do Nursing Mothers Need?

DHA: Take a supplement containing 400 mg DHA daily.

ARA: No supplement necessary.

Iodine: Take a supplement containing 150–200 mcg of iodine daily.

Iron: Take a supplement containing 40–50 mg of iron per day.

THE BEST FORMULA FOR YOUR BABY'S BRAIN

The gold standard for infant formula is breast milk and the best formulas are those that come closest to approximating breast milk. The primary proteins in human breast milk are whey (60–65 percent) and casein (35–40 percent). The ideal whey-to-casein ratio in infant formula should therefore be around 60:40. Whey-based protein, which is derived from cow's milk, is the most similar to that found in human breast milk. Although whey-based protein comes from cow's milk, it is substantially altered to make it more like breast milk. It is not the same as using pure cow's milk, which should not be given to children under 12 months old. Whey protein is more easily digested and easier on the kidneys. If your infant cannot tolerate whey-based formulas, your options are goat's milk formula or soy formulas. Goat's milk–based formula is more easily digested for some infants than cow's milk because it has smaller fat particles and forms smaller curds. Soy formula contains soy protein that has been modified to include all the essential amino acids necessary for the body to manufacture protein.

SOY FORMULA AS A LAST RESORT

As a rule, I don't recommend soy protein unless an infant absolutely can't tolerate other forms of formula. First, soy formula is quite different from breast milk in terms of its fat and protein content. Moreover, soy formula contains much more manganese than milk-based formula, and based on animal studies, some researchers believe that an excessive amount of this mineral may harm the developing brain and cause serious behavior problems. High levels of manganese appear to primarily affect the concentration of the important neurotransmitter dopamine, particularly in the area of the brain involved in problem solving. I'm particularly concerned about the high level of estrogen-like compounds in soy called *phytoestrogens.* As their name suggests, they have well-documented hormonal effects on the body. Children who drink soy formula are exposed to very high levels of these plant estrogens. Although long-term studies of soy formula–fed children have not shown any problems in terms of physical development, I will still worry that there is a potential for harm until there are more studies that confirm these findings. So the bottom line is, whey-based formula is best, goat's milk–based formula is a good alternative, and soy formula is a distant third. Use it if you must.

Infant Formula: How Much Is Optimal?

There are several excellent brands of infant formula on the market. Ultra Bright Beginnings, which also offers an organic product, has the highest levels of DHA, as well as optimal amounts of iron and iodine and is sold at major stores including CVS, Albertson's, Pathmark, and Walgreen's. Other good brands include Parent's Choice (Wal-Mart's brand) and Member's Mark (sold at Sam's Club).

Key Nutrients per 5-Ounce Serving of Formula

DHA: 19 mg
ARA: 34 mg
Iron: 1.8 mg
Iodine: 9 mcg

CHOOSE A NONTOXIC BABY BOTTLE

Choosing the right baby bottle is nearly as important as choosing the right formula. Use only opaque plastic or glass bottles. Avoid clear plastic bottles, which are made of polycarbonate plastic. One of the chemicals used to manufacture these bottles, bisphenol A (BPA) is an estrogenic endocrine disruptor, a chemical that adversely affects the endocrine system in humans and animals. In laboratory studies, this chemical has been shown to inhibit the formation of synaptic connections, particularly in the hippocampus, the memory center of the brain. It has also been shown to alter the regulatory effects of thyroid hormones on brain development. This obviously leads to concerns about its effects in humans. *Consumer Reports* tested hard plastic baby bottles and found that even after multiple washings, they continued to give off BPA. Why take a chance? This is one risk you can avoid simply by not using these bottles. You do have a choice. You can switch to opaque and pastel baby bottles (Evenflo and Gerber are two brands that offer a wide variety of nontoxic bottles), or you can use old-fashioned glass bottles.

CHAPTER EIGHT

Smart Eating for Smarter Kids

As your child moves from infant to toddler, she needs a nutrient-rich diet to feed her developing brain. Half of all energy consumed by young children is utilized to fuel brain activity.

- Your child's brain continues to need optimal amounts of DHA, iron, and iodine.
- During these formative years, allergies and food sensitivities can cause or aggravate learning and behavior problems.

Breast milk or formula should be your infant's only source of nourishment for the first four months. At 4 to 6 months old, however, your baby is ready to be introduced to solid foods. You may have heard that starting your baby on cereal earlier will help him sleep through the night. This is simply not true. When your child begins to sleep for longer periods depends on his development and bedtime routine, not how full he is. Before age 4 to 6 months, your baby's digestive system is not ready to handle solid foods. Too-early introduction of solids will only cause problems, such as increasing his risk of food allergies and obesity, two problems that can ultimately impact your child's mental function.

Cereal: Timing Is Everything

Introduce Cereal Between 4 and 6 Months

A baby's first solid food should be cereal. The timing of when you introduce baby cereal is extremely important. If you do it too early (before 4 months) or too late (after 6 months) you increase the odds of your child developing a sensitivity to gluten, a protein found in grains including wheat, barley, and rye. Gluten sensitivity can interfere with the absorption of important nutrients in children, resulting in unexpected weight loss as well as learning and behavior problems. Gluten sensitivity tends to run in families, but it can also strike out of the blue. Every parent should be aware of this potential problem. (Please turn to Chapter 12 for more information on how gluten sensitivity can affect brain development.)

Start with a single-grain, iron-fortified cereal such as rice or barley cereal or oatmeal, and introduce new cereals only once every four days so you can gauge how your child reacts to each grain. Mix dry cereal with an ounce of formula or breast milk, stirring to reach a thin, runny consistency. Do not use cereals that are premixed with formula because they may contain a mixture of grains and a formula your baby is not used to. Also, don't add sweeteners or salt to your baby's cereal. You might think it tastes bland, but it's not made for your palate. Begin with just a teaspoon of dry cereal once a day, and as your child gets used to solids, gradually increase the serving size to three tablespoons of cereal twice a day.

Pureed Food Is Next

At five to seven months, start your baby on pureed or strained vegetables and fruits. Begin with vegetables, since humans have an innate preference for sweet foods and your child may be reluctant to try vegetables if he's given fruit first. Some pediatricians recommend starting with orange vegetables such as carrots, squash, and sweet potatoes first, followed by peas, green beans, and other green vegetables. As with cereals, stick with single-ingredient baby vegetables. Start with one to three teaspoons, building up to four tablespoons a day. Again, wait four days after starting one food before introducing another and observe how your child tolerates each one. After your child has been introduced to vegetables, start on fruits such as bananas, applesauce, pears, apricot, peaches, and plums in a similar manner.

WHY ORGANIC IS BETTER

Whether you're buying prepared baby foods or making your own, always use whole, natural, preservative-free, additive-free, organic foods whenever possible. Not only do whole foods contain more vitamins, minerals, fiber, and healthful fats as compared to processed foods, but they also bypass the pesticides, additives, and toxins that impair concentration and increase hyperactivity in some children. Good brands of infant cereals and baby foods include Healthy Times and Earth's Best certified organic baby foods. There are a number of excellent infant cereals and canned baby foods sold in supermarkets and health food stores, or better yet, you can make your own.

Fresh food is always more nutritious than canned, processed food, and whipping it up is easier than you might think. All you have to do is puree vegetables, fruit, and other healthful foods you eat in a blender, food processor, or coffee grinder (for dry foods). As your child gets older and his culinary repertoire expands, you can offer a greater selection of home-cooked foods. By the time he is 9 to 12 months old, he will be eating a variety of regular table foods, including fish, poultry, beans, meat, and mixed dishes.

FOOD ALLERGIES

As I mentioned earlier, an important consideration in the timing and method of introducing solids is food allergies. Six percent of American children under the age of 3 have food allergies, and many more have sensitivities to foods that create problems. Food allergies are caused by an overactive immune system that goes into overdrive when exposed to an offending food. This results in the release of histamine and other chemicals that can cause a variety of symptoms.

Allergies tend to run in families, so if a child's parent has allergies, her chances of developing them are dramatically increased. This is why it is so important to take care to start your child on solids slowly and methodically. Do not give your baby several new foods all at once. The recommended interval between the introduction of new foods is four days. This way, if your child has a reaction to something, you can determine what caused it.

While the most prevalent symptoms of food allergies in children are crying, colic, rashes, eczema, diarrhea, and respiratory symptoms, other symptoms such as sleepiness, concentration difficulties, irritability, and temper tantrums (sometimes referred to as "allergic irritability syndrome") are also quite common. I believe that sensitivities to food and environmental allergens are a significant yet overlooked cause of hyperactivity, impulsivity, concentration difficulties, and inability to control emotions and impulses. This is why our clinic uses a food allergy blood test as part of our evaluation of children suspected of having ADHD (see Chapter 17).

The foods most often associated with allergies in children are milk, eggs, peanuts, wheat, soy, and tree nuts such as pecans and walnuts. Beyond being allergic to milk and dairy products, some children don't tolerate these foods because they lack a specific enzyme (lactase) needed to digest a specific milk sugar (lactose). For these children, lactose-free dairy products, which are widely available, are well tolerated. As a child's digestive and immune systems mature, he may outgrow allergies to milk, eggs, and soy.

The food allergy issue gets even thornier as children get older and you have less control over their diet as they are exposed to more outside influences. If you suspect that allergies are a factor in your child's emotional, behavioral, or intellectual function, consult an environmental medicine specialist. And keep in mind that there are now blood tests available to assist in uncovering food allergies.

TODDLERS AND BEYOND

Once your child starts eating regular food—along with the rest of the family at home or in restaurants, and at the homes of relatives and friends—the real challenges begin. We live in a junk food culture. The bulk of the foods targeted for children are high in sugar, fat, and/or calories with little real nutritional value. These foods have a devastating effect on the brain and adversely affect both intelligence and behavior.

The average American child spends at least twenty hours a week in front of a television, and almost two-thirds of all kids under the age of 2 watch a couple of hours of TV a day. And what do they see? Well, among other things, thirteen advertisements for food each and every day, and I guarantee they aren't touting apples or spinach.

Princeton researchers conducted a national survey of the food intake of more than three thousand children ages 4 to 24 months and came up with some appalling statistics. Among children ages 9 to 24 months, 25 to 30 percent ate no fruit on any given day, and 20 to 25 percent ate no vegetables. (The number one vegetable consumed by toddlers was french fries.) On the day of the survey, 69 percent of the kids 19 to 24 months old ate candy or dessert, 44 percent drank sweetened beverages, 27 percent ate hot dogs, bacon, or sausage, 27 percent consumed salty snacks, and 26 percent ate french fries. Even among babies 7 to 8 months old, 46 percent consumed some type of sweetened drink, dessert, or other sweets daily.

You're up against some pretty strong cultural influences, but never forget that the strongest influence on your child's eating patterns is you. This may require you to reevaluate your own diet because children are great mimics. If your family eats balanced, healthful meals, so will your child. If she has access to a kitchen full of soft drinks and sugar-coated cereals, that's what she'll want. Lifelong eating habits are learned and adopted during childhood. This is the time your child is becoming habituated to the types of foods that she will enjoy for the rest of her life. Therefore, the food preferences you instill in your child will not only affect her intelligence and behavior in the short term but will impact all aspects of her health throughout her life.

FATS TO AVOID

Just as important as including brain-building fats, such as DHA, in your child's diet is restricting bad fats. Bad fats are harmful to everyone but are particularly hazardous for young children, whose brains are under construction. When the brain doesn't have access to DHA and other essential fatty acids, it has to make do with the dietary fats that are available. And most of the foods marketed to young children contain bad fats. The most harmful of these are trans fats. When trans fats are incorporated into neurons, they interfere with normal cellular function, resulting in a slower, less efficient brain. To make sure your child avoids trans fats, read food labels carefully. As of January 2006, food manufacturers must list the presence of trans fats in foods. Stay away from fried foods such as french fries and chicken nuggets (the mainstays of children's fast-food meals), cookies, crackers, and other foods made with partially hydrogenated oils that are converted into trans fats. You should also go easy on saturated fat, avoiding concentrated sources such as bacon, hot dogs, and sausage.

PROTEIN TO POWER THE BRAIN

Amino acids, the building blocks of protein, play many crucial roles in the human body, and one of them is the formation of neurotransmitters. Neurotransmitters are specialized chemical messengers that allow brain cells to "talk" to one another. They include acetylcholine, involved in learning and memory; dopamine, which affects movement, balance, and emotion; norepinephrine, known to increase alertness; and mood-, sleep-, and appetite-regulating serotonin, to mention a few. Imbalances and inadequacies in neurotransmitters are linked to mood and emotional disorders, so it's important to supply the brain with the raw materials necessary for their synthesis.

The best sources of animal protein are poultry, eggs, lean beef, pork, lamb, and occasional servings of fish with low mercury content. I know that fish has been touted as "brain food," but I am so concerned about the mercury content and other pollutants in our fish supply that I recommend that children eat no more than one fish meal a week. Beans, nuts and seeds, and whole grains are also protein rich, but they may not contain all the essential amino acids. For children on a healthful, varied diet, getting enough protein is easy. Protein intake can be an issue, however, when parents attempt to raise their children on a strict vegan or macrobiotic diet. Such a diet can cause deficiencies not only in protein but also in iron and vitamin B_{12}, which may lead to significant cognitive decline.

This doesn't mean that a vegetarian diet can't be a brain-friendly diet. Children can absolutely thrive on a vegetarian diet provided that parents are careful about ensuring (1) adequate amounts of vitamin B_{12} and iron, and (2) the proper combination of vegetarian sources of protein along with grains to ensure that the complete amino acid building blocks for protein are provided.

CARBOHYDRATES: ENERGY FOR YOUR CHILD'S BRAIN

Although carbohydrates have taken a beating in recent years with the popularity of low-carb, high-fat diets, they are an essential nutrient. Just as you should not restrict fat from your child's diet, neither should you restrict carbohydrates. Carbohydrates are converted into glucose, which is our primary source of energy. The brain utilizes massive amounts of glucose—up until the age of 3, half of all energy produced by the body goes to fuel the brain. Obviously, an enormous amount of nourishment is required to help young children reach their full intellectual potential.

As with fats, there's a world of difference between different types of carbohydrates. Stay away from rapidly metabolized processed and refined carbohydrates like sugar and white flour. Foods made with these simple carbohydrates provide a rapid rise in blood glucose, which translates into a quick burst of energy followed by a precipitous drop. Children are particularly sensitive to these fluctuations in blood glucose, and they can cause concentration and attention problems, irritability, and mood swings. What your child's brain really needs is a steady source of energy, and this is provided by slow-burning carbohydrates, such as those found in fiber-rich vegetables, fruits, legumes, and whole grains.

Unfortunately, many of the foods our culture trains kids to like are loaded with sugars and other refined carbohydrates: sodas, fruit juices, high-sugar breakfast cereals, cookies and crackers, white bread, fruit-sweetened yogurt, ice cream—the list goes on and on. It's okay to let your child have a piece of birthday cake at a party, but these foods should not be standard fare. The best thing to do is simply keep junk food out of the house.

SMART MEALS FOR SMARTER KIDS

Breakfast

The old saying that breakfast is the most important meal of the day is particularly true for children. The morning meal jump-starts metabolism and supplies the brain with much-needed glucose and other nutrients. Studies show that children who eat breakfast perform better in school in areas such as language, recall, and problem solving. Breakfast should include slow-burning carbohydrates to fuel the brain, as well as protein, which tides kids over and keeps them going through the morning. DHA-enriched eggs and high-quality, whole-grain toast, cereal with fruit and milk, yogurt and fruit, or toast with nut butter and jam are kid-friendly breakfasts that will start your child's day off right.

Lunch

Lunches, whether they're eaten at home, preschool, or on the run, tend to be an informal affair. Like breakfast, they should include both carbohydrates and protein. Unfortunately, many on-the-run foods are low in protein and may cause kids to run out of mental, emotional, and physical steam a couple of hours later. Sandwiches are good lunch fare for kids, but make sure they include an adequate amount of protein-rich filling such as lean chicken, turkey, or roast beef, organic, unsweetened peanut butter without trans fatty acids (sold at many health food stores and some supermarkets), or egg salad made with omega-3-enriched eggs. Soup or leftovers (in a thermos if necessary) are also satisfying lunch items. Rather than serving these items with chips or crackers, give your children raw vegetables, along with fruit slices or yogurt for a sweet treat.

Dinner

Dinner is the meal when the family should sit down together, enjoy one another's company, and eat food that will help wind children down for the evening. Carbohydrates stimulate the production of serotonin, a neurotransmitter that promotes a feeling of calmness and relaxation. Therefore, whole-grain pasta, brown rice, and potatoes make good dinner carbohydrate selections, rounded off with vegetables and lean protein.

Snacks

Kids need snacks. Their stomachs are small but their nutrient needs are big. Providing healthful snacks between meals ensures that a child's growing brain receives a steady supply of glucose throughout the day. About 20 percent of a child's daily calories should come from between-meals snacks. Although it's easy to reach for prepackaged snack foods, most of them, as we've discussed, are low in nutrients and high in sugar, fat, and/or calories. Here are some healthful, easy snack suggestions that kids love.

- Plain organic yogurt with a little chopped fruit, or mixed with whole grain cereal or nuts
- Raw carrot, celery, snow peas, red peppers, and other vegetables cut into small pieces
- Guacamole with raw veggies
- Hummus with crackers
- Peanut butter on celery sticks
- Almond butter on apple slices
- Fruit smoothie (mixed in the blender with whole fruit, ice, and protein powder, if desired)
- Part-skim milk mozzarella cheese sticks
- Low-fat cheese and whole-grain crackers
- Healthy cereal, with or without milk
- Air-popped popcorn
- Applesauce—no sugar added
- Hard-boiled DHA-enriched egg
- Slices or small cubes of turkey or chicken
- Whole-grain toast with nut butter or natural jam

The best way to teach your child the healthy eating habits that will facilitate learning and optimal behavior is to set a good example. Bring only "smart" foods into your kitchen, prepare nutritious meals and snacks for your family, and be very selective when dining out. Getting your child off on the right nutritional footing is one of the greatest gifts you can give him, for it will give him a mental edge that will last a lifetime.

There are a number of other vitamins and minerals that have definitive functions in brain development, attention, and behavior. Antioxidants such as vitamins A, C, E and selenium protect the brain against free-radical damage. B-complex vitamins are required for the synthesis of neurotransmitters and overall nervous system function, and inadequate intake may result in poor concentration and memory. Deficiencies in magnesium and calcium, which help relax nerve and muscle cells, may make children edgy and irritable, and zinc deficiencies have been linked with behavioral and intellectual problems. The best way to ensure that your child receives optimal levels of these and other vital nutrients is to provide a high-quality children's daily multivitamin and mineral supplement. (See Appendix A for recommendations.)

Smarter Child Tip Toddlers and small children also need adequate amounts of iron to fuel their brains. Children between the ages of 2 and 3 require 18 milligrams of iron daily from food and/or supplements; children between the ages of 4 and 8 need 10 milligrams of iron daily from food or supplements. Lean beef, chicken, turkey, soybeans, and iron-fortified cereals are the best sources of iron. See the following food chart to make sure that your child is getting enough iron-rich food.

Iron Is a Key Nutrient for Brain Health

Selected Food Sources of Heme Iron	
Food	***Milligrams per serving***
Chicken liver, cooked, 3½ ounces	12.8
Oysters, breaded and fried, 6 pieces	4.5
Beef, chuck, lean only, braised, 3 ounces	3.2
Clams, breaded, fried, ¾ cup	3.0
Beef, tenderloin, roasted, 3 ounces	3.0
Turkey, dark meat, roasted, 3½ ounces	2.3
Beef, eye of round, roasted, 3 ounces	2.2
Turkey, light meat, roasted, 3½ ounces	1.6

Chicken, leg meat only, roasted, 3½ ounces	1.3
Tuna, fresh bluefin, cooked, dry heat, 3 ounces	1.1
Chicken, breast, roasted, 3 ounces	1.1
Halibut, cooked, dry heat, 3 ounces	0.9
Crab (blue), cooked, moist heat, 3 ounces	0.8
Pork, loin, broiled, 3 ounces	0.8
Tuna, white, canned in water, 3 ounces	0.8
Shrimp, mixed species, cooked, moist heat, 4 large	0.7

Selected Food Sources of Non-Heme Iron

Food	*Milligrams per serving*
*Ready-to-eat cereal, 100% iron fortified, ¾ cup	18.0
Oatmeal, instant, fortified, prepared with water, 1 cup	10.0
Soybeans, mature, boiled, 1 cup	8.8
Lentils, boiled, 1 cup	6.6
Beans, kidney, mature, boiled, 1 cup	5.2
Beans, lima, large, mature, boiled, 1 cup	4.5
Beans, navy, mature, boiled, 1 cup	4.5
Ready-to-eat cereal, 25% iron fortified, ¾ cup	4.5
Beans, black, mature, boiled, 1 cup	3.6
Beans, pinto, mature, boiled, 1 cup	3.6
Molasses, blackstrap, 1 tablespoon	3.5
Tofu, raw, firm, ½ cup	3.4
Spinach, boiled, drained, ½ cup	3.2
Spinach, canned, drained solids, ½ cup	2.5

Black-eyed peas (cowpeas), boiled, 1 cup	1.8
Spinach, frozen, chopped, boiled, ½ cup	1.9
Grits, white, enriched, quick, prepared with water, 1 cup	1.5
Raisins, seedless, packed, ½ cup	1.5
Whole-wheat bread, 1 slice	0.9
White bread, enriched, 1 slice	0.9

*Be aware that while infant cereals are iron fortified, most of the cereals advertised for adults and older children are not.

Source: U.S. Department of Agriculture, Agriculture Research Service, 2003.

THE BEST FOOD FOR THE BEST BRAINS

Portion Size

For toddlers and small children, portion size varies according to age. Below I list some guidelines for portion sizes.

For children ages 1 to 3

For *any* food (meat, cereal, fruit, dairy) one serving size is equal to 1 tablespoon for every year of life:

1 serving size for a 1-year-old = 1 tablespoon
1 serving size for a 2-year-old = 2 tablespoons
1 serving size for a 3-year-old = 3 tablespoons

One toddler meal should consist of two to four different types of foods, depending on how receptive your toddler is to food variety. For example, breakfast could be cereal and fruit; lunch could be pureed chicken and vegetables with cut-up fruit pieces, and dinner could be pasta with small turkey meatballs, green peas, and pudding. Toddlers should be offered two to three snacks daily.

For children ages 4 to 5

Serving sizes for children 4 and over are as follows:

1 serving of meat, fish, poultry = 2–3 ounces or the size of a deck of cards
1 serving of nut butter = 2 tablespoons or 1 golf ball size
1 serving of eggs = 1–2 eggs
1 serving of bread = 1 slice
1 serving of cooked cereal, rice, pasta, mashed potato = ½ cup
1 serving of low-fat cheese or yogurt = 1½ ounces (1 standard slice) or ½ cup cottage cheese or yogurt
1 serving of fruits or vegetables = ½ cup, cooked or fresh, cut in pieces

Poultry

Servings per week: Daily consumption is fine

Chicken and turkey are popular protein foods that kids can eat every day. Poultry is lean (if you remove the skin, which contains a lot of saturated fat), and it's a good source of the amino acid tryptophan, which is a precursor to serotonin, a neurotransmitter that promotes calmness. Look in your supermarket or health food store for free-range, hormone-free, organic poultry. These birds are raised in much more humane, cleaner conditions than mass-produced poultry, fed a more natural diet, and are guaranteed to be free of antibiotics and hormones. Keep bags of frozen, skinned chicken breasts on hand for quick and easy broiling, grilling, baking, or sautéing, but stay away from frozen or fast-food chicken nuggets.

Recommended:

Chicken
Turkey
Ground chicken or turkey
Chicken or turkey sausage
Chicken or turkey bacon

Avoid:

Fried chicken
Fried, breaded chicken nuggets

Meat

Servings per week: 2–3

Meat contains abundant supplies of protein, zinc, and easily absorbed heme iron, a mineral that is critical for optimal brain development. It is also a prime source of saturated fat, so select lean cuts, as noted in the list below, and trim excess fat. Because feedlot animals are routinely given hormones to facilitate growth and antibiotics to ward off disease, I recommend you purchase only antibiotic- and hormone-free organic meat. It's best to get into the habit during childhood of eating red meat no more than two or three times a week and avoiding processed meats as much as possible. Processed meats are loaded with bad fat and other chemicals that, once in the body, are broken down into toxins that can cause inflammation and other problems that disrupt optimal brain function.

Recommended:

Beef tenderloin
Flank, round, or sirloin steak
Lean ground sirloin or round steak
Top round or rump roast
Lamb leg, roast, or chops
Pork tenderloin
Lean boiled ham

Avoid:

Bacon
Sausage
Hot dogs
Deli meats
Ribs
Prime rib

Seafood

Servings per week: 1

Fish and seafood are good sources of lean protein, essential fatty acids, iodine, zinc, and other brain-boosting nutrients. There are some special considerations, however, when selecting fish. First, include in your child's diet cold-water species with a high DHA content, as noted in the following list. Second, avoid types of fish that are most likely to be contaminated with mercury and other brain-damaging toxins. Just to be on the safe side, I recommend kids eat no more than one serving of fish a week. To make fish more appealing to children, cut fillets up into small chunks, quickly sauté, and serve with your child's favorite dipping sauce. Or add a little homemade mayonnaise and turn salmon or another DHA-rich fish into "tuna" salad.

Recommended:

*Wild Pacific salmon
*Sardines
*Herring
Pollock
Cod
Sole
Shrimp

*High in DHA

Avoid:

*Shark
*Swordfish
*Large tuna
*King mackerel
*Tilefish
Farmed salmon
Breaded, fried fish
Frozen fish sticks

*Large predatory species, which are likely to contain unacceptable levels of mercury.

Eggs

Servings per week: Daily consumption is fine for children

Eggs provide all the essential amino acids and are a good source of choline, a key component of phosphatidylcholine. This phospholipid is abundant in the membranes of brain cells, and it is a precursor to the "learning" neurotransmitter, acetylcholine. The idea that eggs increase risk of heart disease has largely been discounted, so feel free to serve your child eggs. Most kids like eggs, and although they're usually reserved for breakfast, they make good snacks or protein sources at any meal. Do note that eggs are among the most common food allergens.

Recommended:

*DHA-enriched eggs

*One good brand is Gold Circle Farms. Each enriched egg contains 150 milligrams of DHA. (Regular eggs average 18 milligrams.)

Avoid:

*Egg substitutes

*Egg-white products such as Egg Beaters (not egg substitutes) are acceptable, but because egg yolks contain a number of brain-building nutrients, I recommend whole eggs for children.

Dairy

Servings per week: 2–3 servings of low-fat dairy products daily are fine.

Frankly, I'm not crazy about giving kids cow's milk at any age, but children younger than 1 year of age should not drink cow's milk. It is low in iron, hampers absorption of this mineral, and is linked to iron-deficiency anemia, which may delay intellectual development. Milk is also a primary allergen in children. Regardless of age, if you suspect that your child is intolerant of milk, take the time and effort to confirm whether or not she has an allergy and, if necessary, remove dairy products from her diet. As mentioned earlier, your child may be sensitive to milk not because of allergy, but because of lactose intolerance. Alternatives to milk include rice milk and almond milk, available at health food stores. There is even a rice-based frozen dessert, Rice Dream, that's perfect for milk-sensitive children. If you do give your child milk, always choose no-fat or low-fat organic milk and dairy products such as yogurt and cottage cheese. Nonorganic dairy products can be loaded with toxins, especially pesticides. Although even organic dairy products may have trace amounts of toxins, they are still lower in toxins than nonorganic products. Organic products are now widely available even in mainstream grocery stores. And since toxins accumulate in fat, it's best to use only no-fat or low-fat dairy products to reduce toxic load.

Recommended:

*No-fat or low-fat plain, unsweetened yogurt (1% fat)
No-fat or low-fat cottage cheese (1% fat)
No-fat or low-fat ricotta cheese (1% fat)
Low-fat cheeses (1% fat)

*Fruit-flavored yogurt contains a lot of sugar. Buy plain yogurt and add fruit and the healthy sweetener of your choice.

Avoid:

Don't eat any full-fat or nonorganic dairy products. These products are high in saturated fat and environmental toxins that are stored in fat.

Nuts, Seeds, and Nut Butters

Servings per week: Daily consumption is fine

Because of allergy considerations, tree nuts should not be introduced into a child's diet before age 2 and peanuts before age 3. This is because nuts are among the most common food allergens, and nut allergies can cause severe, even life-threatening symptoms. Allergies aside, nuts and seeds have a great amino acid and fatty acid profile and contain brain-nurturing omega-3 fats. Roasting nuts and seeds, however, damages these fragile oils. Therefore, it is best to eat nuts and seeds raw and to purchase nut butters made from raw, organic, unroasted nuts and seeds. Other considerations regarding nuts are choking risk for young children and the high fat and calorie content for kids with weight issues.

Recommended:

Almonds
Brazil nuts
Cashews
*Pumpkin seeds
Sunflower seeds
Sesame seeds

Peanuts
Pecans
*Walnuts
†Peanut butter
†Almond butter

*A good source of omega-3 fatty acids
†Unsweetened, nonhydrogenated brands only

Avoid:

Roasted nuts and seeds
Regular peanut butter

Beans and Legumes

Servings per week: Daily consumption is fine

Beans are a terrific food for kids, rich in fiber, slow-burning carbohydrates, protein, and brain-boosting minerals and B-complex vitamins. Cooking beans from scratch requires a little effort—soaking overnight and cooking for several hours—but you can make them in quantity and store them in the freezer. Canned beans are also nice to have on hand, but make sure they aren't loaded with sugar and salt, and rinse in a colander before using.

Recommended:

Pinto beans
Black beans
Navy beans
Kidney beans
Lentils
Garbanzos (chickpeas)
Refried beans (fat-free)
Baked beans (low-sugar)
Soybeans
Edamame (cooked green soybeans)
Tofu
Tempeh

Cereals, Grains, Pasta, and Breads

Servings per week: Daily consumption is fine

This is a category that ranges from the sublime to the terrible. Whole grains provide the brain with a steady, constant supply of energy. They increase levels of serotonin, the "feel-good" neurotransmitter, and provide neurons with vital nutrients such as iron, selenium, magnesium, and B-complex vitamins. When whole grains are processed and refined into flour, not only are they stripped of memory-enhancing nutrients, but they cause blood sugar swings that leave children irritable and foggy. If you're buying whole grains and making your own cereals and baked items, you're feeding your child the right types of these foods. However, most of us in this busy world depend on prepackaged, prepared cereals and breads, so you have to be particularly vigilant about what you're bringing into your home. Read labels carefully, and don't buy into the buzzwords such as "made with whole grains" or "all natural." If there's under three grams of fiber in a serving of cereal or if the first ingredient in a bread is white or wheat flour, it's not a good source of whole grains. Also check labels for sugar and trans fat, which manage to sneak into just about every category of prepared food.

Recommended:

Brown rice
Buckwheat
Oatmeal (old fashioned or steel cut)
Quinoa
Millet
Amaranth
Sprouted grain bread (Ezekiel is a good brand)
Sprouted grain bagels and pita bread
100% rye bread
*100% whole-wheat bread
Low-fat, whole-grain crackers
†Spelt pasta
‡‡Whole Kids Organic macaroni and cheese
Corn tortillas
*Whole-wheat tortillas
Kashi Mighty Bites cereals
Healthy Times Teddy Puffs cereals
‡‡Whole Kids Organic Morning-O's cereal
‡‡Whole Kids Organic Quack'n Bites crackers

*Wheat is another common allergen. Carefully observe your child's reaction to wheat, and if it is not well tolerated, substitute other grains.

†Better tolerated than wheat pasta.

‡Sold in Whole Foods Market stores.

Avoid:

White bread
Baked goods made with partially hydrogenated
Cold breakfast cereals made with highly refined flour and sugar

oils (most crackers, frozen waffles, etc.)
Bisquick
Infant cereals that are not fortified
Instant oatmeal

Packaged and Prepared Foods

I'm all for convenience foods, and there are some good ones out there. However, for every organic, nutrient-rich, frozen meal made with whole grains and healthful oils, there are a hundred that contain refined white flour, trans fats and/or saturated fats, excess sodium, preservatives, and artificial flavorings. The bottom line: Read labels carefully.

Recommended:

Organic, low-sugar marinara sauce (for pasta and pizza)
Amy's frozen meals and snacks
Amy's canned soups

Avoid:

Chicken nuggets
Fish sticks
Frozen pizzas
Most frozen snack foods
Most frozen meals

Desserts and Sweet Snacks

Servings per week: A daily treat is fine as long as it's from the recommended list that follows.

Prepackaged desserts and sweetened snack foods are another nutritional land mine because sugar, white flour, trans fats, and loads of calories are the order of the day. Not only do high-sugar snacks and desserts replace nutrient-dense foods, but sugar does a number on blood glucose levels. Many parents can attest to the "sugar high," the surge of energy following consumption of these foods fueled by a quick rise in blood glucose, followed by the inevitable low, marked by irritability, inattention, and fatigue—plus sugar is a player in dental cavities and weight gain. Keeping your child away from candy and other junk food can be a battle. Although you can't always monitor what he eats away from home, you can control what you bring into the house. Do not get into the habit of offering dessert after every meal or rewarding children with sweet treats. The best place to shop for dessert and snack foods is your health food store, and even there, you must read labels carefully.

Sugar by Any Other Name

Pay particular attention to sugar, for it comes in many guises, including high-fructose corn syrup, sucrose, dextrose, maltose, and other ingredients whose names end in *-ose*. Corn syrup, corn sweetener, fruit juice concentrates, invert sugar, malt syrup, molasses, and syrup are all sugar. Even so-called good sugars like honey and brown sugar can cause a rapid rise in blood sugar levels that can affect mood and behavior. Avoid all artificial sweeteners, including aspartame, sucrilose, saccharin, and xylitol. Kids don't need any extra chemicals in their bodies. Moreover, there's some evidence that aspartame contains chemicals called excitotoxins that can cross the blood–brain barrier, which may disrupt the production of neurotransmitters and promote the formation of dangerous chemicals called free radicals that can damage brain cells.

Recommended:

- Healthy Times Arrowroot Cookies
- Earth's Best Cereal Bars
- Earth's Best Organic Crunchin' Blocks
- Earth's Best Kidz Organic Whole Grain Bars
- Clif Kids Organic Z Bars
- Dark chocolate (in moderation)

Avoid:

- Packaged cookies
- Candy
- Doughnuts and pastries
- Cake

Vegetables

Servings per week: 3 servings daily is ideal

Your child just can't get too many vegetables. They are among our best sources of brain-boosting vitamins, minerals, phytonutrients, and slowly metabolized carbohydrates. Offer your child a wide range of vegetables from the complete color palate. Fresh is best and organic even better: more nutritious, better taste, and no pesticides. If you are unable to purchase organic vegetables, make sure you wash and peel your produce carefully. Frozen vegetables are also acceptable, but canned vegetables as a rule are nutritionally inferior and may be loaded with sugar, salt, and additives. You may need to explore creative ways to get kids to eat vegetables. Children often find raw vegetables cut into small pieces more attractive than cooked vegetables, and serving them with a healthful dip such as hummus or flavored yogurt may make them more appealing yet. You can also sneak veggies into your child's favorite soups and casseroles. If he adamantly refuses to eat certain vegetables, don't let it turn into a major battle, but reintroduce them later. Remember, it may take several tries before a child "bites."

Recommended:

Artichokes (kids love the mechanics of eating these)
Broccoli
Carrots
Celery
Lettuce
Peppers
Cabbage
Cauliflower
Asparagus
Onions
Spinach
Kale and other leafy greens
Corn
Eggplant
*Purslane
Snow peas
Green beans
Sweet potatoes
Squash
Zucchini

*Purslane, a newcomer to supermarket shelves, is a chewy, sweet-sour "weed" with a crunchy texture that's a good source of omega-3 fatty acids.

Avoid:

Canned and frozen vegetables prepared with presweetened syrups or sauces containing added preservatives

Fruits

Servings per week: 2–3 servings daily is fine

Fruits are also extremely nutrient dense and are a particularly good source of vitamin C, selenium, and an array of phytonutrients. In addition to functioning as a potent antioxidant, vitamin C also increases the absorption of iron, so encourage your child to eat citrus fruits to boost stores of this brain-building mineral. A whole apple or orange is a handful for a small child, not to mention hard to eat, so peeled and sliced fruit is preferable. As with vegetables, organic fruit is strongly recommended, and if it is not organic, wash well and peel before eating.

Recommended:

Apples
Pears
Oranges
Grapefruit
Peaches
Apricots
Nectarines
Plums
Bananas
Berries
Melons
Papayas
Pineapple
Jams and jellies (no sugar added)

Cooking Ingredients and Condiments

The best oil for cooking is olive oil, with canola oil, which is highly processed, a distant runner-up. Other expeller-pressed oils may be used in salad dressings, but polyunsaturated oils should never be heated. Avoid the mass-produced, chemical- and heat-extracted vegetable oils you find on supermarket shelves, margarine containing trans fats, and lard. For other cooking ingredients and seasoning suggestions, see the following list.

Recommended:

Olive oil
Canola oil
*Almond, walnut, and other expeller-pressed oils
Organic butter (in moderation)
Whole-grain flour
Mustard
Low-fat mayonnaise made with canola oil
Low-sugar ketchup (in moderation)
Iodized salt (in moderation)
Low-sodium soy sauce
Salsa

*Never heat polyunsaturated vegetable oils as they break down into undesirable compounds.

Avoid:

Corn, peanut, soy, and other polyunsaturated oils
Lard
Margarine made with trans fats
White flour
High-sugar sauces and condiments

Beverages

Children should get into the habit of drinking water, preferably filtered water, when they're thirsty—nothing else. Sodas, regular or diet, should be off limits to your kids. A single can of regular soda contains about ten teaspoons of sugar, which is more than your child should get in a whole day. Many also contain caffeine, which revs kids up, depletes them of water-soluble nutrients, and further disrupts blood glucose levels. Diet sodas are no better, as artificial sweeteners such as aspartame (NutraSweet) have been linked to hyperactivity, mood swings, and poor memory. Many parents think they're doing the best by their children by allowing them free access to 100 percent pure fruit juices. The reality is that such juices are an extremely concentrated source of sugar that can wreak havoc on blood glucose. Kids who get too many of their calories from fruit juice at the expense of other foods are also at increased risk of obesity.

Recommended:

Pure filtered water (distilled or reverse osmosis)
*Diluted 100 percent organic fruit juices
†No-fat or low-fat organic milk
Homemade lemonade sweetened with stevia
Sparkling water

*The American Academy of Pediatricians recommends no more than 4 to 6 ounces of 100 percent fruit juice daily for kids through age 6, and no more than 8 to 12 ounces for those older than 7.

†See Dairy.

Avoid:

Regular and diet sodas
Kool-Aid
Frozen or bottled lemonade and other sweetened fruit drinks
Fruit drinks with added sweeteners

PART IV

CREATING A BRAIN-ENHANCING ENVIRONMENT FOR YOUR CHILD

CHAPTER NINE

Avoiding Toxins That May Deplete Your Child's Brain Power

From the moment they are conceived and for the rest of their lives, children are exposed to innumerable toxins that are potentially harmful to their brains, including lead, pesticides, plastics, solvents, and other industrial substances. And even things that you may think are perfectly safe for your baby, from his teething ring to the cuddly toys you put in his crib to the pajamas he wears every night, could pose a potential threat to your child's brain.

Children's developing brains, along with their immature reproductive and immune systems, are unable to adequately detoxify the scores of chemicals to which they are exposed. Because of children's smaller size and lower body weight, chemicals have the potential to pack a one-two knockout punch to their nervous systems. Pound for pound of body weight, children consume more food, breathe more air, and drink more fluids than adults. Because children's metabolisms are faster than adults', they also absorb toxins faster. For example, children absorb approximately half of the lead they swallow, while adults absorb only about one-tenth. These toxins affect their neurological development at the most critical stages of brain growth, resulting in lowered IQ levels, behavioral problems, and learning disabilities that can last a lifetime.

If you think that government regulatory agencies are going to keep your child safe from toxic overload, think again. Even when the government attempts to regulate toxins, these regulations are based on research that typically gauges the effects of the toxin on the physiology of a 155-pound adult male, which bears little resemblance to that of children with young brains that are still rapidly developing.

In all fairness, U.S. government agencies, such as the Environmental Protection Agency (EPA), U.S. Consumer Product Safety Commission (CPSC), and Food and Drug Administration (FDA), have taken steps to lower our exposure to many toxins to more acceptable levels. But many critics—including me—feel strongly that the legal levels are still far too high, especially for children. What's even more alarming is the fact that government agencies regulating levels of toxic substances estimate the exposure for one chemical at a time, and, for that matter, one chemical at a time for an average-size young male. But children are exposed to multiple toxins in varying mixtures throughout their development and have immature detoxification systems that are easily overloaded.

THE PRICE OF LIVING IN A TOXIC WORLD

What is the price we pay for living in a toxic world? Estimates show nearly 12 million children in the United States under age 18—an astonishing 17 percent—have one or more learning, developmental, or behavioral disabilities. Attention deficit hyperactivity disorder (ADHD) affects 8 to 10 percent of all school-age children (a conservative estimate—the prevalence may be as high as 17 percent). Learning disabilities may affect up to 10 percent of schoolchildren in public schools. Some 1.5 million children take Ritalin or a similar medication for ADHD, with the number taking this type of drug doubling every four to seven years since 1971. As parents, teachers, and physicians, we struggle so desperately to help children affected by these developmental and emotional problems that we forget to focus on the fact that environmental substances might have caused these problems in the first place. And the scientific community is now certain that complex interactions between genetic and environmental factors cause the bulk of these neurocognitive and developmental problems. Most important, we now know that exposure to environmental toxins is preventable.

The Toxics Release Inventory (TRI) showed that during 1997, a total of 2.58 billion pounds of toxic chemicals were released in the United States by the large industrial companies required to report under the

TRI. Of the Top 20 TRI chemicals (those twenty with the largest total releases), some *75 percent* are either known or suspected to be neurotoxins. More shocking is that nearly a billion pounds of these neurotoxins were released by facilities into the air and surface water, allowing them to be inhaled, absorbed, or ingested through air, food, and water.

Fortunately, savvy parents can substantially reduce their child's exposure to potentially dangerous toxins, especially to the most damaging ones. We know we can't keep our children free from all chemical exposure, but we can certainly try to minimize their exposure to the worst offenders, especially during the most critical—and vulnerable—period of brain growth.

THE WORST OFFENDER LIST

Which toxins are the worst offenders that children are most likely to be exposed to at home? Here are the ones that worry me the most from the point of view of your child's developing brain: PVC (polyvinyl chloride), pesticides (such as organophosphates), lead, mercury, dioxins and PCBs, solvents, flame retardants, arsenic (in pressed wood found in playgrounds and decks manufactured before 2004), and secondhand cigarette smoke.

PVC (Polyvinyl Chloride)

Primary Sources

Many types of soft plastic toys
Teething rings
Ingredients in some skin lotions

It's soft and cuddly, but is it safe for your baby? Many parents may be unaware that some of the most popular soft plastic toys contain PVC and are also laced with toxic additives, paints, and finishes. Nor do they know that many of these products, including toys for children of all ages, contain higher toxic chemical levels than the safe levels established by the CPSC.

One of the worst offenders, PVC (also known as vinyl), may be the most toxic plastic of all. It is commonly used in soft children's products such as bath toys, squeeze toys, some books for infants, and yes, even teething rings that babies put in their mouths. PVC may also contain additives, such as lead, phthalates (pronounced THAL-ates, which are discussed at length in Chapter 11), and cadmium, all of which can leech out of the toy. Phthalates are added to make the PVC soft and squishy for use in infant toys that are chewed and sucked primarily to relieve teething irritation. Heavy metals like lead and cadmium are added to make the rigid type of PVC more durable for use in older children's toys and other consumer products. Phthalates are also added to cosmetic products such as nail polish and skin lotions to make them more spreadable.

We don't have very much solid scientific information on how phthalates may affect human health. From animal studies we do know that phthalates are endocrine disruptors, meaning that these chemicals may mimic the action of estrogen in the body, thereby interfering with hormone systems that regulate normal growth and reproductive development in children. Phthalates have been linked to kidney damage and cancer in children. Lead and cadmium have been linked to brain damage. All these chemicals have the potential to harm developing brain cells. So when our children put these toys in their mouths and chew on them, as kids normally do, they are almost certainly ingesting pthalates and other chemicals.

In recognition of the potential danger of phtalates, the European Union recently banned their use in children's toys and personal care products. Here in the United States, Greenpeace petitioned the CPSC to ban PVC in children's toys but was turned down. As a parent, you have a choice not to buy products that contain PVC, and I recommend that you keep your children away from these products. Some manufacturers have shown sensitivity to the issues surrounding PVC and have stopped using PVC in any of their products. As of this writing, the following companies have stopped using PVC in most or all products: Brio, Early Start, Gerber, Lego, Primetime Playthings, Safety First, Sassy, Small World Toys, and Tiny Love.

Other companies have taken PVC out of toys for children under 18 months of age. These include American Girl, Battat, Chicco, Fisher-Price, Mattel, and Shelcore (Little Tikes). Still other companies, such as

Disney, Evenflo, First Years, Hasbro/Playskool, Galoob, Kids II, and Lamaze Infant Development, have removed phthalates only from toys designed to be put in the mouth, such as teething toys.

Make sure you check the labels on the toys to see if they contain PVC, as the list of the companies that remove PVC from one or more products will undoubtedly change.

Alternatives to Toys Made with PVC

Look and ask for toys made without PVC. Alternative, nonchlorinated plastics include polypropylene, polyethylene, EPM, EPDM, EVA, and biobased plastics. These plastics don't require the extensive use of toxic additives as vinyl does, and none contain any considerable levels of reactive chlorine. If it's not labeled, I wouldn't buy it. In addition, manufacturers have successfully used traditional materials such as wood, metal, and cloth for years.

You might also want to get in touch with the large toy retailers such as Toys "R" Us, Kmart, Wal-Mart, Target, and others, and tell them you want them to buy only non-PVC toys, or at least toys that have labels showing the type of plastic used. In addition, you can contact Greenpeace, the worldwide organization that works to protect our planet. (See Appendix F.)

The following are some of the toy manufacturers that have shown a commitment to PVC-free toys. Nonetheless, you should always check labels and check with the manufacturers as well:

Small World Toys
Early Start
BRIO Corporation
APRICA Kassai Incorporated
Lamaze Infant Development
Little Tikes (Rubbermaid)
Ravensburger
Turner Toys
Lego Toys

In November 1998, Toys "R" Us announced its immediate plans for the worldwide removal of all direct-to-mouth products for infant use containing phthalates, such as teethers, rattles, and pacifiers.

Pesticides

Primary Sources

Weed and pest killers

Pesticides on fruits and vegetables

Bug repellent

Pesticides are one of the most common—and potentially dangerous—hazards in the home. There are an estimated 1,400 pesticides in consumer products as part of the ingredients. Of the 1,400 pesticides, at least 37 registered for use on foods are neurotoxic organophosphate insecticides. These substances are closely related chemically to even more toxic nerve agents used in conducting warfare that were developed at the beginning of the twentieth century.

What's particularly alarming is the fact that pound for pound, children eat more fruits and vegetables in relation to their body weight than adults do. Some 20 million American children, ages 5 and under, eat an average of eight different pesticides every day through their food. (This is why I believe that organic produce is well worth the extra cost, as discussed in Chapter 8.) Pesticides are especially dangerous to children because the residue is stored in fat cells and remains in the body indefinitely. Therefore, the younger the exposure, the more lethal and toxic the buildup.

Organophosphates are a widely used class of pesticide that is particularly toxic to the developing brain. They belong to a class of toxic organic molecules containing phosphate, and often fluoride, that are used in both insecticides and nerve gases (such as sarin). Many of these molecules block the action of an enzyme (acetylcholinesterase) that recycles an important brain chemical called acetylcholine. Acetylcholine is a neurotransmitter that controls the actions of skeletal and smooth muscle in the peripheral nervous system and that may also regulate memory (it is severely diminished in the brains of people with Alzheimer's disease). Because the enzyme is inhibited, acetylcholine builds up in the system, causing nervous system dysfunction.

The substances many people use to control pests at home, especially in the lawn or garden, are also the organophosphates. When there is acute exposure (high levels all at once), they have been shown in some cases to cause permanent damage to the workings of the brain. Some behavioral effects have been seen even when the exposure is brief, or at a low level. Studies on newly born mice showed that a single dose of an organophosphate ten days after birth—a stage that is similar to the stage of humans during the last trimester of pregnancy—was linked to hyperactivity in the same mice at 4 months of age. In a comparative study in Mexico, children exposed to pesticides in the 1960s and '70s demonstrated decreases in stamina, coordination, memory, and the ability to draw familiar subjects.

Other organophosphates include chlorpyrifos (Dursban) and diazinon, both of which are linked to neurochemical and behavioral changes in lab animals. In the late 1990s, after it had been used in homes and schools for the previous thirty years, the EPA and Dow AgroSciences agreed to phase out chlorpyrifos, one of the most commonly used insecticides in schools, because of its high risks to children.

I live in a warm, humid climate and we are endlessly challenged by insects and pests in and out of our home. We have never used toxic pesticides around our home or outdoors and never will. There are natural and safer alternatives that can help control pests and weeds without putting the health of your family at risk.

A Safer Bug Repellent

Although we spend a great deal of time outdoors, I have never used chemical bug repellents on me or my children. Many commercial bug repellents contain DEET (N, N-diethyl-m-toluamide), which is a neurotoxin. Animal studies show that DEET can damage brain cells in the hippocampus, the portion of the brain responsible for memory. Although DEET is considered safe for humans, I worry about the long-term side effects, which could include learning and memory problems later in life. Moreover, once again, I'm concerned that the developing brains of small children may be particularly sensitive to chemicals such as DEET. Therefore, I recommend using a natural herbal-based bug repellent such as Bug Off (which contains, among other ingredients, lemon, eucalyptus oil, and karanja oil), Bite Blocker (a soy-based bug repellent), or Burt's Bees Herbal Insect Repellent (see Appendix F). Children under 3 should not use any bug repellent product because they are likely to rub their eyes or put their hands in the mouth. Instead, put a screen over their stroller to keep bugs out the old-fashioned way.

If your children go outdoors in areas that are infested with mosquitoes or ticks, be sure that they are wearing long sleeves and long pants that are tucked into their socks. I know that kids like to wear shorts in the warm weather, but if they are playing in wooded areas they still need to wear lightweight clothing that covers their bodies.

Keep Pests Out the Natural Way

Take steps to make your home, and especially your kitchen, an inhospitable place for pests. For example, when possible, clean up food spills immediately and keep all areas as clean as possible, especially the hard-to-reach areas where pests can hide. Pests can also hide in clutter, so try to remove as much as you can. Keep food that attracts pests in the refrigerator, including flour. Remember that water attracts pests, so have any leaks repaired immediately. Keep screens on doors and windows, and clean and air your clothes regularly. Store the clothes that are out of season in airtight containers to prevent moth infestation.

Control Indoor Insects

You can make insect repellent with foods that attract insects mixed with food that is poisonous to them, but nontoxic for you. For example, mix equal parts of oatmeal and plaster of Paris or equal parts of flour with borax. Sprinkle these mixtures directly on the areas where you have seen insects and on the doorways where insects gain entry in your home. Or try using old-fashioned flypaper. Although these mixtures are nontoxic, they can still make you sick, so don't allow them to come in contact with food. And clean up the exposed areas before allowing your child to crawl on the floor.

Keep the Outdoors a Great Place to Play

Read the labels of any substance you use in your home or garden to make sure that it does not contain any of the toxic pesticides mentioned above. Look in hardware stores for the newer insecticides that use soap-and-water solutions to rid your garden of aphids. At least one company, Agro Logistic Systems, makes such a product.

There are several pesticides that are naturally derived and have varying levels of toxicity to humans. From most toxic to least toxic (to humans), these are: nicotine, rotenone, pyrethrum, and sabadilla. I don't recommend that you use them, especially if you have small children.

There are no safe herbicides. If you are determined to live a weed-free existence, the safest way is to pull weeds by hand.

Unfortunately, pesticide residue remains in the ground for decades, which means even if you are scrupulous about not using neurotoxic chemicals, you can't be sure what the past owners did. If you suspect that your backyard has ever been treated with pesticides, I don't recommend allowing small children to crawl around the yard because their faces are literally in the dirt. It's fine for older children to play outdoors, but make sure they wash their hands and face very well when they come into the house.

For ideas on combating specific pests, see the resource section.

Mercury

Primary Sources

Fatty fish (such as swordfish, tuna, king mackerel, and shark)

Vaccines containing thimerosal, a mercury-based preservative

Many of you have undoubtedly heard about a mercury-based preservative called thimerosal, which was used in vaccines given to infants and which may be linked to an increased incidence of autism among children. (See Chapter 15, "Vaccinations: Making Intelligent Choices for Your Child.") I also want to caution you about *methylmercury,* a highly toxic chemical that accumulates in people and wildlife and is damaging to the brain and nervous system. How does methylmercury find its way into our bodies? Mercury is emitted into the environment from coal-powered plants, trash incinerators, and medical waste incinerators. Once it is released into the air, it falls back to earth and into waterways with rain. It then builds up in fish, and its levels can get to be 100,000 times higher in the fish's system than they are even in the water where the fish live. Since methylmercury accumulates in the muscle tissue of fish, it can't be trimmed away before cooking, nor does it evaporate in the cooking process. And that's how methylmercury ends up on our plates and in our bodies.

So many of our bodies of water have been found by researchers to be contaminated by mercury that forty states have issued health advisories warning pregnant women and women of childbearing age to either avoid or severely limit their consumption of many types of fish. Fully eleven states (Alabama, Florida, Georgia, Louisiana, Maine, Massachusetts, Mississippi, North Carolina, Rhode Island, South Carolina, and Texas) have issued statewide methylmercury poisoning advisories covering their entire coastal area for at least one species of fish, with Rhode Island being the most recent state to issue such advisories.

It's not just pregnant women and nursing mothers who need to be careful about limiting mercury intake. I strongly urge everyone to avoid eating fish that contains the highest levels of mercury and even limit consumption of fish that contains lower levels of mercury. For more guidelines on safe fish consumption, see page 141.

At room temperature mercury is a liquid, but it readily vaporizes and is easily and quickly absorbed through the lungs. Researchers have found a consistent link between people who have been repeatedly exposed to even low levels of mercury vapor over long periods of time and a higher incidence of tremors, irritability, impulsiveness, drowsiness, impaired memory, and sleep disturbances. For children, these potential side effects occur with much lower levels of exposure than for adults.

We know that babies exposed in utero to large amounts of methylmercury show neurocognitive deficits (resulting in mental retardation), problems with gait, and visual problems. Babies in utero who were exposed to even small amounts of mercury have shown lifelong learning disabilities, including language, attention, and memory deficits.

Researchers using information from the Centers for Disease Control and Prevention (CDC) found that as many as 630,000 children in the United States may be exposed annually to mercury in utero at levels high enough to be associated with a loss of IQ. These same researchers suggested that the birth of hundreds of thousands of babies with lowered IQs hurts the U.S. economy through lost productivity. This represents one of the major economic costs of methylmercury toxicity.

In fact, mercury is so toxic that if the amount of mercury contained in a typical fever thermometer (0.7 grams) were to be released into a twenty-acre lake each year, it would be enough to contaminate all the fish in that lake after only a few years. And if we were to stop industrial mercury emissions today, it would still take some fifteen years to substantially reduce the mercury in our environment.

To add to these frightening facts, mercury is found in countless consumer products, including thermometers (fever, candy, fry, oven, and any indoor and outdoor thermometer with a silvery temperature indicator), fluorescent lamps, thermostats, some athletic shoes with lights on their heels, dental fillings (amalgams), some oil-based paints, latex paint manufactured before August 1990, chemistry sets, batteries (some of the "button" batteries), calculators and small appliances, medical laboratory chemicals, mercury vapor lamps, hearing aids, pilot lights, some medicines, and even in some common household cleaners.

When mercury-containing products are thrown away, they are often incinerated, and this further increases the amount of mercury in the atmosphere. For the sake of the environment, if you are disposing of a product containing mercury, contact your local EPA office or town recycling center to see what procedure your city or town has in place to dispose of it safely.

As reported in the *Wall Street Journal*'s series, "Toxic Traces, New Questions about Old Chemicals" (August 2005), a battle has raged since 1979, when the FDA issued an initial advisory about the levels of mercury considered "safe" for consumption. In 1979, the advisory said it was safe to consume 4 micrograms of mercury a day per twenty-two pounds of body weight. That level is four times the level the EPA now describes as safe, although clearly most scientists feel the EPA level remains too high.

Hold the Tuna

Ninety percent of American households consume canned tuna; it accounts for a full 20 percent of U.S. seafood consumption. Moreover, children eat more than twice as much tuna as they do any other fish, especially canned white tuna, which has been found to have the highest level of mercury of any canned fish. Yet many people still consider it to be healthy for adults and kids alike. Recently, the *Wall Street Journal* reported the compelling story of a 10-year-old boy who

continued

had consumed 3 to 6 ounces a day of canned tuna for about a year. Over time, he developed severe learning disabilities, along with compromised motor skills. He went from being a hardworking student at the top of his fourth-grade class to a child with no interest in school who labored at even the most basic tasks such as performing simple addition problems. His parents eventually traced the dramatic change to their son's high level of canned tuna consumption. When a neurologist tested the boy's blood for mercury, the results showed a mercury level nearly double what the EPA considers a safe level. Once his parents realized the source of the problem, their son stopped eating albacore tuna and after two years the boy's mercury level normalized and he regained his previous levels of academic and sports achievement.

In March 2004, the EPA and FDA issued a joint statement advising nursing mothers, pregnant women, and women of childbearing age who may become pregnant to eat only chunk light tuna, on the assumption that it is lower in mercury than albacore, and no more than 12 ounces a week. But the FDA and EPA remain divided on what they deem safe for consumption of tuna and other high-mercury-level fish.

Even if the boy's family had followed the joint advisory suggesting recommended safe levels and given the child just half a can of albacore a week, their son still would have consumed 60 percent more mercury than the EPA can confidently declare safe for his weight.

Dioxins and PCBs (polychlorinated biphenyls)

Primary Sources

Fatty fish
Full-fat dairy
Fatty cuts of meat
Breast milk

Dioxin is a toxic by-product produced through several industrial processes, including the incineration of city and medical waste, the chlorine-based bleaching of pulp and paper, and a particular form of copper smelting. The main source of dioxin exposure is through food, but traces of dioxin are commonly found in disposable diapers and even tampons. Dioxin is an endocrine disruptor and in animal studies it has been shown to compromise the production of a variety of important hormones. That is why the scientific community is so concerned about this toxin—as am I. The effects of dioxin on hormones has the potential to seriously impair the growth and development of the young brain.

Once it is emitted into the air, dioxin, like mercury, can travel via airborne particles, sometimes as far as thousands of miles. Eventually it lands on pastures and bodies of water that are used in the production of food consumed around the world.

PCBs (polychlorinated biphenyls) were banned as health hazards and carcinogens in 1977. Before the ban, PCBs were used in many products commonly found in the home, including fluorescent lights or appliances (such as those lights found on many stoves), insulation, and insecticides. Outside of the home, on the industrial front, PCBs were used in building transformers and capacitors, and in lubricant oils. Like dioxins, PCBs can travel over long distances via airborne particles. Also like mercury, PCBs are bioaccumulative, meaning that they accumulate along the food chain, and are thus found in the most concentrated levels in higher animals, such as mammals (especially whales and humans), birds, and predatory fish.

Although PCBs can be absorbed through the skin, as for example when skin comes into contact with contaminated soil, the most common route of exposure to PCBs for humans is through food consumption. Dioxin, on the other hand, is not readily absorbed through the skin, but typically ends up in our bodies via the food we eat. (Nevertheless, there is concern about the use of products that contain even trace amounts of dioxin, such as disposable diapers, which many children may use for at least the first three years of life, and tampons, which are inserted inside a woman's body.) Once PCBs enter the body, they are stored in body fat and remain there, accumulating over a lifetime. This explains why older people have higher levels of PCBs. And unfortunately, there is no "treatment" for ridding the body of PCBs; all we can do is prevent them from getting into our systems in the first place.

High Levels in Breast Milk

Since PCBs and dioxin are stored in and carried by fat, not only are they passed from mother to fetus during pregnancy, but they are also carried in breast milk to the nursing infant. This is a dramatic example of how industrial chemicals move from "factory to fetus," a phrase coined by environmental researchers. As these toxins accumulate and pool in fatty tissue (like the breast), when the infant nurses, he or she is exposed at the beginning of life to a large quantity of the toxins that have accumulated in the fatty breast tissue of the mother.

Research conducted on monkeys that were exposed to dioxin in utero through their mothers' diet (at the level that nursing human infants are exposed via breast milk) showed that the animals had obvious learning deficits as compared to nonexposed animals. Monkeys fed from birth to 20 weeks on the same concentration of PCBs found in human breast milk showed impaired learning when tested between the ages of 2½ and 5. They also showed behavioral anomalies at PCB levels that are similar to those found in the general human population (2 to 3 parts per billion).

According to Dr. Arnold Schecter, an international medical expert on dioxins and an advisor to the World Health Organization, a baby in the United States can, on average, consume the EPA's maximum lifetime dose of dioxin in just six months of breast-feeding because of the potential for dioxin concentration in human breast milk, which is very fatty. Dr. Schecter believes that the levels of chemicals that could interfere with a child's normal development may be as low as 1 part per *trillion,* or the equivalent of a single drop of liquid placed in the center car of a ten-kilometer-long cargo train.

Dr. Schecter conducted two studies in the late 1990s that were published in the British journal, *Chemosphere.* Dr. Schecter's thesis: We can avoid foods highest in PCBs and dioxin by eating more low-fat foods such as fruits and vegetables, and by avoiding high-fat foods, where dioxins and PCBs accumulate in the highest concentrations.

According to Dr. Schecter, scientists in the field now agree that every person in industrialized countries has dioxins in his or her blood. But Schecter and his team set out to see if certain kinds of food contained more dioxins than others. They looked at grocery store foods, as well as fast-food items (Big Macs, Kentucky Fried Chicken, ice cream) across the United States and concluded that all of the high-fat foods contained trace amounts of dioxin that actually exceeded many government regulations. While vegetables and fruits also contained trace amounts of these chemicals, the levels were significantly lower than those in the high-fat foods.

So far, scientists have not specifically uncovered exactly how PCBs impair brain function. Recent studies have shown an association with the disruption of calcium signaling in nerve cells, which could account for the learning and memory problems found in laboratory animals, children, and, most recently, adults exposed to PCBs.

A 2001 study revealed that adults with high blood levels of PCBs also have more memory and learning problems than people with lower blood levels of the toxins. The study evaluated people who consumed PCB-contaminated sport-caught fish on a regular basis and found that they displayed more learning and memory problems than people of the same age who had lower levels of PCBs in their bodies. Sport-caught fish were defined as fish caught from the Great Lakes.

The benefits of breast-feeding your baby still outweigh the potential risk from PCBs and dioxin. There are still many beneficial ingredients in breast milk, such as immunity-boosting proteins, that have not been duplicated in even the best infant formula. However, it's wise to try avoiding additional exposure to these toxins whenever possible. Carefully restricting your child's intake of fish, as recommended on page 141, is a good way to reduce his exposure to dioxins and PCBs (as well as mercury). Although they are a bit more expensive, dioxin-free diapers are available at health food stores and even some supermarkets. (See the resource section for more information.) If you want to be really kind to the environment, you can use cloth diapers, which are not only good for your baby, but don't contribute to our growing disposable waste nightmare.

Long-Term Effects of PCBs and Mercury Together

In a long-term, ongoing study of children born to mothers who ate fish from Lake Ontario, results show that prenatal PCB and mercury exposures interacted to reduce performance by 3-year-olds on a test called the McCarthy Scales of Children's Abilities. While the exposure to mercury was extremely low, when combined with exposure to PCBs, the impact on neurocognitive development was dramatic.

continued

Studies such as these demonstrate the inadequacies of federal advisories based on analyses of single chemical substances (such as mercury or lead). In too many areas of the country, freshwater fish are contaminated with multiple toxins: mercury, PCBs, dioxin, and many others. So it's hard to imagine how any public advisories about fish consumption that are based on analysis of only one substance can truly be protective.

Lead

Primary Sources

Tap water

Chipped paint

Ceramic dishes and pottery made overseas or in the U.S. prior to 1971

Toys

Lead, a heavy metal, is classified as a developmental neurotoxin, which means that it can directly interfere with a child's normal brain development processes, including cell division, synapse formation, and myelination. At any level, lead is poisonous to the human body. Lead interferes with normal neuron development in young children, resulting in *lifelong* learning and behavioral effects. And it's important to remember that neurotoxins may interfere with brain development and subsequent functioning in children at levels of exposure that have little or no effect on the adult brain.

Since lead is virtually indestructible and nonbiodegradable, manufacturers have used lead to make many different products including paint, batteries, gasoline, pipes, and solder. Lead is also used in vinyl miniblinds, ceramics, dishes, toys, water and sewer pipes, solder, and lead crystal. And since these products are ubiquitous in both residential and commercial buildings, lead contamination or toxicity is not uncommon.

It is shocking that an estimated 200,000 children in the United States suffer from lead poisoning each year, making it the number one preventable disease among children up to age 7. Even more alarming is the fact that 1 million children in the United States exceed the currently accepted threshold for lead exposure, which affects behavior and cognition (a blood level of 10 micrograms per deciliter). And if we were to update the toxic threshold to correlate with results in the most recent studies, the result would be the addition of millions more children.

For example, lead from paint dust and drinking water has harmful effects on adults even at low levels, causing headaches, mood changes, sleep disturbances, a decrease in fertility (men), high blood pressure, digestive problems, nerve disorders, joint pain, and muscle disorders.

According to the U.S. Department of Housing and Urban Development (HUD), although the use of lead-based paint was banned in 1978, some 57 million homes still contain some lead and 75 percent of all private housing built before 1978 contain some lead paint. An estimated one out of every eleven people in the United States is affected by lead poisoning from lead-contaminated paint and dust, the most common source of lead exposure.

Lead-based paint can be on windows, doors, wood trim, walls, cabinets, porches, stairs, railings, fire escapes, old furniture (cribs), and even children's toys. Children may swallow paint that has cracked, chipped, or peeled, or has been sanded or scraped, breaking down into tiny particles that are often invisible. Children can also swallow lead dust in their normal hand–mouth activity, especially if they are crawling. Other household items that may create paint dust include moving parts of windows and doors. Lead exposure may increase during remodeling and renovation projects.

Elevated blood lead levels (as measured by simple blood tests) in infancy and all phases of childhood have been linked to increased impulsiveness, attention deficits, lowered performance at school, aggression, and delinquent behavior. The behavioral consequences of elevated blood lead levels have been reported since the 1940s, and since then, researchers have suggested that increasingly lower and lower levels of exposure to lead can produce behavioral changes and cognitive impairment.

While the level of lead exposure that is safe for both children and adults continues to be a moving target, effects on learning have been seen at blood lead levels below even the current safety standards. In fact the difference in IQ levels between children who have been exposed to lead and those who have not (as measured by blood lead levels) can be as many as 4 to 5.8 IQ points.

Have Your Child Tested

Health officials recommend that children receive a blood test for lead contamination by the age of 1 and continue testing every couple of years. You could also get your child tested by taking a lock of his or her hair and sending it in to a medical testing laboratory. (See Appendix F.)

However, if you suspect that your home may be contaminated with lead, have your child tested at 6 months old. It is estimated that as many as one in four children under the age of 7 have lead in their blood. Contact your local health department for the location of testing facilities in your area.

Sources of Lead in the Home and Reducing the Risk of Lead Contamination

The major sources of in-home contamination are lead-based paints, tap water, colorful ceramic dishes, soil, airborne lead particles, and lead-based ceramic containers, which present a particularly high risk for leeching lead into food. Dishes and pottery made in the United States after 1971 are generally safe because they must comply with federal safety guidelines, but overseas manufacturers may still sell ceramic products with lead levels that exceed U.S. safety standards. Be cautious about using dishes made overseas unless they are from a reputable manufacturer who guarantees the product is lead free. Because you can't see, taste, or smell lead, everyone is potentially at risk. Even a baby's crib may have been painted with lead-based paint. If children ingest even small chips of lead-based paint, it could lead to serious lead toxicity.

The water you drink may contain lead, which can be harmful even with short-term exposure. Plumbing systems often may include lead-containing materials that can contaminate tap water, posing a potentially serious health threat. According to the EPA, approximately 20 percent of public water systems, serving 32 million people, were found to have lead levels exceeding the EPA's safety standard of 15 parts per billion. As you probably know, young children and pregnant women are the most at risk. In fact, water coolers in nursery schools and kindergartens may spout water that contains lead. Always check with the school to find out if they have systems in place to check for lead in water. And don't assume that because you don't live in an inner-city apartment building you are free from the threat of lead contamination. Lead contamination from tap water can occur in *any* neighborhood. The *Washington Post* recently reported on lead contamination in the tap water in the upscale areas of both northeast and northwest Washington, D.C., two of the most affluent neighborhoods in the area.

How to Reduce the Risk of Lead Contamination in Your Home

Strategies to reduce the risk of lead contamination include:

Flush your water pipes before use Prior to using water for cooking or drinking, run the tap water until it becomes as cold as it will get.

Use only cold water for drinking and cooking Hot water is likely to contain higher levels of lead.

Inspect your plumbing system to detect lead Lead pipes and solder are dull gray; when scratched they will look shiny.

Practice good hygiene That is, keep the children's crib, playpen, and play areas as dust free as possible. Wash toys often.

Wash the walls If lead paint is present on your walls, you will want to wash them, at the very least. It's a better idea to cover walls with paneling or wallpaper.

Check product labels Look for the presence of lead, and avoid using products such as hair dyes and lipsticks that may contain lead.

Test your home and water for lead-based paint An at-home test created by Pro-Lab provides an accurate measurement of lead content. The in-home test is usually under $20 or $25 with a small lab processing fee (also under $20). For more information, see the resource section or go to Pro-Lab's Web site at http://www.prolabinc.com (or call 800-427-0550).

Leave it to the experts If your home is found to contain lead-based paint, don't try to remove it on your own. If you can, hire a professional to remove it, preferably while you stay somewhere else.

Solvents

Primary Sources

Paint and adhesive fumes

Varnish strippers

Dry-cleaned clothes

Walk into a nail salon, a dry-cleaning facility, or even your own living room, and you may be getting a lungful of toxic fumes from chemical solvents. A solvent is a liquid used to dissolve other substances. Not all solvents are toxic—water is a solvent—but many can be quite dangerous, especially if they are inhaled. As you may know, there has been an epidemic rise in teenagers abusing solvents as inhalants to get high. This is an incredibly dangerous practice, as acute effects of inhaling solvents include depression of the central nervous system, skin and mucous membrane irritation, and some cardiovascular side effects as well as permanent neurological disorders. As yet, the research exploring the neurological consequences of long-term, low-level solvent exposure is inconclusive. In my opinion, however, the devastating brain changes seen with high-level exposure certainly supports the contention that lower-level exposure likely has negative neurological effects.

So, it makes sense to keep your home and your child's environment as free of toxic fumes as possible and that means using solvents cautiously. There are many solvents in our homes, from the backyard to the kitchen to the bathroom. Household solvents include substances such as ethanol (alcohol), turpentine, kerosene, and acetone. Other solvents used as ingredients in consumer products include toluene, xylene, styrene, and trichloroethlylene, and they are found in adhesives in glue, paint and varnish strippers, carriers for pigment in paint and ink, and fuels. Products that are almost 100 percent solvent include paint thinner, furniture stripper, dry-cleaning fluid, spot remover, degreaser, turpentine, and acetone-based nail polish remover. Products that are composed partially of solvents include furniture oil, glues, aerosol sprays, shoe care products, rug cleaners, and oil-based paints.

As is true with many other toxins, solvents are used extensively in manufacturing processes, and most of what is released into our environment comes from factories. Nonetheless, we are most commonly exposed via indoor sources including household cleaners, recently dry-cleaned clothes, insecticides, paints, glues, and fuels.

Reducing Your Child's Likelihood of Exposure to Solvents

My best advice is to keep all cleaning agents, gasoline, paints, glues, thinners, and other household products in locked or inaccessible cabinets, and to use the entire can or bottle. If you discard any leftover solvents, treat them as hazardous waste and dispose of them through a licensed hazardous waste handler. Call your local sanitation department to find one in your area.

Ideally, try not to expose your child to any solvent if at all possible, even if you feel there is adequate ventilation. If you can't completely avoid having solvents around the home, follow these guidelines to further protect you and your children:

- Never use any solvent in closed spaces.
- Thoroughly air out any space in which you have used a product.
- Avoid taking children to nail salons.
- Keep children out of newly remodeled rooms that may be outgassing (giving off) solvents from carpet or wallpaper glues.
- Air out dry-cleaning in outdoor spaces for one day before bringing it into the house; whenever possible, car windows should be open when transporting freshly dry-cleaned clothes.
- Check with your child's school to make sure any art supplies they may use are nontoxic.
- Recognize that your hobbies may be exposing your children to solvents. The hobbies that would involve solvents include silk-screening, furniture restoration, model building, painting, and automobile restoration.

Flame Retardants

Primary Sources

Children's pajamas

Home furniture

First introduced in the 1970s, brominated flame retardants are chemicals that prevent a fire from spreading. Manufacturers of consumer products add these chemicals to plastic and fabric products—including children's pajamas, home furniture, computers, TVs, radios, and other furniture and electronics to keep a fire from spreading if one should ignite. Like other neurotoxins I have mentioned in this chapter, these flame retardants are bioaccumulative, which means they accumulate in the body—in the fatty tissues, blood, and breast milk.

Specifically, it is the polybrominated diphenyl ether, or PBDE, flame retardants I want to focus on, because research indicates they may be particularly harmful during a critical window of brain development, during pregnancy and early childhood. Recent research in laboratory mice shows that PBDE may mimic thyroid hormones in the body, and that can interrupt the brain's delicately choreographed development, leading to permanently impaired learning and abnormalities of coordination. Thyroid hormone is critical for normal brain development and any abnormality in thyroid expression could be detrimental to a young brain. And while PBDEs are still not regulated, I believe there are no safe levels of exposure at which humans will not suffer at least some damage if they are sufficiently exposed during early development.

Because they are so widely used, PBDEs are the brominated flame retardants that have been studied the most. PBDEs escape into the environment during their manufacture, use, and disposal.

In just one year—1999—manufacturers in North America used some 74 million pounds of PBDEs, which is more than half of all PBDEs used around the world. In fact, initial studies of PBDE contamination of breast milk indicate that U.S. levels are 40 to 60 times higher than those found in Sweden. Scientists have reported that levels of PBDEs in animal and human tissues are growing exponentially, doubling every two to five years. If levels of PBDEs in people's bodies continue rising at current rates, within a few years, the average child in California may be exposed to levels known to cause brain damage in lab animals. The most serious health effects are likely to be impaired learning, memory, and motor skills caused by exposure during critical windows of brain development in children.

In random testing, researchers have found shockingly high levels of

PBDEs in humans. Writers at the *Oakland Tribune* in California set out to write a series of articles on environmental toxins in the wake of state legislative activity to take action to protect citizens against the chemicals. They sent scientists to Berkeley to test a family of four for toxins: metals, flame retardants, plasticizers, and the chemicals that combine to create Teflon and Scotchgard. Their results were astounding and frightening: Researchers found "measurable amounts" of these toxins in all four family members. But most shocking was that both children, and in particular, the 2-year-old boy, tested surprisingly high for the presence of flame retardants.

Flame-Retardant Sleepwear

In 1972, the U.S. government passed the Flammability Fabrics Act, which required that all children's sleepwear be made of flame-retardant material that would self-extinguish when exposed to an open flame. Under 1972 regulations, polyester and other synthetics already complied with these regulations, but natural fibers such as cotton, which were flammable, had to be treated with flame retardant. As most parents know, once cotton is treated with flame retardant it becomes stiffer and not as comfortable. Moreover, there was growing fear that the intense exposure to flame-retardant chemicals was harmful to children. Clothing manufacturers got around the safety standards by offering parents cotton "play" clothes that looked a lot like pajamas, and many parents opted to use them as pajamas.

Under pressure from environmental and parent groups, in 1998 the Consumer Product Safety Commission amended the flammability standard for children's sleepwear, allowing for the use of natural fibers in all sleepwear for infants under 9 months old and in snug-fitting pajamas for children up to 14 years. The rationale was that in the event of a fire, while long, flowing cotton nightgowns or loose pajamas could easily catch fire if you had to run past flames, close-fitting garments had a tendency to self-extinguish primarily because there was less air trapped in the fabric for combustion. Flame-retardant pajamas are still available, but they are now sold side by side with those made of natural fibers. This was a very controversial decision and some fire safety experts feel it was the wrong one, but there's no evidence that wearing nontreated snug-fitting sleepwear is any more dangerous than wearing treated sleepwear. For the record, my wife, Leize, and I never put our children in flame-resistant sleepwear.

Similar to PCBs, PBDEs are stored in body fat, making the effects on the developing brain more and more lethal because it takes so long to get rid of them. The most highly exposed people have been shown to have twice the levels shown to damage the developing brains of laboratory mice. Moreover, it took about forty years after researchers discovered that PCBs might cause harm to humans until they were actually banned in this country. And just as predicted, researchers are finding that even if people were exposed to PCBs at low levels, decades later there is evidence they may have caused harm. In the case of PBDEs, even while they are not yet regulated in the United States, we can take action now to reduce our children's and our own exposure to them.

The European Union reduced the use of PBDEs in the late 1990s after research showed increasing levels in the breast milk of Swedish mothers along with evidence of toxic effects. Since 1998, when the use of PBDEs was reduced in the EU, concentrations of PBDEs in breast milk of Swedish women have declined steadily. The European Union has acted on early warnings of a significant health threat by banning several toxic flame retardants. In early 2003, it officially banned the use of PBDEs and other toxic chemicals in the manufacturing of electronics (such as computers and lighting) after mid-2006.

One piece of good news for the United States: In 2003, the California legislature banned two forms of PBDEs in that state; they'll be phased out entirely in California by 2008.

Still, the Environmental Protection Agency maintains it has found no proven risk to human health associated with PBDEs; but neither does the agency maintain data on whether the profound effects seen in PBDE-exposed lab animals can occur in humans.

How to Reduce Your Family's Exposure to PBDEs

Some manufacturers of furniture, plastic, and electronics have already begun to make products that meet fire safety standards without using PBDEs. These companies include Apple, Ericsson, IBM, IKEA, Intel, Motorola, NEC, Panasonic, Phillips, SONY, and Volvo.

For example, Volvo makes entirely PBDE-free cars. IKEA, the furniture chain, recently replaced brominated flame retardants in fabrics with less toxic chemicals; the electronics company Toshiba replaced toxic flame retardants in casings for electronic parts by switching over to a nonflammable plastic that didn't need any chemical additives.

Here are some other ideas for reducing your exposure to bioaccumulative chemicals:

- Avoid eating farm-raised salmon and rainbow trout—they have been found to have the highest concentrations of PBDEs.
- PBDEs are present in the fat of every animal, so especially limit your consumption of high-fat dairy products, fish and beef.
- If you choose to give your child milk and dairy products, opt for organic products such as Horizon Organic Dairy brand.
- Choose low-fat protein sources such as free-range, antibiotic-free, hormone-free chicken breasts.
- Mattresses have historically been a source of PBDEs for obvious reasons, given that PBDEs are added as flame retardants. According to the Sleep Products Safety Council (www.safesleep.org), manufacturers are phasing out mattresses with PBDEs in them and now using other technology for fire resistance. IKEA (www.ikea-usa.com) hasn't used PBDEs in children's mattresses for at least fifteen years. Other manufacturers of PBDE-free mattresses include European Sleep Works (www.sleepworks.com), The Natural Bedroom (www.naturalhome products.com), and Lifekind mattresses (www.lifekind.com). For chemical-free mattresses and bedding, consult www.nontoxic.com. Keep in mind that you will have to be extra vigilant about fire prevention if you use mattresses with no flame retardants.

Arsenic

Primary Sources

Wooden playground equipment

Outdoor wooden decks

If your child plays outdoors on a wooden deck or on wooden playground equipment or eats lunch on a wooden picnic table, chances are she is being exposed to arsenic, a known neurotoxin. Although arsenic has been virtually banned by the EPA as a pesticide since the 1980s, the wood treatment industry was able to get an exemption to this rule. Except for cedar and redwood, virtually all the outdoor wood sold in the last thirty years was pressure treated with an arsenic-containing compound to prevent rot and repel insects and other animals.

Arsenic occurs naturally in soil and is widely found in the earth's crust. In industry it is combined with oxygen, chlorine, and sulfur to form inorganic arsenic compounds, the most harmful kind—the kind that is used to preserve wood. Many common arsenic compounds are water soluble and can be deposited in soil.

Copper Chromate Arsenic (CCA)

The most common arsenic formulation used in the United States is chromate copper arsenate (CCA). CCA consists of chromium (a bactericide), copper (a fungicide), and arsenic (an insecticide) and is often sold under the trade name "Wolmanized" wood. (Ammoniacal copper zinc arsenate, or ACZA, is a very similar arsenic formulation sold primarily on the West Coast as Chemonite.) ACA and ACC are less widely used arsenic treatments.

CCA is used to make pressure-treated lumber, such as the wood used in playground equipment, picnic tables, decks, fences, boat docks, and benches. Wood treated with arsenic is resistant to decay. CCA is no longer used in the United States for residential purposes; but it is still used in industrial applications.

Some researchers have found that even very low levels of CCA can change hormonal functions, and this can have significant impact on the developing brain. When children touch arsenic-treated wood and put their hands in their mouths, the arsenic gets into their bodies. A number of recent studies have confirmed that high levels of arsenic can be released to children's hands by direct contact with arsenic-treated wood. A University of Florida study of soil below CCA wood decks found that surface soil arsenic concentrations below the decks were elevated on average by 2,000 percent.

In addition, evidence suggests that long-term exposure to arsenic in children may result in lower IQ scores, as they are less efficient than adults at converting inorganic arsenic to the less harmful organic forms.

For this reason, children may be more susceptible to health effects from inorganic arsenic than adults.

There is also evidence that inhaled or ingested arsenic can injure pregnant women as well as their unborn babies, although the studies are not definitive. Studies in animals show that large doses of arsenic that cause illness in pregnant females can also cause low birth weight, fetal malformations, and even fetal death. Arsenic can cross the placenta and has been found in fetal tissues. Arsenic is also found at low levels in breast milk.

What can you do to protect your child?

- Don't allow your children to play in the soil or sand below or around arsenic-treated wood structures. The arsenic leaches into the surrounding soil and contaminates the soil. Typically, arsenic pressure-treated wood has a greenish tint and is often unpainted or unfinished.
- Don't store toys underneath an arsenic-treated structure like a pressure-treated wood deck or patio.
- In addition, always make sure children wash their hands immediately after playing on an arsenic-treated playset and never allow them to eat on an arsenic-treated picnic table without a tablecloth.

What to Do with Existing Wood

Test it If you don't know if the wood is arsenic treated, you should test it (see the Healthy Building Network website at www.healthybuilding.net/ for testing kits).

Replace it There are many safer alternatives available (see the list that follows).

Seal it If you can't replace it, thoroughly coat it at least every two years (annually or better in high-traffic areas) with a waterproof sealant such as polyurethane or an oil-based penetrating sealer. Do not use acid deck wash or brighteners as these are suspected to accelerate the release of arsenic from arsenic-treated wood.

Never sand arsenic-treated wood This spreads arsenic-laden wood dust and increases exposure. If the wood surface has become rough and splinters are an issue, we strongly recommend replacing the structure with a less toxic alternative. Remember, splinters from arsenic wood can be very dangerous.

Don't burn it Never burn treated wood. I repeat, never burn treated wood! Arsenic-treated wood is *extremely* hazardous and should be disposed of properly according to local environmental regulations. Call your local sanitation department for more information.

Less Toxic Alternatives to CCA

There are some excellent alternatives to arsenic-treated wood today. Here are some of the compounds available:

- ChoiceDek by Advanced Environmental Recycling (www.choicedek.com)
- Nexwood (www.nexwood.com)
- PermaDeck by Cascades (www.perma-deck.com)
- Polywood (www.polywood.com)
- Trex (www.trex.com)
- Carefree by US Plastic Lumber plastic and fiberglass (www.carefree-products.com)

See Appendix F for a list of alternative products. Read the labels and ask questions. Let your lumberyard know that you care about the materials you put in your home. If your lumberyard does not stock a nonarsenic alternative, ask them to order one.

Despite a voluntary labeling agreement between the EPA and manufacturers, pressure-treated wood is often unmarked or poorly labeled in stores. If you're not sure or the label is unclear, ask if the lumber has been treated with CCA, ACZA, or another arsenic compound. If the store clerks can't tell you exactly what it is, don't buy it.

Cigarette Smoke Is a Brain Toxin

There are many toxins in the environment that are difficult to avoid no matter how hard you try. PCBs, perchlorate (from rocket fuel), and PBDEs are so prevalent in our environment that nearly everyone living in an industrialized country will have traces of these toxins and countless others in their bodies. But there's one toxin that you can absolutely keep away from your child: secondhand smoke.

Unfortunately, more than 40 percent of children in the United States are exposed to cigarette smoke in their homes. Secondhand smoke is especially harmful to children, being responsible for between 150,000 and 300,000 lower respiratory tract infections in infants and children under 18 months of age, and between 7,500 and 15,000 hospitalizations each year. In this age group, secondhand smoke has also been linked to 1,900 to 2,700 cases of sudden infant death syndrome (SIDS) in the United States annually. Secondhand smoke exposure may cause buildup of fluid in the middle ear, and can also aggravate symptoms in children with asthma (estimated to be between 200,000 and 1,000,000 children).

Secondhand smoke is not only a threat to a child's body, but to his mind as well. In a recent six year study, scientists found that approximately 50–75 percent of children in the United States have detectable levels of *cotinine,* which appears in the blood as a result of the breakdown of nicotine. Moreover, researchers found a link between exposure to tobacco smoke and cognitive as well as intellectual deficits, along with behavioral problems in children. For example, they saw reduced vocabulary and reasoning abilities, and significant numbers of children who were held back a grade early in their educational experiences.

The solution is so simple: Don't allow anyone to smoke cigarettes in your home or around your child.

d Toxins That May Deplete Your Child's Brain Power

PVC (Polyvinyl Chloride)
Primary Sources
Many types of soft plastic toys
Teething rings
Ingredients in some skin lotions

Pesticides
Primary Sources
Weed and pest killers
Pesticides on fruits and vegetables
Bug repellent

Mercury
Primary Sources
Fatty fish (such as swordfish, tuna, king mackerel, and shark)
Vaccines containing thimerosal, a mercury-based preservative

Dioxins and PCBs (Polychlorinated Biphenyls)
Primary Sources
Fatty fish
Full-fat dairy
Fatty cuts of meat
Breast milk

Lead
Primary Sources
Tap water
Chipped paint

Ceramic dishes and pottery made overseas or in the U.S. prior to 1971

Toys

Solvents

Primary Sources

Paint and adhesive fumes

Varnish strippers

Dry-cleaned clothes

Flame Retardants (PBDEs)

Primary Sources

Children's pajamas

Home furniture

Arsenic

Primary Sources

Wooden playground equipment

Outdoor wooden decks

Cigarette Smoke

Primary Sources

Firsthand and secondhand smoke

PART V

THE BRAIN–BODY CONNECTION

COMMON MEDICAL CONDITIONS AND VACCINATIONS THAT CAN AFFECT YOUR CHILD'S BRAIN

CHAPTER TEN

Asthma

Asthma is one of the most common diseases of childhood, affecting more than one in ten children. And it's on the rise—the incidence of asthma has doubled since 1980. Asthma disproportionately affects young children, with fully half of all children who get asthma developing symptoms before the age of 5 years. Among older children, asthma is the number one cause of missed days at school and poor academic performance.

Asthma is characterized by an allergic reaction of the bronchial tubes, causing these small air passages to go into spasm and making it difficult to breathe. Symptoms of asthma include attacks of wheezing, shortness of breath, excessive mucus production, and a feeling of tightness in the chest. A child who is in the midst of an asthma attack typically experiences a rapid heartbeat and appears distressed and anxious.

When a child has an asthma attack, the amount of oxygen carried in the blood is reduced, thereby compromising oxygen supply. This kind of oxygen deprivation in the brain—even when it's very brief—can harm your child's brain development. Because of breathing difficulties associated with asthma, the amount of oxygen in the blood is frequently reduced when the disease is active. The effect of even mild levels of oxygen depletion associated with asthma on development, behavior, and academic achievement has recently been described in an article appearing in *Pediatrics.* In this report, Harvard researchers found a clear correlation between abnormalities of brain function at all levels and reduced blood flow to the brain. They noted, "Adverse impacts of chronic or intermittent hypoxia on development, behavior, and academic achievement have been reported in many well-designed and -controlled studies in children."* They further noted that adverse effects were found even at mild levels of oxygen depletion. This study underscores how asthma can impair a child's ability to succeed.

ASTHMA TRIGGERS

What triggers an asthma attack? Common allergens are likely culprits, including pollen, dust mites, food allergies (especially to eggs), exposure to animal dander, and tobacco smoke. Environmental pollutants such as household chemicals may also trigger asthma, as well as certain medications, including aspirin. Physical activity is also a trigger, and exercise-induced asthma (EIB for "exercise-induced bronchospasm") is seen in up to 90 percent of all asthma sufferers. Exercise-induced asthma is more likely to occur in cold, dry air. If your child is asthmatic, plan indoor exercise for days that are likely to trigger attacks. Warming up before exercise can help reduce the risk of having an asthma attack.

Finally, emotional stress may also be a trigger.

Children who suffer from a serious respiratory infection in the first two years of life are at much higher risk of developing asthma and the same is true for children who suffer from frequent ear infections. There is also a genetic link: Children who have one or more parents with a history of asthma have double the risk of developing asthma, compared to children with no immediate family member with the disease.

In recent years, the rise in the incidence of asthma among children has prompted researchers to examine what has changed over the past decade or so to bring on such a dramatic increase. Some researchers speculate that the indoor, sedentary lifestyle typical of modern Western society may increase the exposure to indoor asthma triggers. In one groundbreaking study, Swedish researchers working with their American counterparts at Rutgers University found a strong association in children between both asthma and allergic symptoms and exposure to a group of chemical compounds commonly found in house dust called

*Bass, Joel L., et al, "The Effect of Chronic or Intermittent Hypoxia on Cognition in Childhood: A Review of the Evidence." *Pediatrics* 114(3):805-06, 2004.

phthalates. The researchers found a stunning relationship between the concentration of phthalates in dust collected in children's homes and the children's risk for asthma. Phthalates are widely used in industry and are virtually everywhere: They are used as additives to hair spray, plastic softeners, in wood finishes, perfumes, fragrance-containing soaps, nail polish and other beauty products, and most frightening, in a large number of soft plastic toys. Phthalates are endocrine disruptors, which means they adversely affect hormone production in the body, which in turn affects the development and function of all organ systems, including the nervous system. There are lots of good reasons to try to reduce your child's exposure to these chemicals, including their association with asthma. (I cover phthalates in more detail in Chapter 9.)

There is also evidence that early exposure to fumes emitted from cleaning products and other chemicals (including paint, floor adhesives, and room fresheners) commonly found around the house may increase the risk of a child developing asthma. Needless to say, children should not be exposed to potentially dangerous fumes. Children who are asthmatic may find their asthma is irritated by any strong chemical odor, even those that don't necessarily affect other people. If you are using cleaning supplies around the house, keep your child away from the immediate area and make sure the entire house is well ventilated.

THE HYGIENE HYPOTHESIS

Although it seems counterintuitive, children who are exposed early in life to animals and natural allergens (such as plants) do not have a higher incidence of asthma—in fact, their risk is reduced. Some scientists believe that the exponential increase in allergy and asthma is due to our modern intolerance of dirt. We're simply too clean! No kidding. They point out that prior to the twentieth century, most people lived on farms, where kids had close contact with farm animals and dirt, the kind you grow things in. Back then, the immature immune system of a child was taught early on how to tell a true enemy from a foe. Through experience, the immune system of a nineteenth-century child knew that pollen from a flower was nothing to fear, or the dander of a cat was harmless. It didn't go into overdrive every time it was exposed to something new, triggering an allergic reaction. Deprived of these early lessons, the immune systems of children today are more prone to allergy, which can lead to asthma. Moreover, we load our children up with antibiotics, which over time may hamper normal immune function.

Smarter Child Tip Breast-feeding, which is beneficial to your child in so many other ways, also appears to offer strong protection against asthma. According to a study published by the National Institutes of Health evaluating children ages 3 to 5, a history of being breast-fed was associated with a 59 percent reduction in the risk of developing asthma. Interestingly, children who were breast-fed showed a reduction in risk for asthma even if they were exposed to environmental tobacco smoke. (This doesn't mean that it's okay to smoke around your child. We know that there is a greater risk of asthma and other health problems in kids who have been exposed to secondhand smoke, but the risk is somewhat diminished if your child is breast-fed.)

CORTICOSTEROIDS ARE NOT GOOD FOR THE BRAIN

The most common treatment for childhood asthma is the use of corticosteroid drugs, synthetic versions of the hormone cortisol, which is normally produced by the adrenal glands. Corticosteroids can be inhaled or taken in pill form and are powerful drugs with potentially devastating side effects. In particular, I am concerned about the effect of inhaled corticosteroids on BDNF, the growth hormone in the brain that is critical for brain development. German researchers recently found that asthmatic patients who used inhaled corticosteroids had significantly lower levels of BDNF than asthmatic patients not treated with these drugs. The long-term use of inhaled corticosteroids can cause other worrisome nasty side effects, specifically including damage to the hippocampus, the memory center of the brain, not to mention a slew of other physical problems including blood sugar abnormalities and thinning of bones.

The best way to offset the reduction of BDNF caused by the use of steroid medication is to make sure your child takes a DHA supplement each day. Due to the antiinflammatory effect of DHA, I think it's wise for all children with asthma to take extra DHA whether or not they are taking steroids.

- Children between the ages of 6 months to 2 years should take 200 milligrams of DHA daily.
- Children between the ages of 2 and 5 should take 400 milligrams of DHA daily.

A SAFER DRUG

In my opinion, a much safer medication choice than steroids for treating asthma is montelukast (Singulair). This new medication is safe for 2- to 5-year-olds, and the dosage is one milligram chewable tablet each evening. While I am not a big proponent of medication, especially in children, Singulair is highly effective and well tolerated, especially in exercise-induced asthma.

The best approach is for parents to help their child manage his or her asthma so that it doesn't become a major problem. Try to keep your child away from the environmental triggers that cause the attacks whenever possible. Reduce your child's exposure to stress. Key factors that increase stress in young children include inappropriate television programs, interaction with violent children, and exposure to family conflict.

CHAPTER ELEVEN

Ear Infections

More than 10 million children are treated each year for ear infections, and chances are, your child is one of them. If an ear infection clears up quickly, it's no more of a problem than the common cold. In many cases, however, ear infections become chronic, which can cause permanent hearing loss in small children.

The first two years of life are critical for the development of language skills and obviously hearing function plays the pivotal role in this achievement. Hearing impairment is thus a fundamentally important issue, as it is related to significant delays in speech and language development, both of which affect academic performance as well as social and emotional growth. It's also important to note that children with hearing impairment often demonstrate emotional and behavioral problems that, in and of themselves, can result in poor academic performance.

Despite the fact that ear infections are so common and that they often lead to hearing problems, hearing impairment is generally not recognized until a child is between 2 and 2½ years old. But it is imperative to identify hearing loss much earlier. As many as 80 percent of children get middle ear infections, technically known as otitis media, by the age of three. These middle ear infections can affect a child's hearing when they become chronic, or when fluid builds up behind the eardrum. A middle ear infection that includes fluid buildup behind the eardrum is called *otitis media with effusion* (OME). These middle ear infections, especially OME, are the most common causes of inadequate hearing in children.

Smarter Child Tip A recent study showed that infants who used pacifiers had a 40 percent increase in the risk of ear infections; interestingly, when parents were counseled to reduce use of the pacifiers, the study demonstrated a 29 percent decrease in the rate of ear infections. The study authors suggest that parents reduce the use of pacifiers, and use them only when the child is falling asleep. They added that since ear infections are so common in childhood, even a slight change in habits that reduces their frequency would be extremely beneficial in preventing infections. But don't throw out the pacifier yet. A recent study suggested that babies who sucked on pacifiers while falling asleep were at a dramatically reduced risk of sudden infant death syndrome (SIDS). So the sensible solution seems to be reserving the use of pacifiers to calm your baby at bedtime.

It is also important to recognize that most middle ear infections (about two-thirds of uncomplicated infections) will clear up on their own within twenty-four hours, and in more than 80 percent of uncomplicated infections, symptoms will diminish or disappear within one to seven days. Since many middle ear infections are caused by viruses, antibiotics, which fight bacterial infections, do not help to clear up the primary infection, nor do they eliminate middle ear fluid. Antibiotics, which are widely overused in treating ear infections, are thus frequently unnecessary, and can even be harmful in some cases, as overusing antibiotics can breed antibiotic-resistant strains of bacteria. Perhaps even more important is the fact that frequent use of antibiotics in children has been linked to a higher incidence of attention deficit hyperactivity disorder (ADHD). Of course, it's up to your doctor whether or not to prescribe an antibiotic, but all too often, doctors succumb to the pleading of anxious parents who feel that an antibiotic will solve the problem quickly. The reality is, it makes better sense to monitor the problem for a week or so to see if it resolves on its own. As noted earlier, in most cases, it will. Save the antibiotic for the rare ear infection so severe that it doesn't clear up on its own.

As for removing the adenoids of children suffering from recurrent ear infections, recent evidence has shown the benefit of this procedure with respect to reducing frequency of ear infections to be so small that many doctors now do not recommend this approach as a primary treatment in children up to 2 years of age.

THE IMPACT OF EAR INFECTIONS ON CHILDREN'S LANGUAGE SKILLS

Most of the research both on otitis media and OME over the past ten years has focused on the effects of temporary hearing loss on the development of language skills in children younger than 3 years old. One study examined a group of 3 to 8-year-olds who had histories of chronic ear infections and OME, all of whom got ear infections before 18 months of age. The study found that although these children did misarticulate more consonants than children without histories of ear infections, both groups made errors on the same sounds.

Several studies suggest a direct relationship between educational achievement and occurrence of otitis media and OME. Interestingly, a few of these studies also suggest that children with intermittent hearing loss may have more difficulties with speech and language than children with steady mild-to-moderate hearing impairment.

But one study of 698 children of diverse backgrounds showed that prolonged or chronic otitis media or OME, especially in children between 6 to 12 months, may put children at risk for cognitive delays at around 3 years of age. Conceivably, if these children were identified and given help when their cognitive deficits were first uncovered, they would be able to get back up to speed, and thus, even by the age of 5, be at reduced risk for negative development effects. These findings provide an even stronger argument for early testing of hearing impairment, especially in at-risk children.

Most importantly, remember that the window during which screening and subsequent therapy will help a child overcome any developmental deficits brought on by hearing loss is brief, and considered by most experts to end at age 3. This is even more reason to have early and frequent testing and pursue corrective therapy if needed.

HOW TO PREVENT HEARING LOSS FROM TAKING A TOLL ON YOUR CHILD'S DEVELOPMENT

With all of this evidence that hearing impairment affects a child's development and performance, I believe strongly in screening children for hearing as early as possible.

In fact, I am very much in favor of screening newborns for hearing problems, which is not now a universal practice. A growing number of professionals, including neonatologists, believe it is imperative to screen infants as early as possible, ideally at birth and certainly by the age of 1 to 2 months at the latest. Each day, some thirty-three infants in the United States are born with total hearing loss, the most common congenital disorder in newborns, and twenty times more prevalent than phenylketonuria, a condition for which all newborns are currently screened. An estimated sixty additional infants per day are born with moderate hearing loss that could be exposed with universal newborn screening and intervention programs. Furthermore, statistics show that 90 percent of hearing-impaired infants are born to parents with normal hearing, and fewer than half of hearing-impaired infants have known risk factors. The infants at highest risk for hearing loss, not surprisingly, are those in the neonatal intensive care unit where the risk of moderate-to-severe permanent hearing loss in both ears is ten to twenty times higher than in the general population.

As advocates of early hearing detection and intervention programs (EHDI) can tell you, universal newborn hearing screening can identify those infants who have even moderate hearing loss, enabling them to receive speech and language therapy, amplification, and family support immediately, before their development falls far behind that of other children of their age. This kind of universal screening even has the potential to reduce the disparity in language skills between deaf and hearing children.

OTITIS MEDIA WITH EFFUSION (OME): THE PERLMUTTER RECOMMENDATION

If your 2- or 3-year-old gets an ear infection (diagnosed by your physician), I recommend not pursuing antibiotic therapy for at least the first forty-eight to seventy-two hours, as the cause may be a virus; in addition, antibiotics typically will not eliminate middle ear fluid. You should ask your physician for an anesthetic eardrop to decrease the pain. In addition, diphenhydramine (Benadryl) often works wonders in terms of "taking the edge off" and allowing you and your child to get some much-needed rest. The specific products I recommend are Children's Benadryl Dye-Free Allergy Liquid or Benadryl Dye-Free Allergy Liqui-Gels. Make sure to read the package so you use the appropriate dosage for your child.

Another excellent choice to alleviate the pain of an ear infection for your child is children's strength ibuprofen, as it will both alleviate pain and reduce inflammation and fever. Again, pay attention to the directions on the package to ensure you give your child the right dosage for his or her weight and age.

Keep your infant well hydrated by increasing the frequency of breast-feeding; for the older child, offer plenty of spring water and diluted fruit juices and avoid dairy products, as they tend to increase the mucous secretions.

I have found Recharge Sports Drink particularly helpful when kids have ear infections, colds, or diarrhea. Recharge is an all-natural product that contains important electrolytes, which, in my opinion, clearly help children feel better sooner. Other helpful ideas include propping your child's head up with a pillow or two to improve drainage of fluid through the eustachian tube. In addition, a warm, moist compress will also often help alleviate pain.

Fluid behind the eardrum (OME) can significantly harm a child's hearing. If the problem persists, children may, in fact require the insertion of ear tubes. This allows drainage of the fluid and ventilation of the region behind the eardrum, allowing hearing to be restored.

Finally, it's also important to remember that ear infections, on rare occasion, can be a sign of other, more serious problems. Call your doctor if your child experiences a severe headache, stiffness of the neck, fever, chills, sudden hearing loss, dizziness, or sudden and severe ear pain with drainage, even if the pain is alleviated upon drainage.

One very useful device is the EarCheck monitor, which uses sound waves to evaluate the eardrum. The EarCheck monitor can signify the degree of infection and help you determine whether or not you need to visit your child's pediatrician. For more information, the telephone number is 888-EAR-CHECK (888-327-2435), or visit www.earcheck.com.

CHAPTER TWELVE

Gluten Sensitivity

Recently, parents of a lovely 9-year-old girl named Karen brought her to see me because she was falling behind in her schoolwork. According to her parents, she was having difficulty thinking and staying focused and having memory problems. Interestingly, they said that at times she was fine, while at other times her mental function seemed to radically change for the worse.

Due to her significant issues with academic performance, Karen's parents elected to homeschool her. Academic testing revealed that she was functioning at or below her third-grade level in a variety of areas, including math skills, reading fluency, story recall, and overall academic skills. She had had no significant medical problems in the past and her overall physical and neurologic examinations were entirely normal. Routine blood studies were not revealing, so I was left to reconsider her history to see if there were any clues as to what might be causing this child's problems.

What was most telling was that her problems were not constant. That indicated to me that basically her brain was intact and something seemed to be influencing her intermittently and causing significant problems with brain function. In considering what would change from day to day for a child, certainly diet would be at the top of the list.

As a physician, and a neurologist, I know that sensitivity to gluten (a protein found in wheat, barley, and rye) is extremely common, so I decided to do a simple blood test to check for gluten sensitivity. As the tests showed that Karen was profoundly sensitive to gluten, I instructed her parents to put her on a gluten-free diet, which meant eliminating all wheat, barley, and rye from their daughter's diet.

While Karen's parents considered the diet to be challenging, they complied. Over the following two weeks, they observed a remarkable change in their daughter's cognitive function. She suddenly was able to focus much more readily on her schoolwork and told her parents that she noticed she was thinking much more clearly. Her parents kept her on a gluten-free diet and over the next several months continued to see further improvements in her schoolwork. At the end of the school year, Karen showed a grade-level equivalent for math calculation skills of 5.1, with reading fluency at 5.6 and story recall at 8.4—the latter score indicating that she was functioning at a normal level for a midyear eighth-grade student!

A brief note from Karen's parents read,

> Karen is completing the third grade this year. Prior to removing gluten from her diet, academics, especially math, were difficult. As you can see, she is now soaring in math. Based on this test, entering the fourth grade next year, she would be at the top of her class. The teacher indicated that if she skipped the fourth grade and went to the fifth, she would be in the middle of her class. What an accomplishment!

Karen is not an isolated case. Current studies indicate that about 1 percent of Americans are gluten sensitive. This is an astounding statistic when you consider that at the time of this writing, there are some 300 million Americans, which means that about 3 million of us are gluten sensitive; and of children up to age 5—who number about 23 million—some 230,000 are gluten sensitive.

"ONE OF THE MOST COMMON CONDITIONS YOU'VE NEVER HEARD OF"

This is the tagline of the Celiac Disease Center at Columbia University, created within the department of medicine in 2001 and dedicated to the study and treatment of celiac disease (gluten sensitivity) in children and adults (www.celiacdiseasecenter.columbia.edu).

If your child has gastrointestinal complaints or headaches, along with problems with learning or apparent ADHD or other behavioral problems, and continues to get all clear checkups, it certainly makes sense to be suspicious of gluten sensitivity and bring her to your family doctor for a blood test to check for this condition.

Despite the fact that gluten sensitivity was originally described in 1888, and that some 4 million Americans suffer from it, we hear astoundingly little about celiac disease. Standard medical texts typically describe celiac disease as being primarily a gastrointestinal problem. I remember learning about celiac disease in medical school; we were taught that it was characterized by abdominal pain, abdominal distention with bloating and gas, decreased appetite, diarrhea, nausea, unexplained weight loss, and growth delay in children.

CELIAC DISEASE AND YOUR CHILD'S DEVELOPING BRAIN

New research on celiac disease indicates that it can have a profound effect on the nervous system. In fact a physician in Great Britain, Dr. Maios Hadjivassiliou, who is a recognized world authority on gluten sensitivity, reported in the journal *The Lancet* that gluten sensitivity can actually be at times primarily a neurological disease. Thus, people with gluten sensitivity can have symptoms involving brain function without having any gastrointestinal problems whatsoever.

Researchers in Israel have described neurological problems in 51 percent of children with gluten sensitivity. They also have described a link between gluten sensitivity and ADHD. Actually, the link between gluten sensitivity and problems with brain function, including learning disabilities and even memory problems, is not that difficult to understand. Gluten sensitivity is caused by elevated levels of antibodies against a component of gluten called gliadin. The antigliadin antibody combines with gliadin when a person is exposed to any gluten-containing food like wheat, barley, or rye.

When this happens, protein-specific genes are turned on in a special type of immune cell in the body. When these genes are turned on, inflammatory chemicals called *cytokines* are created. Cytokines, which are the chemical mediators of inflammation, are directly detrimental to brain function. In fact, elevated levels of cytokines are seen in such devastating conditions as Alzheimer's disease, Parkinson's disease, multiple sclerosis, and even autism. Essentially, the brain does not like inflammation and responds quite negatively to the presence of cytokines.

The antigliadin antibody can also combine directly with specific proteins found in the brain that may resemble the gliadin protein found in gluten-containing foods, so the antigliadin antibody just can't tell the difference. The combining of the antigliadin antibody with specific brain proteins, which has been described for decades, also leads to the formation of cytokines. This is an example of turning on genes that ultimately affect brain health and function in a negative way.

TIME GRAINS CORRECTLY

A recent study demonstrates that parents can absolutely influence the likelihood of their child developing gluten sensitivity. In a fascinating report in the May 2005 *Journal of the American Medical Association,* Dr. Jill Norris and her colleagues at the University of Colorado revealed that the timing of the introduction of gluten-containing foods in the diet plays a critical role in determining the risk for gluten sensitivity. In this study, Dr. Norris and colleagues evaluated risk for developing gluten sensitivity (celiac disease) in a group of 1,560 children at increased risk for this problem because they had a relative with insulin-dependent diabetes. In the study, researchers looked at the age at which gluten-containing foods (wheat, barley, or rye) were introduced into the diet. The results were startling:

- The risk of celiac disease increased 500 percent for children who were exposed to gluten-containing foods prior to 4 months of age.
- Children introduced to gluten-containing foods at age 7 months or older had an 87 percent increased risk of the disease.
- Infants who were breast-fed were at an increased risk for gluten intolerance if breast-feeding ended before gluten was introduced into the diet.

Based on this study, the researchers determined that the ideal time to introduce gluten into an infant's diet is between 4 and 6 months. Moreover, according to this study, the risk of gluten sensitivity was reduced by 41 percent if infants were still being breast-fed when gluten was introduced into their diets. Other research has shown that gradual introduction of gluten containing foods also reduces risk of gluten sensitivity.

WHEN SHOULD YOU GET YOUR CHILD TESTED FOR CELIAC DISEASE?

As I mentioned in Chapters 3 and 8, the overall risk for gluten sensitivity in the population is 1 percent. That risk is increased if your child is exposed to gluten-containing foods prior to 4 months of age, receives wheat, barley, or rye after breast-feeding is discontinued, or is exposed to a lot of gluten-containing foods, even during the appropriate time for their introduction (4 to 6 months). Having a primary relative (brother, sister, mother, or father) with insulin-dependent diabetes or gluten sensitivity is also associated with increased risk. In addition to these factors, any child 1 year or older who is in the bottom 5 percent of the growth chart, or who is experiencing headache, unexplained hair loss, or any of the gastrointestinal problems described above, should also be considered at increased risk for gluten sensitivity and tested.

If your child has none of these risk factors, it may seem overly aggressive to perform a diagnostic test for wheat sensitivity. Nonetheless, in light of its significant relationship to brain function, you may want to consider testing your child, even if he or she has no risk factors. Identifying children who are sensitive to gluten/wheat early on and making appropriate changes in diet will clearly have a very positive effect on brain function and academic performance.

A simple blood test is all that's needed to make the diagnosis of gluten sensitivity. If the tests for the IgG and IgA antigliadin antibodies are positive, the likelihood of gluten sensitivity is at least 96–97 percent. If the antiendomysial antibody is added, and the result is positive, the accuracy of gluten sensitivity diagnosis is almost 100 percent. For the antibodies to be present, the child must already have been exposed to the gluten. This is why it makes no sense to check for gluten sensitivity in the newborn.

If gluten-containing foods are introduced at between 4 and 6 months (considered an appropriate time), abnormal levels of antibodies will be detected in the blood by the time the child is 2 years old if he or she is gluten sensitive.

As children generally have blood tests for one or another reason during their early years, it's a good idea to ask your doctor to add the gluten sensitivity blood tests at the same time.

A complete blood screen for gluten sensitivity is provided as part of the Children's Better Brain Profile available from Genova Diagnostics at www.GenovaDx.com, or call (828-210-7433). The panel also includes an extensive evaluation for food allergies as well as a measurement of important brain fats including DHA, and can be performed in a doctor's office.

WHAT TO DO IF THE TESTS FOR GLUTEN SENSITIVITY ARE POSITIVE

If your child's blood tests for gluten sensitivity come out positive and he or she is suffering from one or more of the symptoms described in the charts at the end of this chapter, gluten sensitivity is most likely the correct diagnosis. You will then need to make a continuous, focused effort to eliminate gluten from your child's diet.

While there is currently no cure for celiac disease, it can be managed by changing to a gluten-free diet. The good news is that there are still many basic, nutritious foods you can eat on a gluten-free diet, including fresh fish, poultry and meats, most dairy products, fruits, vegetables, rice, potatoes, and gluten-free flours, such as rice, corn, and potato flours. Fortunately, there are also an increasingly high number of gluten-free products available, including bread and pasta. If you can't find any at your local bakery or grocery store, check with a celiac support group or on the Internet.

In addition to being found in breads, cereals, crackers, pasta, baked goods, gravies, and sauces, grains containing gluten are often used in food additives such as malt flavoring and modified food starch, among others. The principal foods to be avoided are, of course, wheat, barley, and rye (including various types of wheat such as durham, semolina, farina, and graham flour), as well as bulghur, kamut, spelt, and triticale. Amaranth, quinoa, and buckwheat are gluten free, but check package labeling to be sure these products are harvested and processed in a gluten-free environment, since they can be cross-contaminated if they are treated in mills that also treat gluten-containing grains. This can happen with oats as well, though they are, by nature, gluten free. In fact, it is so common for oats to be contaminated with wheat that oats

should generally be avoided, unless their packaging reveals sp
tention to being processed in a gluten-free environment.

There are also many resources available, including two membership-based organizations, dedicated to informing and assisting people with celiac disease. Two places to start are www.glutenfree.org and www.gfcfdiet.com, which offer information on gluten-free products and links to other related Web sites.

Symptoms of Gluten Sensitivity

Typical Gastrointestinal Symptoms of Gluten-Sensitive Children		
Abdominal pain	Abdominal distention	Bloating
Excessive gas	Diarrhea	Constipation
Nausea and vomiting	Foul smelling stools that may float	Unexplained weight loss

Non-Gastrointestinal Symptoms Associated with Gluten Sensitivity		
Anemia	Bone and/or joint pain	Osteoporosis (unexplained bone fractures)
Shortness of breath	Dental discoloration	Tendency to become easily fatigued
Delay in growth	Unexplained hair loss	Mouth ulcers
Muscle cramps	Unexplained skin disorders	Vitamin and mineral deficiency

Neurological Symptoms Associated with Gluten Sensitivity		
Anxiety and depression	Ataxia (poor coordination)	Attention deficit hyperactivity disorder (ADHD)
Autism	Epilepsy	Headaches including migraines

CHAPTER THIRTEEN

Sleep Problems and Snoring

Ever wonder why newborns spend so much time sleeping? While your child is sleeping, some amazing things are happening to her brain. Researchers from the University of Wisconsin at Madison were able to identify an astounding one hundred genes that are actually turned on by the process of sleep. They also found that the proteins made by these genes play important roles in brain function and maintenance. In other words, sleep turns on smart genes.

The flip side is, a lack of sleep can stunt brain growth. Scientists at the University of California in San Francisco monitored the brain changes in young cats allowed to sleep as much as they needed, as compared to those kept in a state of sleep deprivation. They found that the sleep-deprived animals had only half the neuronal connections in key areas as did those who slept. The take-home message is that sleep is vitally important for brain development—it is essential for normal synaptic pruning and the consolidation of neural connections necessary to build a faster, stronger brain. When your child doesn't get enough sleep, his brain cannot do the important work it needs to, robbing your child of brain power.

Sleep is no less important for toddlers and older children. Numerous studies have shown that children who experience difficulty sleeping during the first five years of life have lower IQ scores and do worse in school than children who do not have sleep problems.

So, what's preventing children from getting a good night's sleep?

WHEN BREATHING DURING SLEEP IS DISTURBED

Breathing disorders are one of the most common problems that disrupt a child's sleep. Two of the most common include snoring and obstructive sleep apnea. Breathing problems cause daytime sleepiness and are directly correlated with deficits in learning, memory, and intellectual function.

But the role of breathing disorders in children has only recently been explored. It turns out that even simple snoring, observed in about 12 percent of children, has a profound effect on mental function. Researchers have demonstrated that children who snore are at a significantly increased risk for such problems as aggression, behavioral changes, inattentiveness, hyperactive behavior, and daytime sleepiness.

Just like children who have asthma, children who snore are reducing the oxygen that flows to their brains, even if it is just momentarily. As has been seen in young children with asthma, children who snore show changes in cognitive function. In fact, researchers in Australia found a dramatic drop in IQ when comparing age-matched children who snored to those who didn't. Children who snored had Verbal IQ scores an incredible 17.6 points lower than those of children who didn't snore, and Global IQ scores 13.5 points lower than children who didn't suffer from snoring. And equally if not more significant, memory testing showed that children scored a full 16.9 points lower if they snored than if they did not.

A relationship between snoring and attention deficit hyperactivity disorder (ADHD) is clear; one-third of children with ADHD are habitual snorers, compared with only 9 percent of children who don't have ADHD.

Another study, by David Gozal, a professor of pediatrics at the University of Louisville School of Medicine, looked at two thousand 13- and 14-year-olds. Dr. Gozal and his researchers found that according to parents' reports, children who snored between the ages of 2 and 6 years of age were three times more likely to have behavioral and/or intellectual problems and perform badly in middle school classes. In fact, the middle school students who snored as youngsters performed in the bottom twenty-fifth percentile of their class. They were also more than three times as likely to have had their tonsils and/or adenoids removed at a very young age.

Smarter Child Tip Here is yet another reason to keep your child away from secondhand smoke: According to Dr. Gozol, children who were exposed to smoking had an increased risk of snoring and showed learning, memory, and behavior deficits. Moreover, researchers in New Zealand who evaluated infants discovered snoring in nearly 16 percent during the first four weeks of life. Snoring in later infancy increased to 26 percent and was found to be related to maternal smoking, as well as to the number of respiratory infections.

While historically parents and physicians believed that children who suffered from breathing disorders such as snoring were simply sleepy during the day, and thus less attentive, the new research shows there is much more to this story. The evidence shows that because these disorders interrupt sleep, they have profound biochemical effects on your child's brain. In other words, if your child's sleep is interrupted by breathing disorders, important genes that are turned on during normal sleep and serve to enhance synaptic pruning and synaptic plasticity become less functional, building a brain that is slower, below average in memory capacity, and less efficient. Stated in another way, unless your child gets good-quality, uninterrupted sleep, she will not fully benefit from the creative, mind-expanding activities she experiences throughout the day when she is awake. We now know that sleep actually turns on smart genes in the brain, so identifying and treating snoring (or any other disordered breathing problems such as sleep apnea) in your child can have profound, measurable lifelong benefits.

WHY DO CHILDREN SNORE?

Snoring is not just something kids do, nor is it, by any means, an indication of deep sleep. Snoring in young children should always be considered a sign of a physiological problem with behavioral, cognitive, and neurocognitive implications, as we've seen.

Logically, the reasons kids snore are similar to the reasons adults snore. These include asthma and allergy, colds, sinus infections, enlarged tonsils, enlarged adenoids, and, sadly, obesity, along with smoking by the mother and general exposure to smoking and smokers.

OBSTRUCTIVE SLEEP APNEA

Obstructive sleep apnea (OSA) in children is characterized by sudden cessation of breathing because of an obstruction in the airway that can be caused by swollen nasal passages, enlarged tonsils, or excessive relaxation of throat muscles. This causes the child to awaken frequently, gasping for breath. Some children suffer from OSA as a result of a variation in jaw structure.

In a recent report in the *Journal of Pediatrics*, the authors suggest the prevalence of OSA in children may be as high as 10 percent. The report showed that approximately 84 percent of children with OSA suffer from excessive daytime sleepiness, while 76 percent have some behavioral disturbance; 42 percent are classified as hyperactive, and 16 percent have decreased school performance. Moreover, the researchers estimate that neurobehavioral problems may be as much as 300 percent higher in children with sleep apnea than in those without this disorder. But the study also showed that inattention and hyperactivity almost uniformly improved following surgery.

The danger of OSA to the developing brain is that it causes frequent interruptions in sleep, preventing children from experiencing the important stages of REM sleep and non-REM sleep. Children with OSA display an exaggeration of the same symptoms noted in children who snore (significant inability to learn, and drowsiness during the day). OSA is an even more significant problem, as it increases a child's risk not just for these brain-related problems, but for pulmonary and even cardiovascular disease.

DIAGNOSING OSA

The polysomnogram, a noninvasive and painless test in which a device is attached to a child's finger, is considered the gold standard for diagnosis of obstructive sleep apnea. The test is usually performed in a sleep clinic under the direction of a physician specializing in pulmonary medicine (treatment of breathing disorders). Ask your pediatrician or local hospital to recommend a breathing disorder specialist. The polysomnogram measures activities such as brain waves (which show the quality of sleep) and air flow through the nose and mouth, providing information about how effectively and efficiently the child is breathing, as well as blood oxygenation levels (how much oxygen is being carried by the blood). These elements are measured in an effort to learn both the cause as well as the severity of sleep-related breathing problems. Some physicians may recommend audiotaping and videotaping the child at home while he or she is sleeping. While these methods have some value for diagnosing snoring problems, they have not been proven useful in reaching a definitive diagnosis.

If your child sweats heavily during sleep, complains of headaches, feels worse in the morning, is irritated and shows aggressive behavior, seems sleepy during the day, or suffers from daytime behavioral problems, you should be suspicious that he or she may be suffering from obstructive sleep apnea.

Physiological abnormalities associated with OSA include decreased growth and cardiovascular problems, such as heart dysfunction and hypertension. But interestingly, growth accelerates following surgery for the problem. Cardiovascular problems appear to improve following the removal of the adenoids and tonsils.

TREATING OBSTRUCTIVE SLEEP APNEA AND SNORING

Not surprisingly, there is a strong correlation between obesity and OSA. So I believe initial efforts to treat OSA should be directed toward weight loss. Despite the bewildering array of weight-loss diets so popular today, keep in mind that weight loss and weight gain are simply a function of the difference between calories taken in and calories burned. To help your child shed excessive weight, steer him away from calorie-dense foods such as high-sugar snacks, sodas, and junk food. Turn off the TV, take away the joystick, and encourage him to get more physical activity. For many children, simply revving up physical activity and cutting back on candy, chips, and other "empty calories" are all it takes to lose the extra pounds. Review Chapter 8 for more information on what you should be feeding your child.

I also believe that while many ear, nose, and throat doctors feel the best approach to treatment of OSA is removal of the tonsils and adenoids, surgery should not be the first-line therapy. Like any surgical procedure, removing the tonsil and/or adenoids can be complicated by infection and bleeding, as well as unexpected reactions to anesthetic medications. Moreover, it is important to remember that the tonsils are part of the immune system and serve as the first line of defense against dangerous bacteria in the mouth and throat.

Rather, I agree with the approach that Dr. Francis McNamara of the University of Sydney, Australia, suggests. Dr. McNamara advocates the use of a technique called nasal continuous positive airway pressure (nCPAP), which involves the placement of a small plastic mask over the nose with an infusion of air to maintain positive pressure. This positive pressure tends to keep the airway open and has proven extremely effective in adults, children, and, most recently, in infants. In fact, the nCPAP technique has dramatically reduced daytime sleepiness in children and improved academic performance. Children who have shown these kinds of significant improvements in alertness and schoolwork have also improved behaviorally.

HOW MUCH SLEEP IS NORMAL?

Since good-quality, uninterrupted sleep that cycles through all stages is so fundamentally important to your child's developing brain, it's important to focus on how your child develops good sleep habits.

In terms of how much sleep is normal, there are many changes that occur throughout the first several years of life. Newborns generally may sleep seventeen to eighteen hours a day, typically divided into three- to four-hour segments during both daytime and nighttime. An infant will eventually adapt to a day–night sleep cycle, often as early as the first month of life.

By 6 months, nighttime sleep approaches six hours, with a progressive decline in total sleep time from seventeen to eighteen hours a day to about thirteen hours per twenty-four-hour period (including a daytime nap) by 12 to 24 months. By age 3, most children have stopped their afternoon nap, and by 5 years of age, children sleep an average of eleven to eleven and a half hours per day.

Although you should expect your infant to awaken once or even twice during the night, by 5 to 6 months, most babies are sleeping through the night. In fact this may even happen as early as 3 months of age. Keep in mind that even in children up to 2 years of age, it is normal to awaken once or twice during the night and then go back to sleep without any intervention on the part of a parent.

TEACHING YOUR CHILD TO DEVELOP GOOD SLEEP HABITS

Make Sleep a Priority

Remember that an infant needs to sleep to develop her brain. Your infant needs to sleep about sixteen to eighteen hours a day. Try not to keep your baby awake for longer than a few hours at a time, and put your infant to sleep at the first signs of drowsiness.

Create a Regular Sleeptime Routine

This can't be overstated, and it is important for people of all ages, but especially for infants and toddlers. Your baby will quickly learn to respond to specific routine signals such as rocking, stroking, or singing to her and know that it is time for sleep. Her body will naturally respond to these activities by relaxing if they are repeated at bedtime each night.

Be Consistent

Routine means . . . routine. Sometimes it means adjusting your schedule so your child can keep his nap time and bedtime. But you will be helping your child tremendously by training his physiology to know what to expect at specific times of the day.

Accept That Your Child May Cry

By about 9 months or thereabouts, many infants begin to have separation anxiety issues at bedtime. Remember that as your baby grows into a toddler and learns to go to sleep on her own, there may be some tears over being on her own at bedtime. If you feel it is really "protest crying" (vs. distress for another reason that does require your attention) as your baby learns healthy sleep habits, keep in mind that it is completely normal, and difficult though it may seem it is part of the process. While you may want to rock your baby to bed each night, ultimately infants and children can become dependent on this activity and not gain the ability to settle themselves enough to fall asleep. So be careful not to unwittingly create dependency when your child needs to learn to train herself to fall asleep.

CHAPTER FOURTEEN

Traumatic Brain Injury

The National Center for Injury Prevention and Control estimates there are some 1.5 million cases of traumatic brain injury (TBI) in the United States every year. In fact, a traumatic brain injury occurs every 15 seconds. What's even more alarming is the fact that the two age groups at highest risk for TBI are children from birth to age 4 and 15- to 19-year-olds.

And babies are especially vulnerable to injury. Incredibly, in a report published in the *Journal of the American Medical Association,* it was observed that the most common cause of serious or fatal traumatic brain injury in children 2 years of age or younger was physical abuse—that is, injuries inflicted by others. In fact, child abuse is believed to be responsible for at least *half* of infant brain injuries.

TBI occurs when the head is struck with force, the head strikes an object, or the brain undergoes movement within the skull, even with no visible trauma to the outside of the head. Children tend to land head first, as their heads are proportionately larger than adults' heads, so brain injuries tend to be particularly serious in children.

While the injury can be severe or mild, an injury to the head should never be ignored, especially with a child, whether or not you can see any visible symptoms. Even milder traumatic brain injuries can have long-term residual effects, so it's important that you seek medical care when a child receives an injury to the head.

The good news is that a child's brain has the ability to recover from trauma better than an adult's due to the ability of other, noninjured parts of the brain to take over the function of the injured neurons. This is called neural *plasticity.* And more good news: Children rehabilitate better and more quickly than do adults.

A BRAIN IS A TERRIBLE THING TO INJURE

The exquisite complexity of our brains sets the stage for serious consequences as a result of an injury. The brain can be damaged by trauma from motor vehicle accidents, sports injuries, falls, abuse, and other causes, as well as situations that can deprive it of blood and/or oxygen (such as carbon monoxide poisoning, strangulation, suffocation, choking, and near-drowning).

Direct trauma that injures the brain is a leading cause of death and disability not only in children, but in adolescents as well. Head injuries affect more than 1 million American children annually, and about 16 percent of these children require hospitalization. Although the brain is protected by the skull, permanent impairments in one or more areas of brain function are relatively common following head trauma. Of course, the types of deficits that occur as a result of TBI depend on which area of the brain was damaged. Common problems include difficulties with communication, behavioral issues, and a wide variety of cognitive difficulties, along with physical handicaps. Specific cognitive problems that may persist after TBI include memory dysfunction (both short- and long-term), impairments in reading and writing skills, and difficulty concentrating, as well as emotional control problems. Depression is common, along with mood swings and problems in interpersonal relationships.

As a practicing neurologist, I can tell you that treating brain-injured children is among the most challenging and heart-wrenching tasks I encounter. Because head injuries can be so devastating to brain function, it is important to look at how these injuries occur, and, more importantly, what you can do to prevent them.

PREVENTING INJURIES TO YOUR INFANT OR TODDLER AT HOME

You don't need a neurologist to tell you that your baby's greatest risk factor in her first two years is her own curiosity. This is true, of course, because a baby learns to move around and explore the environment first by crawling, then by pulling herself up on furniture, and ultimately by walking.

Children have a natural tendency to want to climb up on objects, including furniture and windowsills. It is when they get to the climbing and walking stages that their risk for injury multiplies. Your quest to prevent head injury in your child starts immediately, though, even if she is just barely able to roll over. She is at great risk for injury if, for example, she is left unattended on a changing table. At this stage, your child is actually safer in the middle of the floor or in a playpen.

Use Safety Restraints

When your child is in a stroller or high chair, remember to always use safety restraints. Once your child is able to pull herself up on furniture, she and you face new hazards that include sharp corners on chairs and tables, lamps and mirrors that can fall over—in fact, anything in your home that is not tied down.

Furniture

As your baby is learning to walk (or, ideally, even before her first steps), take a look around your home while you're sitting on the floor, as this will help you get a toddler's-eye view of your home, and will help you identify sharp corners than can harm her if she falls. If you see sharp corners that could hurt your toddler, make sure to pad them before your child begins to dart around. Be sure that furniture is sturdy and that children can't pull over things like bookshelves and dressers when climbing on them. You should have bookshelves that are bolted to the wall, rather than free-standing pieces.

Rugs

Rugs should either have nonskid pads under them or be tacked down to the floor; they should not be left loose on the floor.

Bathtubs and Swimming Pools

Put special nonskid tape strips in bathtubs to prevent slipping while bathing; also, children should be encouraged not to stand up in the bathtub, except for getting in and out, and even then they should be assisted by an adult. Under no circumstances should a baby be left unattended in the bathtub or even in his small washing basin. And an older sibling should not be left to watch your baby if you are called away. Toilet seats should be locked in the down position using a lid-locking device, and it's a good idea to keep the bathroom door closed at all times, since bathrooms can pose many risks to young children, even beyond drowning.

Some one thousand children in this country drown each year, with most of these deaths occurring in swimming pools. All pools should be protected by a fence that's at least five feet in height with a self-closing and self-latching gate that can be locked. Always remove toys from the pool after your child has been swimming to reduce the chance of your child trying to retrieve them when you are not around. *Commercially available pool alarms can be effective for older children, but they have not specifically been proven to reduce the risk of drowning for very young children.* Don't count on them to ensure the safety of your toddler.

I feel strongly that any parent who spends time with children at a swimming pool, a lake, or at the beach, should take the time to learn cardiopulmonary resuscitation (CPR), and should insist that any babysitter or anyone left in charge of children in or around water have CPR training as well. Tragically, children can also drown in the bathtub, so it's best that you and all babysitters get trained in CPR. Remember, when children are around water, they need *constant* supervision. Impress upon babysitters or caregivers that they should never take their eyes off your child when they are near water. We all recognize the dangers of lakes, the beach, and the swimming pool, but other potential hazards include fountains, buckets, the toilet bowl, hot tubs, and even small, inflatable wading pools with only one or two inches of water.

Stairways

Stairways present an all too common and potentially devastating risk for small children. My strong opinion is that parents should never consider a gate across a stairway to be adequate protection; children can climb over these gates and fall down the stairs. Check your stair banister to make sure your child can't fit through the rails. Better yet, purchase a protective guard and install it on the banister to further reduce the risk that your child could squeeze through and fall.

Windows

Check every window in your house to be sure it is childproof. Even windows above and behind dressers can present a hazard, again because of children's natural tendency to climb up on furniture. A window screen does virtually nothing to protect a child from falling out of a window. There are a variety of window protection devices that can help prevent your child from opening the window and falling out. Keep in mind that a child can conceivably fall through a window open as little as five inches.

Baby Walkers

Despite their significant risk, there is still a tendency for parents to choose baby walkers in an attempt to teach their babies to walk earlier. Each year, more than fourteen thousand children have to go to the hospital as a result of injuries related to falls from using baby walkers. Baby walkers have caused children to drown in swimming pools, be burned by heaters and stoves, and roll down flights of stairs. I urge parents not to use a baby walker. Your child will learn to walk just fine without it.

OUTDOOR SAFETY

Of course children should be encouraged to play outdoors. But this presents its own set of potential hazards. Perhaps one of the most dangerous activities, which is unfortunately becoming more and more popular in America, is the use of the home trampoline. Children 5 years and under should absolutely not use a trampoline, even if there is adult supervision, because of the overwhelming risk of injury. The play area should be free of rocks and other hard surfaces. Children will be running—and falling down—so soft surfaces are a must (including sawdust, woodchips, and sand).

Bicycles and Scooters

Bicycle riding is a wonderful activity for adults and kids, and is certainly something you as parents will want to share with your children. So my most important message to you for riding bicycles, scooters, skateboards, in-line skates, and anything else with wheels is this: You and your child should wear a helmet at all times when riding or learning to ride, even when he is using training wheels. Helmets save lives (as do seat belts and the proper placement of child safety seats, which I will discuss later). Whether or not your state has a mandatory helmet law, you should have and enforce a mandatory helmet law in your family—and that includes you. I can't tell you how horrified I am when I see an adult riding with a child, and only the child is wearing a helmet. It makes no sense and gives a very confusing and dangerous message to the child when the adult doesn't wear a helmet and sets a terrible example.

Make sure your child's helmet fits properly: It should not be so tight that it is uncomfortable, or so loose that it easily moves around on his head. When the strap is fastened correctly, there should be no more than a finger's width between the strap and your child's chin. Make sure the helmet is either CPSC or "Snell" certified. The Snell Memorial Foundation is a nonprofit organization founded in 1957 that is dedicated to research, education, testing and development of helmet safety standards.

Here are some statistics about bike riding in the United States: Seventy-five percent of all bike accidents involve a head injury, which, as I have mentioned, can lead to lifelong impairment in brain function. Bike accidents account for some 250 deaths in children each year, and over 500,000 injuries as well. Incredibly, only about 20 percent of children wear a helmet when biking, despite the fact that the use of bicycle helmets can reduce the risk of serious injury by approximately 75 percent.

Children under age 15 are the group that uses scooters the most. Not surprisingly, about 90 percent of the injuries sustained in scooter crashes happen to children in this age group, with nearly one-third of scooter injuries since 2000 involving children under the age of 8. In the year 2000, almost forty thousand injuries associated with scooters were treated in emergency rooms. And here's perhaps the most shocking statistic: Proper use of helmets can reduce brain injuries associated with scooters by 85 percent.

Automobile Safety Seats

Child automobile safety seats have been proven to make babies and toddlers safer. It is critical to the safety of your child that she be put in a child safety seat as an infant, and in a booster seat until she is no longer under 80 pounds, under 58 inches tall, or under a sitting height of 29 inches, per current federal recommendations.

Researchers at the University of Washington in Seattle studied a group of 149 children, ages 4 to 8, to determine how parents and caregivers used booster seats. They found that only 10 percent of children 6 to 8 years old were restrained with booster seats, when all should have been. When parents were questioned about why they didn't use the booster seat, most thought the child was large enough to use the regular lap-shoulder belt system. The researchers discovered that a parent's or caregiver's misconceptions about the safety of adult-sized seat belts was the most common reason why the children were not properly and safely restrained.

When choosing a safety seat for your child, make sure you look for a label showing that the seat meets or exceeds Federal Motor Vehicle Safety Standard 213. Especially if you have gotten a used child safety seat from someone, it's a good idea to call the manufacturer with the model number to see if it has been recalled. In fact, recall of children's auto safety seats is not uncommon!

It is critical to the safety of your child that you choose the right size seat. "Infant only" seats are designed for infants up to 20 or 22 pounds. These seats are specifically designed to face the back of the car so that the baby is not thrown forward into the restraining device if an accident should occur. Even if your baby weighs more than 20 pounds, but is less than 1 year of age, he should still be positioned facing the back of the car. The ideal position for an infant car seat is facing backwards, in the middle of the back seat of the car. Make sure your baby's head is at least two inches below the top of the car seat. The harness strap should fit securely but should never be twisted.

When your child is a year old and weighs between 20 and 40 pounds, it is time to get a larger car seat; this may be positioned in the back seat, but facing forward.

Car owners' manuals actually give good information on car seat placement. In addition, you will receive a lot of information when you purchase an infant car seat, and it is critically important that you read and understand the safety seat instruction manual.

At 40 to 80 pounds, your child is ready for a booster seat. Booster seats are specifically designed to safely restrain the child who is still too small for the standard car seat belt. They also face forward, like the seats for children between 20 and 40 pounds. But booster seats should still be in the back seat as well.

Airbags present a significant danger for babies in rear-facing car seats; this is why babies in rear-facing seats should never be in the front seat of a car that has a passenger-side airbag.

CHAPTER FIFTEEN

Vaccinations: Making Intelligent Choices for Your Child

Do the standard childhood vaccinations against diseases such as polio, tetanus, and whooping cough increase your child's risk for autism or ADHD? There has been a great deal of controversy reported in the mainstream press as well as medical and academic publications about the safety of various vaccines, as well as their impact on the developing brain.

I want to be clear that I believe most of the childhood immunizations are essential. Compared with the risks to your child's health of the actual illnesses the immunizations are designed to prevent, immunization makes good sense. Having said that, I have to add that the process of immunization creates a considerable challenge for the immune system and occurs at a time when both the immune and nervous systems are undergoing rapid development. I also feel that there is a better, safer way to immunize children than the way it is commonly done today.

Infants are born with temporary immunity to certain diseases because their mothers' antibodies are transferred to them through the placenta. A breast-fed child gets the continued benefits of additional antibodies from his mother's breast milk, which provides additional immunity.

But there are many diseases for which even breast-fed infants and children need to be immunized. Immunization entails using small amounts of a killed or weakened microorganism that otherwise could cause a particular disease. The microorganism might be a virus, such as the measles virus, or bacteria, such as pneumococcus. These microorganisms stimulate the immune system to react as if there were a real infection. The immune system then fights off the "infection" and remembers the organism (in the form of antibodies), creating what it needs to fight it off quickly if it enters the body in the future.

The two critical issues surrounding childhood immunization are: (1) the problems created for children and their immune systems by combining vaccines; and (2) the debate surrounding mercury in vaccines and whether or not it contributes to the increasing incidence of autism in children.

THE PROLIFERATION OF IMMUNIZATIONS OVER THE DECADES

In the early 1950s, children in the United States routinely received only four vaccines: tetanus, diphtheria, pertussis, and smallpox. Diphtheria, tetanus, and pertussis were combined into one injection, called the DTP shot.

By the 1980s, in addition to the DTP vaccine, children were also receiving immunization for mumps, measles, and rubella in one shot (MMR), as well as a polio vaccine. Smallpox was no longer required beginning in the early 1970s.

In the past twenty years, several more immunizations have been mandated for children, including the *Hemophilus influenza* type b (Hib), hepatitis B, and varicella (chicken pox) vaccines, along with changing the oral polio vaccine to an inactivated polio virus injection (IPV). And over the past several years, pneumococcal conjugate vaccine (PCV) has also been added to prevent pneumonia and meningitis caused by this bacterium. Today, the immunization schedule recommended for children by the Department of Health and Human Services is almost bewildering. Children receive as many as twenty vaccines by 2 years of age, and may get as many as *eight* injections in a single doctor's visit.

The relationship between the tremendous increase over the past thirty years in the number of vaccinations children receive and the dramatic rise in the various neurological problems we're seeing in children—including learning disabilities, ADHD, and a frightening increase in the diagnosis of autism—is impossible to ignore.

Immunizations work by stimulating the immune system. In response to this stimulation, white blood cells dramatically increase their production of chemicals called cytokines, which produce inflammation that can damage delicate neurons. The more immunizations at a given time, the higher the cytokine surge and subsequent risk of neuron damage. Scientific research now reveals a direct relationship between brain cytokines and a variety of brain disorders, including ADHD, autism, and even Alzheimer's disease. My feeling is, better to be safe than sorry.

According to the Centers for Disease Control, there is actually a range of times (such as between 1 and 4 months, or between 6 and 18 months) that is acceptable for children to receive each particular immunization. You can create a brain-friendly schedule by reducing the number of immunizations your child receives at each doctor's visit. Be sure to request single-dose vials of each vaccine. This means that you will have to return to the doctor for more doses of the vaccine, as only one dose of that particular vaccine is administered at each visit. Of course, this not the most convenient suggestion, as it means several more visits to the doctor's office. But I truly believe that separating immunizations to reduce the amount of vaccine your child receives at any one time will definitely reduce the risk of serious reactions. The chart at the end of this chapter lists all the immunizations that your child needs, along with my recommendation for when your child should receive each vaccine and the follow-up boosters.

MERCURY IN YOUR CHILD'S VACCINES

Many researchers believe that the use of thimerosal (a form of ethylmercury, a known neurotoxin) as a preservative in vaccines is directly related to the meteoric rise in the rate of autism. Since 1991, the incidence of autism has increased *1,500 percent,* from one in every 2,500 children, to one in every 166. Interestingly, it was in 1991 that the CDC and the FDA recommended giving three additional vaccines (all of which contained thimerosal) to extremely young infants, often in the first month of life. After studying the controversy extensively, I must tell you that I do believe there is a relationship between the thimerosal in vaccines given to infants and very young children and the surge in cases of autism in our country.

There is a simple way to avoid exposing your child to harmful mercury: requesting that only single-dose vials of all immunizations be used for your child. Thimerosal is added as a preservative to multidose vaccines to prolong their shelf life. Single-dose vials do not use thimerosal as a preservative, although they still may contain trace amounts from the manufacturing process. According to FDA guidelines, these vaccines are still considered "thimerosal-free," and the minute amount of thimerosal they contain does not pose a risk to your child's brain. You will likely have to pay a little extra for the single-use, thimerosal-free vial of the vaccine, but I encourage you to spend the extra money and take the time for the extra doctor visits. The immunization schedule that follows is based on the use of single-dose vaccines. Single-dose versions of each vaccine are available and your doctor should be able to provide them to you upon request. By using this approach, we can maintain the benefits of immunization for our children, while reducing the risk of damaging a developing brain. (See the resource section for more sources of information on mercury and vaccines.)

Immunization Schedule from Birth to Age 6

	birth	1 month	2 months	4 months	6 months	12 months	15 months	18 months	24 months	4–6 years
Hepatitis B	X	X			X					
Prevents hepatitis B, a liver disease. Be sure to request the *monovalent* form of this vaccine, which requires fewer doses.										
DTaP (Diphtheria, Tetanus, and Pertussis)			X	X	X			X		
Diphtheria is an acute form of tonsillitis. Tetanus is a bacterial disease that affects the nervous system. Pertussis is whooping cough.										

	birth	1 month	2 months	4 months	6 months	12 months	15 months	18 months	24 months	4–6 years
Hib (Hemophilus influenza type b)			X	X		X				
Prevents a potential cause of serious disease, including pneumonia and meningitis. Request either the PedVaxHIB or ComVax brands, as they require fewer doses.										
IPV (Inactivated Poliovirus)			X	X			X			X
Prevents polio										
MMR (Measles, Mumps, and Rubella)						X				
Prevents measles, mumps, and rubella (German measles).										

	birth	1 month	2 months	4 months	6 months	12 months	15 months	18 months	24 months	4–6 years
Varicella								X		
Prevents chickenpox.										
Pneumococcal			X	X	X		X			
Protects against infection by *Streptococcus pneumoniae*, a bacterium that can cause meningitis, pneumonia, and otitis media (ear infection).										
Hepatitis A						X		X		
Prevents the liver disease hepatitis A.										

Note: I recommend that parents discuss influenza immunizations separately with their pediatrician. This schedule will reduce the number of immunizations given at any one visit to the pediatrician's office. It is meant as a general guide. The specific schedule required for your child should be determined by your pediatrician.

PART VI

FIGHTING ADHD BY BUILDING A BETTER BRAIN

CHAPTER SIXTEEN

ADHD

Overdiagnosed and Overdrugged

Several times each week I see parents in my office who are worried sick about their children. Typically, they tell me things such as "His teacher says he can't sit still—not even for a minute" or "He's disruptive in the classroom" or "His babysitter says he's always hitting other kids." What's particularly alarming is that more often than not, a teacher or caregiver goes as far as to tell these parents that their child "is ADHD." Visibly upset, these parents will ask, "Could it be true? Do you think our child is ADHD?"

WHAT IS ADHD?

There are three major symptoms of ADHD: inability to maintain attention, hyperactivity, and impulsivity. Children with ADHD have difficulty concentrating and therefore are easily distracted and thrown off task. Due to their inattention, these children may suffer from an inability to organize thoughts and activities, or to complete tasks on time. Moreover, they have difficulty learning new material and cannot fully attend to details involved in planning and organizing their activities.

Hyperactivity, the second major symptom of ADHD, is, quite simply, being unable to sit still. Hyperactive children squirm around in their seats, seem to move their feet excessively, and appear restless and fidgety. Often, they engage in multiple activities at the same time but have difficulty in actually completing any of their tasks.

The third common characteristic of ADHD is impulsivity, characterized by the inability to think before acting. Impulsive children may immediately respond in a physical manner when they are frustrated or feel wronged. They may strike other children and become essentially out of control in situations requiring them to take their turn, such as waiting in line or playing a game.

Although the terms "attention deficit disorder" (ADD) and "attention deficit hyperactivity disorder" (ADHD) have been used for about the past thirty years, similar conditions have been described in the scientific literature dating back at least 120 years, under at least twenty-five different names. Recently, ADHD has become a national phenomenon, with countless books, television programs, and therapeutic approaches being devoted to this subject.

Despite the fact that millions of children have been diagnosed with ADHD, I believe that the real incidence of ADHD is probably extremely rare. My guess is less than half of 1 percent of all children actually have this problem. So why are so many of our children being labeled ADHD? I think a lot of it has to do with the fact that we live in a pill-popping culture where the solution to virtually everything is pharmaceutical. If something doesn't quite fit the norm, label it a disease and find a drug to "cure it."

I'm not saying that some children don't have a tendency toward hyperactivity, or that some kids may fidget more than others and have difficulty maintaining attention. By age 3, most children are able to follow simple commands with gentle persuasion, sit still for up to three minutes, and take out a toy and put it away. These are kids who do well in preschool and don't challenge a teacher or caregiver's patience. In reality, however, there are lots of kids who even at 4, 5, and beyond may have a great deal of difficulty doing any or all of these things. There is a range of activity level and maturity among kids, and a child who is very active or difficult at 4 or 5 could grow into a more settled child at 6 or 7. Furthermore, all too often, drugs have become our first line of defense against hyperactive behavior to the exclusion of other methods that often work as well or even better without side effects. Of course a child who is disruptive in a classroom, or who can't keep up with her work because she is so distracted, needs to be helped, but in general when parents are told to reach for drugs as the answer, I think they need to take great pains to make sure that every possible alternative has been tried before giving a child these powerful medicines.

TO DRUG OR NOT TO DRUG

I have had parents of children as young as 3 to 4 years tell me that they have taken their child to a pediatrician who felt it would be in their child's best interest to immediately get on medication because he obviously had ADHD. Unfortunately, a great number of parents succumb to the totally baseless argument that somehow their child will be "left behind" if they do not aggressively treat him with one of the popular ADHD medicines on the market today. Parents (and unfortunately a large number of physicians) have somehow bought into the idea that the "biological cause" of ADHD is some failure or abnormality of brain chemistry. Indeed, a booklet for the classroom teacher on ADHD and learning disabilities recently brought to my office by concerned parents stated that "ADHD drugs" "appear to work by correcting for a lack of certain necessary brain chemicals in the nervous system. Parents should be aware that these medicines do not 'drug' or 'alter' the brain of the child. They make the child 'normal' by correcting for a neurochemical imbalance."

The belief that brains of children with ADHD are somehow defective and deficient in certain brain chemicals is pervasive throughout schools and pediatricians' offices in this country. I need to state categorically that this whole concept is completely false. There is simply no evidence to support this claim.

Nonetheless, despite admonition from the prestigious American Medical Association, millions of American schoolchildren have been placed on potentially dangerous drugs (discussed below) for, in my opinion, inappropriate reasons. Indeed as the U.S. Drug Enforcement Agency stated in 1995, "Quite clearly, the United States is the only country in the world that has so thoroughly embraced the notion that a large number of our children are suffering from a 'neurobiological' disorder that needs to be treated with a potent psychostimulant as first-line treatment for behavioral control."* Even beyond the dangers posed by

***Methylphenidate* (a background paper), U.S. Drug Enforcement Administration, October 2005, p. 16.

the medications, the diagnosis itself might have adverse effects, as called to our attention by neurologist F. A. Baughman when he states,

> Invented by a committee of the American Psychiatric Association, ADHD has yet to be validated as a disease, syndrome, or anything biological or organic. Nowhere in the voluminous literature on ADHD is there proof of a biological link. Positron Emission Tomography (PET), MRI, and biochemical assays have yielded nothing. Given the lack of proof of any effective therapy, and more fundamentally the lack of validation of ADHD as a disease, the diagnosis of ADHD in and of itself might have adverse effects.*

In February 2006, an advisory panel to the Food and Drug Administration voted 8 to 7 to suggest adding the agency's strongest warning label to Ritalin, Adderall, and similar medications. The panel based its decision on an FDA report that found that twenty-five children and adults from 1999 to 2003 had died suddenly after taking ADHD drugs.

Despite the fact that no long-term studies have validated the effectiveness of ADHD medication, as well as the fact that there have been no long-term studies supporting their safety, the American Academy of Pediatrics, on its Web site, has published the following statement:

> For most children, stimulant medications are a safe and effective way to relieve attention deficit/hyperactivity disorder (ADHD) symptoms. As glasses help people focus their eyes to see, these medications help children with ADHD focus their thoughts better and ignore distractions. This makes them more able to pay attention and control their behavior.

I find this statement particularly disturbing, especially the parallel that it draws between ADHD and visual problems. Obviously, no parent would deprive a child of glasses if she could not see well, and we are thus led to believe that ADHD drugs similarly should not be restricted. It is fundamentally important to recognize that all the drugs commonly prescribed for children with ADHD do not actually treat ADHD. Ac-

*Baughman, F.A., "Letter to the Editor," *Clinical Psychiatry News* 8 (1996).

cording to the American Medical Association, no drug treatment has ever been demonstrated to be effective in any long-term study. When I interview parents of a child on medication, I often like to ask them, "What are you doing to treat her ADHD?" They, in turn, respond by saying, "We are using Ritalin [or other medication]." I then find it helpful to point out that, in fact, there is no medication available to treat ADHD. Simply stated, what they are doing is treating the *symptoms* of ADHD, not the underlying problem.

THE ROOT CAUSES OF ADHD

Two-time Nobel Prize laureate Dr. Linus Pauling has stated, "It is now recognized by leading workers in the field that behavior is determined by the functioning of the brain and that the functioning of the brain is dependent upon its composition and structure." Simply stated, the brain is made of "stuff" just like every other organ in the human body and, as pointed out by Dr. Pauling, the function of the brain is dependent on the stuff from which it is made. In building a brain, what are the key players that enhance its function, and how do they relate to the risk of ADHD? Dr. L. J. Stevens, reporting in the *American Journal of Clinical Nutrition,* performed a study in which she evaluated blood levels of DHA in 53 boys with ADHD, compared to 43 controls. The results of the study were astounding. DHA levels in the ADHD group were far lower than in the control group of boys without ADHD. As described earlier, DHA plays a fundamental role in building a better brain, paving the way for better cell-to-cell communication, sprouting of dendrites, synaptic pruning, and overall speed and efficiency of brain function. Many researchers have described DHA as the reason behind the "breastfeeding factor"—the profound increase in IQ of children who are breastfed compared to those who are not. Indeed, as researchers at Purdue University have pointed out, the risk of ADHD in children who were not breast-fed is almost double the risk for breast-fed children. Other factors that show a strong correlation with ADHD, according to both Dr. Stevens and the Purdue researchers, include a substantially increased risk of ADHD in children who have taken more than ten antibiotics since birth, or had more than ten ear infections, and a more than threefold increase in the risk of ADHD in children diagnosed with asthma.

HOW TO PREVENT ADHD

Throughout this book, I have provided leading-edge, highly effective techniques for building a better brain, allowing you to raise a smarter child by the time he or she is ready for kindergarten. These recommendations will build a faster, more efficient, and more intelligent brain—and a brain profoundly resistant to ADHD.

DHA

Getting the right fat into the brain is key to preventing hyperactive behavior. As studies have demonstrated, there is a profound correlation between low levels of DHA and risk for ADHD. This provides yet another compelling reason to ensure that your child receives adequate DHA during these critically important years for brain development. As described in Chapter 7, human breast milk is an excellent source of DHA, provided the mother's diet is DHA-enhanced, as described earlier. DHA-containing foods along with DHA supplementation play a further critical role in brain development and resistance to ADHD as your child matures. (For information on DHA supplements, see Chapter 7.)

Breast-Feeding

Breast-feeding remarkably reduces your child's risk for medical conditions that are associated with a higher rate of ADHD, including asthma (see Chapter 10), ear infections (Chapter 11), and gluten sensitivity (Chapter 12).

Get the Excitotoxins off Your Child's Plate

Excitotoxins are chemicals added to food that can cause the brain to become overly stimulated, triggering a surge in brain activity that can harm healthy cells. All children are particularly vulnerable to these chemicals, but children with hyperactive tendencies appear to be especially susceptible to their ill effects. The primary chemicals to avoid are (1) aspartame, an artificial sweetener (NutraSweet); (2) MSG (monosodium glutamate), often used in Asian cooking but also in many processed foods; and (3) hydrolyzed vegetable protein, used as a flavoring agent and a filler in processed foods. Read food labels to make sure that these additives are not in your child's diet.

Reduce Exposure to Environmental Toxins

I believe that there is a strong relationship between exposure to various household chemicals and risk for developing ADHD. In particular, exposure to secondhand cigarette smoke increases the risk of ADHD, and also increases the risk of asthma and ear infections which are both associated with this problem. Lead exposure is also related to ADHD, so please review Chapter 9 to learn more about this toxin.

Limit TV

There is a strong correlation between amount of TV viewing between the ages of 1 and 3 and risk of ADHD. In an article appearing in the *Journal of Pediatrics* in 2004, researchers from the Department of Pediatrics at the University of Washington in Seattle evaluated 1,278 children at 1 year of age and 1,345 children at age 3 to determine the number of hours of television viewed per day at those ages. The children were then evaluated at age 7. Ten percent of the children had developed "attention problems" by that age. What the study revealed was a very strong correlation between the amount of television watched at ages 1 and 3 years and the risk of developing attentional problems. These authors' findings further support the view that there are things we can do to reduce the risk of children developing ADHD. As they stated, "Our findings suggest that preventive action can be taken with respect to attentional problems in children. Limiting young children's exposure to television as a medium during formative years of brain development consistent with the American Academy of Pediatrics' recommendations may reduce children's subsequent risk of developing ADHD."*

*Christakis, D.A., et al. "Early Television Exposure and Subsequent Attentional Problems in Children," *Journal of Pediatrics* 113(4):708–13.

THE PERLMUTTER PROTOCOL FOR THE TREATMENT OF HYPERACTIVE CHILDREN

I treat thousands of children in my practice, and a large percentage of them are seen because of problems with hyperactivity and attention deficit. As of this writing, I am using medications to treat the symptoms of ADHD in a total of three children. For the overwhelming majority of these patients, we have been successful in improving their ability to remain attentive in school, focus, and control their impulsivity—without drugs. We use drugs as we believe they were intended to be used, as a last resort, when all else has failed, and the child is still having profound difficulties functioning in the classroom. This is not to say that many of our patients don't still have problems with these issues, but they experience enough improvement that they can function in a regular classroom and not have their teachers writing letters home to parents pleading for them to medicate their child.

During the course of our standard evaluation for children with ADHD-type behavior, we have found the following to be helpful:

I. Medical Evaluation

1. Check for Gluten Sensitivity (see Chapter 12)

Although gluten sensitivity is seen in only about 1 percent of the American population, I have observed this problem to be dramatically increased in children I am evaluating for ADHD. In my office, when I evaluate a child with symptoms of ADHD, checking the antigliadin antibody (a screen for gluten sensitivity) is generally number one on the list of laboratory studies performed in this type of evaluation.

If blood studies show that children are gluten sensitive, this is often a home run. Adopting a gluten-free diet, although somewhat challenging, often produces dramatic and almost immediate results. It's as if the static on the line has been removed and children are better able to focus on the information being presented or the task at hand.

2. Intracellular Vitamin Analysis

This simple blood test can be done in any doctor's office and provides a wealth of information about the nutritional status of your child. The test measures levels of important vitamins including vitamins E, B_1, B_2, B_3, folate, and others, as well as minerals, amino acids, and brain-boosting antioxidants. Parents are often surprised to learn that their child has a specific vitamin deficiency despite the fact that they were providing a "balanced diet." This test helps take the guesswork out of determining a child's specific supplement needs. More information is available at www.SpectraCell.com, or call SpectraCell Laboratory (800-227-5227).

3. Food Allergy Panel

Frequently, parents report behavioral changes when their child eats specific foods. Trying to figure out which foods are responsible could require some challenging trial and error. In these circumstances, especially when a child demonstrates other evidence of allergy like frequent ear infections, asthma, itchy eyes, hives, headaches, or sleep disturbances, we perform a blood test to find out just what foods may be responsible. We use the Children's Better Brain Profile from Genova Diagnostics. This simple blood test measures specific antibodies to eighty-eight common foods. The results allow parents to exclude specific foods to which their child is sensitive, with almost immediate and often dramatic results. Again, this is a test that can be performed in any physician's office. For more information visit www.Genovadx.com.

4. Check Vision

It may surprise you to learn that many children walk around with undiagnosed eye problems. Since they can't see what's going on in the classroom, they appear distracted and disengaged. Often, simply providing them with the right prescription eyeglasses ends the problem.

5. Check Hearing.

Like eye problems, hearing problems can go undetected. If a child doesn't listen to his teacher, it could be he can't hear what's going on.

II. Treatment Protocol

1. DHA Supplements

DHA supplementation plays a pivotal role in our treatment of children with symptoms of ADHD. As noted above, risk for ADHD has been found to be significantly higher in boys with low DHA levels, and this makes sense as DHA plays such an important role in so many areas of brain function. We generally recommend 400 milligrams of DHA daily, using products derived from marine algae. This dosage is 200 milligrams more than we typically prescribe for kids 2 and over. More information on DHA can be found in Chapter 7 and you can visit YourSmartChild.com to learn more.

2. Brain-Specific Nutrients

In addition to DHA, there are five other key supplements that are clinically proven not only to protect the brain, but to enhance function as well. We have had great success with these supplements, which are now the fundamental components of our ADHD program. Here are my supplement recommendations as well as dosages for children ages 4 and over. I have designed my own product, Kids BrainSustain (www.kids BrainSustain.com), which includes all the necessary supplements mentioned below; you can also purchase each supplement separately. For more information, see the resource section.

N-acetyl-cysteine	100 milligrams
Phosphatidylserine	25 milligrams
Alpha lipoic Acid	20 milligrams
Coenzyme Q-10	15 milligrams
Ginkgo biloba	15 milligrams

3. Multivitamin Supplements

I recommend that all children take a multivitamin and mineral supplement, and this is especially important for children with symptoms of ADHD. Information from the Intracellular Vitamin Analysis described earlier is always helpful in further defining a child's specific nutritional needs. There are many good children's multivitamins on the market. In my practice, we use Dr. Perlmutter's Multivitamin for Children, but for information on other products, see the resource section.

4. Engage Your Child in the Right Kind of Brain-Stimulating Activities

Children with hyperactive tendencies do better playing games where they are physically engaged, such as playing with building blocks and putting puzzles together. I urge you to play some of the activities listed in Chapter 3 with your child, but be sure to stop playing before she shows signs of boredom. The second your child begins to exhibit bored or aggressive behavior, stop the game.

5. Music Lessons

Your child may only be able to sit through a ten-minute lesson and not the full half hour, but get him started studying an instrument at age 4, for all the brain-boosting reasons listed in Chapter 5. Listening to relaxing music can also help calm children down, especially around bedtime.

6. Help Your Child Improve Focus

There are a variety of interactive programs now available designed to improve a child's ability to focus and avoid distraction. We have been particularly impressed with The Listening Program, offered by Advanced Brain Technologies. This program is specifically designed to enhance a child's ability to focus on auditory information as well as integrate multiple types of information, including auditory, visual, and tactile. To learn more about The Listening Program visit the Advanced Brain Technologies Web site, www.advancedbrain.com.

LAURA'S STORY

Recently, Laura, a 6-year-old child, was brought to my office by her mother. Laura's mother described her daughter as "frustrated, lacks attention for detail, is disorganized, has temper tantrums, is impulsive, hits people, lacks focus, does not finish tasks aside from watching television and doing art, seems withdrawn, seems overwhelmed, and has problems sharing."

Prior to the office visit, Laura had been evaluated by a psychologist. IQ testing indicated that she was above average in many areas but had some academic deficits nonetheless. Her mathematical composite score was in the forty-fifth percentile, but word reading was only in the twenty-fifth percentile. Weaknesses were observed in reading, decoding, math concepts, math problem solving, written language, handwriting, and behavioral issues involving the classroom. At that time, she was unable to recognize letters by name or sound. Further, the psychological evaluation revealed that the child demonstrated significant problems with self-confidence.

Her medical history was completely unremarkable aside from the fact that she was born two weeks early, and her birth was without complication. She was not breast-fed at all and the mother reported that her child was "colicky." She had received several courses of antibiotics for recurrent ear infections.

When I examined this healthy-appearing child, I did not find any specific abnormalities with respect to the function of her nervous system. She certainly seemed quite active and was unable to sit down for more than a few seconds at a time. She also appeared to be very distracted and was unable to focus on even playing with a toy.

Her parents had been told that she was suffering from "an advanced case of ADHD," and that their only course of action would be to immediately place her on stimulant drugs. In fact, there were statements from teachers also suggesting that this was necessary.

From experience, I knew that it was not really necessary to engage in a series of sophisticated neurodiagnostic studies. Seeing children like this day in and day out allowed me the confidence to formulate a very simple plan. We placed Laura on oral supplementation of DHA and on brain-function enhancement nutritional supplements including N-acetyl-cysteine, coenzyme Q10, alpha lipoic acid, phosphatidylcholine, and ginkgo biloba. (See Brain-Specific Nutrients on page 244.)

I saw her in a follow-up visit three months later. Her parents were overjoyed that she had "written six sentences yesterday with capital letters and periods" and was reading at a first-grade level. Apparently she had written a brief paragraph as to why she should be president of the United States! Teachers reported that her rate of progress was such that six months hence they expected her to be back on track for her age group, and they noted a "remarkable improvement in her mathematical skills." There was good news from the home front as well: Laura's mother reported that her daughter was now actually able to do homework on her own.

A Final Note

Raise a Smarter Child by Kindergarten provides a blueprint for you to help your children develop into smart, capable, and successful adults. As a parent, you have a brief window of opportunity to have a huge impact not only on your child's brain development, but on your child's entire future.

We live in a competitive society and intelligence is a supreme advantage, not only for the obvious direct benefits it imparts, but also because of the self-confidence it fosters. As early as kindergarten, a child begins to develop a keen awareness of how he or she stacks up to peers as well as how teachers and other adults respond to him or her. Children of higher intellect command respect from those around them, and this is a powerful personality builder.

Preschool and kindergarten teachers uniformly agree that identifying children bound for academic success even at this early stage of development is commonplace. These children stand out. Taking advantage of the brain-enhancing games and activities, nutritional considerations, and supplement recommendations, as well as the information on detrimental toxins, overly aggressive immunization schedules, inappropriate medications, and outdated approaches to preschool teaching described in this book, is almost guaranteed to put your child in the winner's circle.

Perhaps the most compelling discovery in the science of brain development is that the single most important factor in boosting brain performance in children is parental involvement. Children learn best when they feel loved, secure, happy, and relaxed. Cherish the time you spend together.

In the pages that follow, you will find additional tools you need to *Raise a Smarter Child by Kindergarten,* including my favorite toys, books, video games, and Web sites for children.

APPENDICES

APPENDIX A

Daily Supplementation Program for Children and Mothers

DAILY SUPPLEMENTATION FOR NURSING MOTHERS*

DHA: 400 mg

A multivitamin containing:
Iodine (150–200 mcg)
Iron (40–50 mg)

*Vegetarians should add an additional B-complex vitamin containing at least 400 mcg of folic acid (800 mcg is preferable), 50 mg of vitamin B_6, and 500 mcg of vitamin B_{12}.

DAILY SUPPLEMENTATION FOR FORMULA-FED TODDLERS

Your baby's formula should contain the following nutrients per 5-ounce serving of formula:

DHA: 19 mg
ARA: 34 mg
Iron: 1.8 mg
Iodine: 9 mcg

DAILY SUPPLEMENTATION FOR CHILDREN 6 MONTHS TO 2 YEARS*

DHA: 100 mg

*Iron: Breast-fed infants should receive 2 mg of iron per 2.2 pounds of body weight until 1 year old.

DAILY SUPPLEMENTATION FOR CHILDREN 2–5

Children's multivitamin
DHA: 200 mg from marine algae

DAILY SUPPLEMENTATION FOR CHILDREN WITH ADHD (AGE 4 YEARS OR OLDER)

Children's multivitamin, Dr. Perlmutter's Children's Multivitamin (www.inutritionals.com or telephone 800-530-1982)
DHA: 400 mg from marine algae
N-acetyl-cysteine: 100 mg
Phosphatidylserine: 25 mg
Alpha lipoic Acid: 20 mg
Coenzyme Q-10: 15 mg
Ginkgo biloba: 15 mg

*The supplements listed above can be purchased separately at your local health food store. They are also available from Kid's Brain Sustain at www.kidsBrainSustain.com or call (800-530-1982).

APPENDIX B

Food Lists

Recommended Foods for a Better Brain

Poultry	
Recommended	***Avoid***
Chicken	Fried chicken
Turkey	Fried, breaded chicken nuggets
Ground chicken or turkey	
Chicken or turkey sausage	
Chicken or turkey bacon	

Meat	
Recommended	***Avoid***
Beef tenderloin	Bacon
Flank, round, or sirloin steak	Sausage
Lean ground sirloin or round steak	Hot dogs
Top round or rump roast	Deli meats
Lamb leg, roast, or chops	Ribs
Pork tenderloin	Prime rib
Lean boiled ham	

Seafood	
Recommended	***Avoid***
*Wild Pacific salmon	**Shark
*Sardines	**Swordfish
*Herring	**Large tuna
Pollock	**King mackerel

Cod	**Tilefish
Sole	Farmed salmon
Shrimp	Breaded, fried fish
	Frozen fish sticks
**High in DHA*	***Large predatory species, which are likely to contain unacceptable levels of mercury*

Eggs

Recommended	***Avoid***
*DHA-enriched eggs	**Egg substitutes
**One good brand is Gold Circle Farms. Each enriched egg contains 150 mg of DHA. (Regular eggs average 18 mg.)*	***Egg-white products such as Egg Beaters (not egg substitutes) are acceptable, but because egg yolks contain a number of brain-building nutrients, I recommend whole eggs for children.*

Dairy

Recommended	***Avoid***
*No-fat or low-fat plain, unsweetened yogurt (1% fat)	Don't eat any full-fat or nonorganic dairy products. These products are high in saturated fat and environmental toxins, which are stored in fat.
No-fat or low-fat cottage cheese (1% fat)	
No-fat or low-fat ricotta cheese (1% fat)	
Low-fat cheeses (1% fat)	
**Fruit-flavored yogurt contains a lot of sugar. Buy plain yogurt and add fruit and the healthy sweetener of your choice.*	

Nuts, Seeds, and Nut Butters

Recommended	*Avoid*
Almonds	Roasted nuts and seeds
Brazil nuts	Regular peanut butter
Cashews	
Peanuts	
Pecans	
*Walnuts	
*Pumpkin seeds	
Sunflower seeds	
Sesame seeds	
**Peanut butter	
**Almond butter	
**A good source of omega-3 fatty acids*	
***Unsweetened, nonhydrogenated brands only*	

Beans and Legumes

Recommended
Pinto beans
Black beans
Navy beans
Kidney beans
Lentils
Garbanzos (chickpeas)
Refried beans (fat-free)
Baked beans (low-sugar)
Soybeans
Edamame (cooked green soybeans)
Tofu
Tempeh

Cereals, Grains, Pasta, and Breads

Recommended	*Avoid*
Brown rice	White bread
Buckwheat	Baked goods made with partially hydrogenated oils (most crackers, frozen waffles, etc.)
Oatmeal (old fashioned or steel cut)	
Quinoa	

Millet	Bisquick
Amaranth	Cold breakfast cereals made with highly refined flour and sugar
Sprouted grain bread (Ezekiel is a good brand)	Infant cereals that are not iron fortified
Sprouted grain bagels and pita bread	Instant oatmeal
100% rye bread	
*100% whole-wheat bread	
Low-fat, whole-grain crackers	
**Spelt pasta	
***Whole Kids Organic macaroni and cheese	
Corn tortillas	
*Whole-wheat tortillas	
Kashi Mighty Bites cereals	
Healthy Times Teddy Puffs cereals	
***Whole Kids Organic Morning-O's cereal	
***Whole Kids Organic Quack'n Bites crackers	

**Wheat is a common allergen. Carefully observe your child's reaction to wheat, and if it is not well tolerated, substitute other grains.*

***Better tolerated than wheat pasta.*

****Sold in Whole Foods Market stores.*

Packaged and Prepared Foods

Recommended	***Avoid***
Organic, low-sugar marinara sauce (for pasta and pizza)	Chicken nuggets
Amy's frozen meals and snacks	Fish sticks
Amy's canned soups	Frozen pizzas
	Most frozen snack foods
	Most frozen meals

Desserts and Sweet Snacks

Recommended	***Avoid***
Healthy Times Arrowroot Cookies	Packaged cookies
Earth's Best Cereal Bars	Candy

Earth's Best Organic Crunchin' Blocks	Doughnuts and pastries
Earth's Best Kidz Organic Whole Grain Bars	Cake
Clif Kids Organic Z Bars	
Dark chocolate (in moderation)	

Vegetables

Recommended	***Avoid***
Artichokes (kids love the mechanics of eating these)	Canned and frozen vegetables prepared with presweetened syrups or sauces containing added preservatives
Broccoli	
Carrots	
Celery	
Lettuce	
Peppers	
Cabbage	
Cauliflower	
Asparagus	
Onions	
Spinach	
Kale and other leafy greens	
Corn	
Eggplant	
*Purslane	
Snow peas	
Green beans	
Sweet potatoes	
Squash	
Zucchini	
**Purslane, a newcomer to supermarket shelves, is a chewy, sweet-sour "weed" with a crunchy texture that's a good source of omega-3 fatty acids.*	

Fruits

Recommended
Apples
Pears
Oranges
Grapefruit
Peaches

Apricots
Nectarines
Plums
Bananas
Berries
Melons
Papayas
Pineapple
Jams and jellies (no sugar added)

Cooking Ingredients and Condiments	
Recommended	***Avoid***
Olive oil	Corn, peanut, soy, and other polyunsaturated oils
Canola oil	Lard
*Almond, walnut, and other expeller-pressed oils	Margarine made with trans fats
Organic butter (in moderation)	White flour
Whole-grain flour	High-sugar sauces and condiments
Mustard	
Low-fat mayonnaise made with canola oil	
Low-sugar ketchup (in moderation)	
Iodized salt (in moderation)	
Low-sodium soy sauce	
Salsa	
**Never heat polyunsaturated vegetable oils as they break down into undesirable compounds.*	

Beverages	
Recommended	***Avoid***
Pure filtered water (distilled or reverse osmosis)	Regular and diet sodas
*Diluted 100% organic fruit juices	Kool-Aid
**No-fat or low-fat organic milk	Frozen or bottled lemonade and other sweetened fruit drinks
Homemade lemonade sweetened with stevia	Fruit drinks with added sweeteners
Sparkling water	

**The American Academy of Pediatricians recommends no more than 4 to 6 ounces of 100% fruit juice daily for kids through age 6, and no more than 8 to 12 ounces for those older than 7.*

***See Dairy.*

APPENDIX C

Dr. Perlmutter's Picks

The Most Beneficial Books, Games, and Toys for Children

Below you will find a partial list of what I consider to be the most beneficial and creative books, games, and electronic toys for children. These selections are available at most retail toy and book stores as well as through online retailers.

MUSICAL SELECTIONS

Advanced Brain Technologies (ABT) *Music for Babies* CD series introduces your baby (from infancy to 36 months) to a wide variety of music, ranging from classical works by Mozart and Beethoven to folk music to traditional old childhood favorites such as "London Bridge Is Falling Down," and "The Farmer in the Dell." There are four CDs in the set: *Playful Baby, Cheerful Baby, Sleepy Baby,* and *Peaceful Baby.* Music for putting your baby to sleep or into a mellow mood has a slow tempo; music for play or cheerful wakefulness has a more upbeat tempo. The *Music for Babies* series is easy on the ears, even for adults! For more information, go to ABTmedia.com or call (888-228-1798).

MUSIC PLAY

Small World Toys offers phthalate-free music blocks of different colors and shapes that increase a child's discrimination skills and encourage experimentation with sound. I also like Sunshine Symphony, a sun-shaped stuffed toy with a variety of textures to stimilate tactile discrimination. I've had this toy in my waiting room for the past year and children love it. It plays four music selections and is available from Neurosmith and SmallWorldToys.com.

BOARD GAMES AND PUZZLES

LeTrend Enterprises offers some terrific educational board games for kids that are fun, yet effective learning tools. My favorites include the Colors & Shapes Match Me Game for ages 3 to 6, which is a useful tool to enhance your child's recognition of colors and shapes. I also recommend their Rhyming Bingo Games for ages 4 to 7, which are great for learning phonics. For more age-appropriate educational games, check out their Web site, trendenterprises.com.

Carson-Dellosa Publishing Company games and puzzles for prekindergarten children are excellent early learning tools. Their Hands-on-Learning puzzles such as Numbers Puzzles, Oceans Puzzles, and Parts of the Body Puzzles not only teach children basic shapes but also reinforce the concept of sorting like groups or objects together, which enhances basic discrimination skills. I also recommend their Learning to Sequence Early Childhood Games starting at age 3 and up and also offering more advanced games for older children. As the name implies, these games teach children how to think sequentially, which is important for honing critical thinking skills as well as basic time management. (For example, one game teaches children the order in which to get dressed.)

This same company makes a wonderful twenty-four piece puzzle for ages 3 and up called Farm Animals and Their Babies. Parents can create a storyline with their children as they put this puzzle together, which encourages creativity and imaginary play. Visit their Web site at carson-dellosa.com.

Small World Toys offers four levels of puzzles in their Puzzibilities line. These unique puzzles make sounds as they are constructed and are bilingual in English and Spanish. Small World Toys IQ Pre School Line provides phthalate-free toys specifically designed to stimulate and challenge young minds.

Contact Small World Toys at 800-421-4153 or go to SmallWorld Toys.com.

COMPUTER GAMES

Shelly's My First Computer Game Goldilocks and the Three Bears by ABT Interactive are terrific ways to introduce children between 3 and 6 to basic computer functions as well as enhance reading, memory, and critical thinking, among other important basic learning skills. For more information, visit ABTmedia.com or call (888-222-1798).

ELECTRONIC GAMES

The following electronic games are good alternatives to standard video games, which are often too intense or violent for young players.

Fisher-Price's InteracTV, an interactive DVD-based learning system, has a console appropriate for age 3 and above. The system offers several different DVDs with different storylines for kids to play along with. Children interact with the program and are asked questions they can answer by using their wireless controller. This is a terrific, fun way for children to learn numbers, colors, and counting as well as early math and memory skills.

Visit fisher-price.com for more information on InteracTV and other games.

LeapFrog's handheld console, the Leapster Learning System, for kids age 4 years and over is a great alternative to the typical video games. There are several game cartridges available for kids ages 4 to 5 that teach letters, phonics, listening skills, and counting and number skills. Children as young as 6 months can use the Little Touch Leappad with their parents. It includes a stylus or pen that allows the child to touch things on the console, enhancing hand–eye coordination and manipulation. At age 3, they can move on to the more advanced Leappad Learning System (for ages 3 to 5), which also includes a stylus and is a terrific way for kids to learn letters.

There are many different LeapFrog products on the market. You can learn more at leapfrogstore.com.

The V.Smile TV learning system includes a console and a joystick similar to those of standard video games and has programs that teach language comprehension, math, vocabulary, phonics, and problem solving. I particularly like the fact that the console has large buttons, making it very easy for kids to manipulate. V.Smile features the Easy Learners Library of games that are appropriate for children ages 3 to 5 and the Junior Thinkers series for ages 4 to 5, which tells stories but is interactive. Similar to standard video games, two players can play against each other, which gives your child more of the video game experience.

RECOMMENDED WEB SITES TO EXPLORE WITH YOUR CHILD

barney.com
bensguide.gpo.gov (no www.)
berenstainbears.com
billybear4kids.com
classicbrain.com
www.crayola.com
cyberkids.com
disney.com
foxkids.com
funbrain.com
funschool.com
kids.com
kidsdomain.com
kidsgardening.com
kidshealth.com
kidssongs.com
mamamedia.com
nationalgeographic.com/kids/
nickeledeon.com
PBS.org
pawisland.com
winniethepooh.com

SOME OF MY FAVORITE BOOKS

Books by Sandra Boynton

Barnyard Dance!, Workman Publishing Company, 1993.
Snuggle Puppy, Workman Publishing Company, 2003.
Hippos Go Berserk, Simon & Schuster Children's Publishing, 1996.
Dinos to Go: 7 Nifty Dinosaurs in 1 Swell Book, Little Simon, 2000.
Horns To Toes, Little Simon, 1984.
One, Two, Three! Workman Publishing Company, 1993.
The Going to Bed Book, Little Simon, 1982.
Belly Button Book, Workman Publishing Company, 2005.
Doggies, Little Simon, 1984.
But Not the Hippopotamus, Little Simon, 1982.
Oh My Oh My Oh Dinosaurs! Workman Publishing Company, 1993.

Blue Hat, Green Hat, Little Simon, 1984.
A to Z, Little Simon, 1984.
Moo, Baa, La La La! Little Simon, 1982.

Touch and Feel Books from DK Publishing

Touch and Feel: Mealtime, 2002.
Touch and Feel: Jungle Animals (Nicola Deschamps, Editor), 2001.
Touch and Feel: Baby Animals, 1999.
Touch and Feel: Wild Animals, 1998.
Touch and Feel: Farm, 1998.
Touch and Feel: Tractor, 2003.
Touch and Feel: Baseball, 2003.

Books by Fiona Watt

That's Not My Monster . . . Usborne Books, 2004.
That's Not My Car . . . Usborne Books, 2004.
That's Not My Truck . . . E.D.C. Publishing, 2002.
That's Not My Puppy . . . Usborne Books, 2001.
That's Not My Tractor . . . E.D.C. Publishing, 2001.
That's Not My Dinosaur . . . E.D.C. Publishing, 2002.
That's Not My Lion . . . E.D.C. Publishing, 2002.
That's Not My Fairy . . . Usborne Books, 2004.

Books by Various Authors

Goodnight Moon, Margaret Wise Brown, Harper & Row, 1947.
The Runaway Bunny, Margaret Wise Brown, Harper & Row, 1942.
Feely Bugs, David A. Carter, Little Simon, 1995.
Five Little Ladybugs, Melanie Gerth, Piggy Toes Press, 2003.
Who's Under That Hat, Sarah Weeks and David A. Carter, Red Wagon Books, 2005.

Storybooks

The Very Quiet Cricket, Eric Carle, Philomel, 1990.
The Cat in the Hat, Dr. Seuss, Random House, 1957.
The Gingerbread Man, Jim Aylesworth, Scholastic Press, 1998.
HarperCollins Treasury of Picture Book Classics: A Child's First Collection, Katherine Tegen (Editor), HarperCollins, 2002.
The Little Engine That Could, Watty Piper, Grosset & Dunlap, 1978.
If You Give a Pig a Party, Laura Numeroff and Felicia Bond, Laura Geringer/HarperCollins, 2005.

APPENDIX D

How to Pick a Brain-Friendly Day-Care Center

You could be doing all the right things at home, but if your child spends a good part of the day in day care, you need to make sure that all your good work isn't being undone.

There are two main types of day care: a standard day-care center, which typically must be licensed by the state, and family care, in which a child is brought to the home of a family care provider who usually watches a small number of children. Depending on the state, family care providers may or may not be licensed.

Before enrolling your child in day care, be sure to visit the site at least twice to check up on the facility. Here are some tips on what to look for:

READ THE INSPECTION REPORT

Depending on the state in which you live, a licensed day-care center will be periodically inspected by state regulators to be recertified. Ask to see the most recent state inspection report, and do call whatever agency regulates day-care centers in your area to make sure that there are no complaints.

CHECK WITH YOUR SENSES

As my friend who has a Ph.D. in education put it, some day-care centers are so bright and noisy, they are the equivalent of "casinos for kids." Needless to say, a frenetic environment can be overwhelming to small children. And when children are overstimulated, their brains shut down and they are not receptive to learning or interacting with other kids. A good day-care center should be buzzing with activity (at least most of the time) but not frantic. When you visit the day-care center, close your eyes and listen. Do you hear lots of screaming, unhappy children, or do you hear the hum of children busily engaged in interesting activities, but not loud, strident noise? Do you hear pleasant music in the background? Does the center pass the "smell test"? Does the food smell good, or do you smell garbage and dirty diapers? Look around carefully. Do the children look happy? Are they well supervised? Are there lots of books and age-appropriate toys around? Are the caregivers or teachers interacting well with the children? Is the TV on all the time? If you don't get a good feeling about the day-care center, leave.

STAFFING

Ask to speak to the teachers or caregivers who will be taking care of your child. Be sure that they are not overworked. Ask the director of the center about the frequency of staff turnover. If there is a high rate of turnover, it's a sign of unhappiness on the staff's part and translates to your child having the added burden of constantly adjusting to new people. The rule of thumb is, children up to around age 2½ should be in groups of no more than 6 to 8 children attended to by two caregivers. The younger the children, the greater their needs are for hands-on care. Children between the ages of 2½ and 3 should be in groups of no more than ten children with at least two caregivers. Children 3 years and older should be in groups with no more than fourteen to fifteen children, with at least two caregivers.

ACTIVITIES

Be sure to ask specific questions about how your child is going to spend her day. Is there time for supervised indoor play? Is there time for outdoor play? Although I personally don't believe in forcing small children into a rigid classroom setting, I think that it's reasonable to expect that caregivers will play some fun math and letter games with your children so that they begin to build a foundation for literacy and math.

They should also spend at least thirty minutes a day reading to your children at the very least. I understand that caregivers need a break, and at times it may be necessary to put on an age-appropriate video for a half hour or so, but TV watching should not be a big part of the day.

SICK CHILD POLICY

If the day-care center allows children to attend when they are sick, be sure that they separate sick children from the well children. Children who attend day care are at risk for more respiratory infections than children who are cared for in their homes, which ultimately means that they may be exposed more to antibiotics. Frequent exposure to antibiotics increases the risk of ADHD, so I think it's important to try to keep your child as well as possible.

WATER

Make sure that children are given purified, filtered drinking water. Ask about any problems with lead in the water. (This is the kind of information that should be in most state inspection reports.) If no information is available, you can check for lead yourself. (See page 170.)

PESTICIDE POLICY

It's pointless to avoid pesticides at home only to have your children crawl in them at day care. Be sure to check the day-care center's policy on pesticide use. Preferably, they are using natural, nonchemical products in the center and the outdoor play area. If they do spray with pesticides, make sure that they are required to notify parents ahead of time. (See page 160.)

PLAYGROUND

Make sure that your child is getting enough outdoor play. Physical activity is extremely important for brain development because it boosts levels of BDNF, the growth hormone that turns on smart genes. But make sure that your child is not playing on equipment made of pressure-treated wood that contains arsenic or eating lunch or doing craft activities on arsenic-containing pressure-treated picnic tables. (See page 179.)

A WORD ABOUT FAMILY CARE

Family care may be a good choice for very small children who may be overwhelmed by a larger day-care facility. The only problem is, family care is only as good as the sole provider, who is usually a mother with a small child herself. You must be certain that the family care provider is not taking in too many children. The ratio of child to caregiver for 2-year-olds should not exceed three to one. During the active years of brain development, children need to be in a stimulating environment with a loving caregiver who is talking to them, reading to them, and making them feel secure. Make sure that the children get to go outside for supervised play, and that they are not spending their days watching TV or videos.

Make sure that the caregiver's home is as toxin free as your own. Ask questions. Make sure that the caregiver's home is not sprayed with pesticides, and that she uses only purified, filtered water and is scrupulous about childproofing the areas in which children are allowed to play.

Once again, you must be diligent about checking references. Ask to speak to several parents of children who have stayed with the home care provider. Spend a day or two observing how the home care provider interacts with children. Take advantage of the fact that you can always drop in to check on your child whenever you like.

APPENDIX E

Resources

CHAPTER EIGHT

DHA Recommendations

Nursing Mothers Take a supplement containing 400 milligrams of algae-derived DHA daily. I recommend Neuromins, Natrol Neuromin DHA Omega-3, and Dr. Perlmutter's DHA which can be obtained from www.smartDHA.com.

Formula-Fed Infants Look for formula containing around 19 milligrams of DHA per 5-ounce serving.

Children 2 and Over From ages 6 months to 2 years, take 100 milligrams daily; from ages 2 through 5, 200 milligrams daily. Depending on your child's age, capsules may be swallowed or chewed, or punctured with a pin or needle and the contents mixed in with cereal or other food. I recommend Neuromins for Kids (100- or 200-milligram capsules) and my own brand, Dr. Perlmutter's DHA for Kids (100-milligram capsules), which can be obtained from www.smartDHA.com.

CHAPTER NINE

For additional information, call the FDA's food information line at 888-SAFEFOOD. For information on the EPA's actions to control mercury, see the EPA Web site, www.epa.gov/mercury.

For information on environmental toxins, contact:

Greenpeace (www.greenpeace.org/usa/)
Physicians for Social Responsibility (www.psr.org)

For information on alternatives to pesticides, contact:

www.organicgardening.org
www.pesticide.org
www.pesticidefreeyards.org

At-Home Lead-Testing Kit

An at-home test created by Pro-Lab provides an accurate measurement of lead content. The in-home test is usually under $20 or $25 with a small lab processing fee (also under $20). Visit Pro-Lab's Web site at: www.prolabinc.com (or call 800-427-0550). Genova Diagnostics (800-522-4762) also offers lead testing.

For information on testing lead levels in your drinking water, go to:

www.leadtesting.org
www.osha.gov/SLTC/leadtest/intro.html

CHAPTER THIRTEEN

For information on gluten sensitivity, click onto the following Web sites:

www.csaceliacs.org/
www.celiac.org/

These two Web sites offer a great deal of information on everything from the basics about the disease to support groups to places to buy gluten-free products. There are also many books offered through these organizations, including cookbooks and self-help and guidance books such as *Guidelines for a Gluten-Free Lifestyle* by the Celiac Disease Foundation.

CHAPTER FIFTEEN

The following organizations can provide information on brain injuries:

Brain Injury Association of America
800-444-6443
www.biausa.org

North American Brain Injury Society
703-960-6500
www.nabis.org

Centers for Disease Control and Prevention
800-311-3435
www.cdc.gov

CHAPTER SEVENTEEN

For a current listing of the mercury concentration in most U.S. licensed vaccines, you can access the Web site of the National Network of Immunization Information at http://www.immunizationinfo.org/vaccine_components_detail.cfv?id =3#concentration.

For a full report on thimerosal in vaccines, go to the FDA Web site at http://www.fda.gov/cber/vaccine/thimerosal.htm#t3.

You can also consult the Johns Hopkins University Institute for Vaccine Safety at http://www.vaccinesafety.edu/thi-table.htm.

Selected Bibliography

CHAPTER TWO

Memory

Fagan, J.F. Relationship of Novelty Preference During Infancy to Later Intelligence and Recognition Memory. *Intelligence* 8:339–46, 1984.

McCall, R.B., et al. A Meta-Analysis of Infant Habituation and Recognition Memory Performance as Predictors of Later IQ. *Child Development* 64:57–79, 1993.

Rovee, Collier, C. The "Memory System" of Prelinguistic Infants. *Annals of the New York Academy of Sciences* 608:517–542, 1990.

Speech and Language

Damasio, A.R., et al. Brain and Language. *Scientific American* 267:88–95, 1992.

Eimas, P.D., et al. Speech Perception in Infants. *Science* 171:303–6, 1971.

Kuhl, P.K., et al. Cross-Language Analysis of Phonetic Units in Language Addressed to Infants. *Science* 277:684–86, 1997.

Lecours, A.R. Myelogenetic Correlates of the Development of Speech and Language. In *Foundations of Language Development: A Multi-Disciplinary Approach, Vol. 1,* ed. E.H. Lenneberg and E. Lenneberg, 121–35. New York Academic Press, 1975.

Newport, E.L. Maturational Constraints on Language Learning. *Cognitive Science* 14:11–28, 1990.

Whitehurst, G.J., et al. Accelerated Language Development Through Picture Book Reading. *Developmental Psychology* 24:552–69, 1988.

CHAPTER SIX

Music

Allman, W.F. The Musical Brain. *U.S. News & World Report,* June 11, 1990.

Kolata, G. Rhyme's Reason: Linking Thinking to Train the Brain? *New York Times,* February 19, 1995.

Rauscher, F., et al. Music Training Causes Long-Term Enhancement of Preschool Children's Spatial/Temporal Reasoning. *Neurological Research* 19:2–8, 1997.

Schlaug, G., et al. Increased Corpus Callosum Size in Musicians. *Neuropsychologica* 33:1047–55, 1995.

Trainor, L.J. Infant Preferences for Infant-Directed Versus Non-Infant-Directed Play Songs and Lullabies. *Infant Behavior and Development* 19:83–92, 1986.

CHAPTER SEVEN

Television

American Academy of Pediatrics/Committee on Public Education. Media Education. *Pediatrics* 104 (2 Pt 1):341–43, 1999. Updated July 2, 2005, available at http://www.pediatrics.org/cgi/content/full/104/2/341.

Christakis, D.A., et al. Early Television Exposure and Subsequent Attentional Problems in Children. *Pediatrics* 113(4):708–13, 2004.

Christakis, D.A. Television, Video, and Computer Game Usage in Children Under 11 Years of Age. *Journal of Pediatrics* 145(5):652–56, 2004.

Kalin, C. Television, Violence, and Children. M.S. Synthesis Paper, College of Education, University of Oregon, June 1997, available online at http://www.interact.uoregonedu/medialit/mir/readings/article/ kalin.html.

Zimmerman, F.J. Early Cognitive Stimulation, Emotional Support, and Television Watching as Predictors of Subsequent Bullying Among Grade-School Children. *Archives of Pediatrics and Adolescent Medicine* 159(4):384–88, 2005.

CHAPTER EIGHT

DHA

Birch, E., et al. A Randomized Controlled Trial of Long-Chain Polyunsaturated Fatty Acid Supplementation of Formula in Term Infants After Weaning at Six Weeks of Age. *American Journal of Clinical Nutrition* 75:570–80, 2002.

Committee on Drugs, American Academy of Pediatrics. The Transfer of Drugs and Other Chemicals into Human Milk. *Pediatrics* 108(3):776–89, 2001.

Dagnelie, P.C., et al. Nutritional Status of Infants Aged 4 to 18 Months on Macrobiotic Diets and Matched Omnivorous Control Infants: A Population-Based Mixed-Longitudinal Study: I. Weaning Pattern, Energy and Nutrient Intake. *European Journal of Clinical Nutrition* 43(5):311–23, 1989.

Hellband, I.B., et al. Maternal Supplementation with Very-Long-Chain N-3 Fatty Acids During Pregnancy and Lactation Augments Children's IQ at Four Years of Age. *Pediatrics* 111(1):E39–E44, 2003.

Hoffman, D.R., et al. Visual Function in Breast-Fed Term Infants Weaned to Formula With or Without Long-Chain Polyunsaturates at Four to Six Months: A Randomized Clinical Trial. *Journal of Pediatrics* 142(6):669–77, 2003.

Kuriyama, S.M., et al. Developmental Exposure to Low-dose PBDE 99: Effects on Male Fertility and Neurobehavior in Rat Offspring. *Environmental Health Perspectives* 113(2):149–54, 2005.

Mojska, H., Influence of Trans-Fatty Acids on Infant and Fetus Development. *Acta Microbiologica Polonica* 52 (Supplement): 67–74, 2003.

Makrides, M., et al. Are Long-Chain Polyunsaturated Fatty Acids Essential Nutrients in Infancy? *Lancet* 345:1463–68, 1995.

Riordan, J. Breastfeeding and Human Lactation. 438–39, Jones & Bartlett, Sudbury, Massachusetts, 2005.

Stevens, L.J., et al. Essential Fatty Acid Metabolism in Boys with Attention-Deficit/Hyperactivity Disorder. *American Journal of Clinical Nutrition* 62(4):761–68, October 1995.

Stevens, L.J., et al. Omega-3 Fatty Acids in Boys with Behavior, Learning, and Health Problems. *Physiology & Behavior* 59(4–5) 915–20, 1996.

Virch, E.E. A Randomized, Controlled Trial of Early Dietary Supply of Long-Chain Polyunsaturated Fatty Acids and Mental Development in Term Infants. *Developmental Medicine and Child Neurology* 42:174–81, 2000.

Wu, A., et al. Dietary Omega-3 Fatty Acids, Normal BDNF Levels, Reduce Oxidative Damage, and Counteract Learning Disability After Traumatic Brain Injury in Rats. *Journal of Neurotrauma* 21(10):1457–67, October 2004.

Iodine

Delange, F., et al. The Role of Iodine in Brain Development. *Proceedings of the Nutrition Society* 59(1):75–80, February 2000.

Kirk, A.B., et al. Perchlorate and Iodide in Dairy and Breast Milk. *Environmental Science and Technology* 39(7):2011–17, April 2005.

Semba, R.D., et al. Iodine in Human Milk: Perspectives for Infant Health. *Nutrition Reviews* 59(8 Pt 1):269–78, August 2001.

Iron

Algarin, C., et al. Iron Deficiency Anemia in Infancy: Long-Lasting Effects on Auditory and Visual System Functioning. *Pediatric Research* 53:217–23, 2003.

Baker, S.S. Iron Fortification of Infant Formula. *Pediatrics* 105:1370–71, 2000.

Barclay, L. Iron Supplementation Beneficial in Healthy, Full-term Infants. Medscape, www.medscape.com, October 6, 2003.

Committee on Nutrition, American Academy of Pediatrics. Iron Fortification of Infant Formulas. *Pediatrics* 104(1 Pt 1):119–23, 1999.

Eden, A., et al. Iron Supplementation for One to Two Year Olds (letter to the editor). *Pediatrics* 106(5):1166, 2000.

Lozoff, B., et al. Long-term Developmental Outcome of Infants with Iron Deficiency. *New England Journal of Medicine* 325(10):687–94, 1991.

Oski, F.A., et al. Effect of Iron Therapy on Behavior Performance in Non-anemic, Iron-Deficient Infants. *Pediatrics* 71:877–80, 1983.

Picciano, M.F. Nutritional Guidance is Needed During Dietary Transition in Early Childhood. *Pediatrics* 106:109–14, 2000.

Van Dusseldorp, M., et al. Risk of Persistent Cobalamin Deficiency in Adolescents Fed a Macrobiotic Diet in Early Life. *American Journal of Clinical Nutrition* 69(4):664–71, 1999.

CHAPTER TEN

Toxins

Baby Alert: New Findings about Plastics. *Consumer Reports Special Report*, April 21, 1999.

Bellinger, D., et al. Longitudinal Analyses of Prenatal and Postnatal Lead Exposure and Early Cognitive Development. *New England Journal of Medicine* 316:1037–43, 1987.

Canfield, R., et al. Intellectual Impairment in Children With Blood Lead Concentrations Below 10 microg Per Deciliter. *New England Journal of Medicine* 348(16):1517–26, 2003.

Breed, C., et al. Increased Migration Levels of Bisphenol A from Polycarbonate Baby Bottles after Diswashing, Boiling, and Brushing. *Food Additives and Contaminants* 20(7):684–89, 2003.

Carta, P., et al. Sub-clinical Neurobehavioral Abnormalities Associated with Low Level of Mercury Exposure Through Fish Consumption. *Neurotoxicology* 24(4–5):617–23, 2003.

Geier, D.A., et al. A Comparative Evaluation of the Effects of MMR Immunization in Mercury Doses from Thimerosal-Containing Childhood Vaccines on the Population Prevalence of Autism. *Medical Science Monitor* 10(3):P133–39, 2004.

Harmon, M.E. This Vinyl House: Hazardous Additives in Vinyl Consumer Products. Greenpeace, June 2001, www.greenpeaceusa.org.

Kohn, D. Solvents Linked to Diminished IQ. *South Bend Tribune,* November 24, 2004.

Longnecker, M.P., et al. Persistent Organic Pollutants in Children. *Pediatric Research* 50(3):322–23, 2001.

Peart, K.N. Chemical Present in Clear Plastics Can Impair Learning and Cause Disease. *Environmental Health Perspectives* 10:1289, 2005.

Schettler, T., et al. In Harm's Way: Toxic Threats to Child Development. Greater Boston Physicians for Social Responsibility (GBPSR), May 2000.

Siddiqi, M.A., et al. Polybrominated Diphenyl Ethers (PBDEs): New Pollutants—Old Diseases. *Clinical Medicine and Research* 1(4):281–90, 2003.

Trasande, L., et al. Public Health and Economic Consequences of Methylmercury Toxicity to the Developing Brain. *Environmental Health Perspectives* 113(5):590–96, 2005.

Waldman, P. Mercury and Tuna: U.S. Advice Leaves Lots of Questions. *Wall Street Journal,* August 1, 2005.

Waldman, P. Toxic Traces, New Questions about Old Chemicals. *Wall Street Journal,* August 1, 2005.

Waldman, P. Common Industrial Chemicals in Tiny Doses Raise Health Issue, Advanced Tests Often Detect Subtle Biological Effects; Are Standards Too Lax? *Wall Street Journal,* July 25, 2005.

Living on Earth: The Secret Life of Lead, available online: http://www.loe.org/

CHAPTER ELEVEN

Asthma

Bornehag, C.G. The Association Between Asthma and Allergic Symptoms in Children and Phthalates in House Dust: A Nested Case-Control Study. *Environmental Health Perspectives* 112:1393–97, 2004.

CHAPTER TWELVE

Ear Infections

Balbani, A.P., et al. Impact of Otitis Media on Language Acquisition in Children. *Jornal de Pediatria* 79(5):391–96, 2003.

DeCasper, A.J., et al. Of Human Bonding: Newborns Prefer Their Mothers' Voices. *Science* 208:1174–76, 1980.

Fernald, A. Four-Month-Old Infants Prefer to Listen to Motherese. *Infant Behavior and Development* 8:181–95, 1985.

Fifer, W.P., et al. Psychobiology of Newborn Auditory Preferences. *Seminars in Perinatology* 13:430–33, 1989.

Margolis, R.H., et al. Effects of Otitis Media on Extended High-Frequency Hearing in Children. *Annals of Otology, Rhinology, and Laryngology* 102:1–5, 1993.

Muir, D.W. The Development of Infants' Auditory Spatial Sense. In *Auditory Development in Infancy,* ed. S.E. Trehub and E.D. Schneider, 51–83. New York: Plenum Press, 1985.

Peters, S.A., et al. The Effects of Early Bilateral Otitis Media with Effusion on Educational Attainment: A Prospective Cohort Study. *Journal of Learning Disabilities* 27(2):111–21, 1994.

Roberts, J.E., et al. Otitis Media in Early Childhood and Later Language. *Journal of Speech and Hearing Research* 34:1158–68, 1991.

Tibussek, D., et al. Hearing Loss in Early Infancy Affects Maturation of the Auditory Pathway. *Developmental Medicine and Child Neurology* 44:123–29, 2002.

CHAPTER THIRTEEN

Gluten Sensitivity

Hadjivassiliou, M., et al. Gluten Sensitivity as a Neurological Illness. *Journal of Neurology, Neurosurgery, and Psychiatry* 72(5):560–63, 2002.

Helms, S. Celiac Disease and Gluten-Associated Diseases. *Alternative Medicine Review* 10(3):172–92, 2005.

Hoffenberg, E.J., et al. Should All Children Be Screened for Celiac Disease? *Gastroenterology* 128:S98–F103, 2005.

Ivarsson, A., et al. Breast-Feeding Protects Against Celiac Disease. *American Journal of Clinical Nutrition* 75(5):914–21, 2002.

Norris, J.M., et al. Risk of Celiac Disease, Autoimmunity, and Timing of Gluten Introduction in the Diet of Infants at Increased Risk of Disease. *JAMA* 293:2343–51, 2005.

Zelnik, N., et al. Range of Neurologic Disorders in Patients with Celiac Disease. *Pediatrics* 113(6):1672–76, 2004.

Traumatic Brain Injury

Prange, M.T., et al. Anthropomorphic Simulations of Falls, Shakes, and Inflicted Impacts in Infants. *Journal of Neurosurgery* 99(1):143–50, 2003.

Ramsey, A., et al. Booster Seat Use and Reasons for Nonuse. *Pediatrics* 106(2):E20, 2000.

CHAPTER FOURTEEN

Breathing and Sleep

Bennington, J.H., et al. Cellular and Molecular Connections Between Sleep and Synaptic Plasticity. *Progress in Neurobiology,* 69(2):71–101, 2003.

Cirelli, C.A. Molecular Window on Sleep: Changes in Gene Expression Between Sleep and Wakefulness. *Neuroscientist* 11(1):63–74, 2005.

Cirelli, C., et al. Gene Expression in the Brain Across the Sleeping-Waking Cycle. *Brain Research* 885(2):303–21, 2000.

Hoban, T.F. Sleep and Its Disorders in Children. *Seminars in Neurology* 24(3):327–40, 2004.

Kennedy, J.D., et al. Reduced Neurocognition in Children Who Snore. *Pediatric Pulmonology* 37(4):330–37, 2004.

O'Brien, L.M., et al. Neurobehavioral Correlates of Sleep-Disordered Breathing in Children. *Journal of Sleep Research* 13(2):165–72, 2004.

Scheers, N.J., et al. Where Should Infants Sleep? A Comparison of Risks for Suffocation of Infants Sleeping in Cribs, Adult Beds, and Other Sleeping Locations. *Pediatrics* 112(4):883–89, 2003.

Stevens, Laura, J. et al. Essential Fatty Acid Metabolism in Boys with Attention-Deficit Hyperactivity Disorder. *American Journal of Clinical Nutrition* 62:761–68, 1995.

Taiship, P., et al. Conditions That Affect Sleep Alter the Expression of Molecules Associated with Synaptic Plasticity. *American Journal of Physiology, Regulatory, Integrative, and Comparative Physiology* 281(3):R839–R845, 2001.

Yilmaz, G., et al. Factors Influencing Sleeping Pattern of Infants. *Turkish Journal of Pediatrics* 44:128–33, 2002.

Schechter, M., Technical Report: Diagnosis and Management of Childhood Obstructive Sleep Apnea Syndrome. *Pediatrics* 109(4), E69, April 2002.

CHAPTER SIXTEEN

Vaccinations

Kennedy, R.F., Jr. Deadly Immunity. *Rolling Stone* 977/978, June 30, 2005.

Parker-Pope, T. Controversial Study Reignites Debate Over Autism and Childhood Vaccines. *Wall Street Journal (Health Journal),* September 7, 2004.

CHAPTER SEVENTEEN

Attention Deficit Hyperactivity Disorder (ADHD)

Armstrong, T. ADD as a Social Invention. First published in *Education Week,* October 18, 1995, available online at http://www.thomasarmstrong.com/articles/ADDinvention/htm.

Brown, R.T., et al. Prevalence and Assessment of Attention Deficit/Hyperactivity Disorder in Primary Care Settings. *Pediatrics* 107(3), E43, 2001.

Dimitri, A., et al. Early Television Exposure and Subsequent Attentional Problems in Children. *Pediatrics* 113(4):708–13, 2004.

Mental health in the United States: Prevalence of Diagnosis and Medication Treatment for Attention Deficit/Hyperactivity Disorder—United States, 2003. *Morbidity and Mortality Weekly Report* 54(34):842–47, September 2, 2005, available online at http://www.cdc.gov/mmwr/preview/mmwrhtml/mm5434a2.htm.

Index

About the Authors

David Perlmutter, M.D., F.A.C.N., a board-certified neurologist, has achieved international recognition as a leader in the field of complementary medicine. The recipient of numerous awards, including the Linus Pauling Award and the Denham Harmon Award, his scientific publications have appeared in the most well-respected medical journals including *The Archives of Neurology, The Journal of Neurosurgery,* and *The Southern Medical Journal.* He is the founder of the Perlmutter Health Center and lives in Naples, Florida.

Carol Colman is the coauthor of numerous bestselling health titles. She lives in Larchmont, New York.